It's Time to Learn

Levels 1, 2, 3
1st Edition

Mia Y. Merritt, Ed. D

Merritt Publishing

ISBN # 979-8-88526-713-7
1st Edition

Library of Congress Cataloging
In-Publication Data

Merritt Consulting, Inc.

First Printing 2024
Printed in the USA

Message to the Teacher:

Teaching English Speakers of Other Languages (ESOL) is a rewarding experience, but your instructional delivery must be strategic and scaffolded. Depending upon the ESOL/CASAS level of your students, your lessons must build upon a foundation already laid in the four language domains in order to ensure student success. With that said, this book is aimed to do just that - ensure student success in the English language!

What this book entails:
Answering questions
Conversation practice
Dialoging with partners
Grammar
Instructional assignments
Parts of Speech
Public Speaking
Reading Calendars
Reading Comprehension
Review & Practice Activities
Skits
Stories
...and so much more!

Mia G. Merritt

Contents

Lesson 1: Basic Communication

Dear ESL Teacher,

As you embark on teaching Lesson 1: Basic Communication, you have at your disposal a comprehensive guide designed to foster language acquisition and proficiency among your students. Through structured activities such as vocabulary introduction, sentence practice, grammar drills, and conversational exercises, students will build foundational skills in English language communication. The instructional procedures outlined include direct instruction, guided practice, and independent practice. They all ensure a balanced approach to learning that supports diverse learning styles and abilities. We encourage you to use this guide as a springboard for engaging and effective teaching, while empowering your students to succeed in their language learning journey.

OBJECTIVES:
1. Students will be introduced to, identify and use vocabulary related to basic communication.
2. Students will construct and practice simple sentences using targeted vocabulary.
3. Students will demonstrate understanding of basic grammar concepts (verbs to be, pronouns, contractions, articles).
4. Students will engage in conversations using learned vocabulary and grammar.
5. Students will comprehend and respond to simple reading passages.
6. Students will participate in dialogues to practice communication skills.
7. Students will demonstrate their learning through a comprehensive assessment at the end of the lesson.

INSTRUCTIONAL PROCEDURES:

DIRECT INSTRUCTION:
- **Objective**: Begin by presenting new vocabulary and grammar concepts clearly and explicitly.

- **Details**: Begin the lesson by introducing the new vocabulary words and explaining their meanings using visuals and contextual examples. Provide clear definitions, pronunciation examples, and use each word in sentences to demonstrate its usage. Use the whiteboard or projector to display visuals that aid understanding, such as images or diagrams illustrating the meaning of each word. Encourage students to repeat and practice pronouncing the words aloud to reinforce retention, then read the sentence that use each word correctly.

GUIDED PRACTICE:
- **Objective**: Help students apply new knowledge in a supportive environment.

- **Details**: After introducing vocabulary and grammar concepts, facilitate structured activities where students practice using these concepts with teacher guidance. For example, provide sentence frames or prompts that incorporate the new vocabulary and grammar structures. Walk around the classroom, offering support and feedback as students work through the activities. Encourage peer collaboration by having students work in pairs or small groups to complete tasks, ensuring everyone has a chance to participate actively.

INDEPENDENT PRACTICE:

- **Objective**: Reinforce learning through individual or paired activities.

- **Details**: Have students take out a sheet of paper, then assign tasks from the book that require students to independently practice foundational English rules such as verbs to be and pronouns. Provide clear instructions and examples to guide students as they work through the tasks. Encourage self-monitoring by asking students to review their work for accuracy and clarity before submitting it. Monitor progress and offer assistance as needed, ensuring that all students have the opportunity to practice and solidify their understanding independently.

DIFFERENTIATION/ADAPTATIONS:

Provide visual aids and simplified instructions for English language learners:

- **Objective**: Support comprehension for students with varying English proficiency levels.

- **Details**: Use visual aids such as charts, diagrams, or illustrations alongside verbal explanations to enhance understanding. Provide simplified instructions and break down complex concepts into smaller, more manageable steps. Offer bilingual dictionaries or picture dictionaries for students who may benefit from additional language support. Adjust the pace of instruction to accommodate slower processing speeds, allowing extra time for comprehension and practice.

Offer additional practice or alternative activities for students with diverse learning needs.

- **Objective**: Address individual learning needs and preferences.

- **Details**: Provide differentiated assignments or activities that cater to different learning styles and abilities. For example, offer extension activities for advanced learners that challenge them to apply vocabulary and grammar concepts in more complex contexts. For students who struggle with written assessments, consider alternative formats such as oral presentations or digital projects that demonstrate understanding. Offer flexible grouping strategies to accommodate social and emotional needs, ensuring all students feel included and supported in their learning journey.

By implementing these instructional procedures and differentiation strategies, you can create a supportive and inclusive learning environment in which all students can actively engage with and master the content of Basic Communication in your ESOL/ELL book.

ACTIVITIES:

Vocabulary Introduction:

- **Objective**: Introduce key vocabulary words essential for basic communication.

- **Details**: Use visual aids such as flashcards, images, or charts to illustrate each vocabulary word. Provide contextual examples in sentences or short paragraphs to show how each word is used in different contexts. Encourage students to repeat and practice saying the words aloud to enhance retention.

Sentence Practice:
- **Objective**: Help students construct meaningful sentences using the new vocabulary and grammar concepts introduced.

- **Details**: Guide students step-by-step in forming sentences that incorporate the vocabulary words and target grammar structures (e.g., verbs to be, pronouns, contractions). Begin with simple sentence structures and gradually increase complexity as students become more comfortable. Provide scaffolded support with sentence starters or frames if needed.

Grammar Drill:
- **Objective**: Reinforce understanding of grammar rules related to verbs to be, pronouns, contractions, and articles.

- **Details**: Conduct focused exercises where students practice using these grammar elements correctly. This can include fill-in-the-blank activities, matching exercises, or creating sentences that demonstrate proper usage. Provide explanations and examples to clarify any misunderstandings as they arise.

Conversation Practice:
- **Objective**: Develop students' ability to engage in spoken communication using the learned vocabulary and grammar.

- **Details**: Pair students or organize small groups for conversational activities. Provide prompts or scenarios that require the use of targeted vocabulary and grammar structures in a meaningful context. Encourage students to take turns speaking and actively listen to their peers, fostering both speaking and listening skills.

Reading Comprehension:
- **Objective**: Enhance students' ability to understand written English through reading passages.

- **Details**: Select age-appropriate reading materials or passages that align with the lesson's vocabulary and grammar focus. After reading, ask comprehension questions that require students to recall details, make inferences, or summarize key points. Encourage students to read aloud to practice pronunciation and fluency.

Dialogue Creation:

- **Objective**: Encourage students to apply learned vocabulary and grammar by creating dialogues.

- **Details**: Guide students in pairs or small groups to develop dialogues that incorporate the lesson's vocabulary and grammar concepts. Provide a scenario or context (e.g., ordering food at a restaurant, introducing oneself) and encourage creativity in dialogue creation. Emphasize natural conversational flow and appropriate language use.

ASSESSMENT:
- **Objective**: Evaluate students' comprehension and application of lesson content.

- **Details**: The assessment is found at the end of each Lesson.

MATERIALS AND RESOURCES:
- It's Time to Learn English book
- Worksheet pages from the book
- Vocabulary cards
- Whiteboard and markers
- Worksheets for grammar exercises
- Audio recordings for listening activities

TECHNOLOGY NEEDED:

- Projector or screen for displaying visuals
- Computer or tablet for accessing digital resources

Laying the Foundation: 2 weeks

T - Think Back (Review)

Activity: Begin by reviewing what was taught and learned in the last lesson (if applicable) and explain the connection to the current lesson. Remind students how to incorporate concepts from the last lesson into their daily lives. Use a brief warm-up activity to engage students and assess their current understanding of the basic communication terms.

Time: 5-10 minutes

E – Entry (Introduction/Beginning)

Activity: Introduce the new vocabulary words essential for basic communication using visual aids such as flashcards, images, or charts. Explain the meanings of the words, provide clear definitions, model correct pronunciation of each word, and use each word and have students read the words in sentence form found at the beginning of the lesson.

- **Time:** 15 minutes

A - Application (Teaching/Presentation/Delivery)

Activity: Present new grammar concepts clearly and explicitly. Use direct instruction to introduce verbs to be, pronouns, contractions, and articles. Provide examples and demonstrate their usage in sentences. Also refer to the activity section on the previous pages.

Time: 20 minutes

C - Collaborative Practice (Student Practice)

Activity: Facilitate guided practice by having students work in pairs or small groups to complete structured activities using sentence frames or prompts. Assign pages from the lesson book for students to work on. Review the answers with students while re-teaching the rules for correct usage.

Walk around the classroom to offer support and feedback.

Time: 25 minutes

H - Highlight (Wrap-up/Closing)

- **Activity:** Summarize the key points of the lesson, highlighting the new vocabulary and grammar rules learned. Encourage students to share what they found challenging or interesting.
- **Objective:** Reinforce the lesson's content and ensure students understand the material.
- **Time:** 10 minutes

E - Evaluate (Assessment/Evaluation)

- **Activity:** Conduct an informal assessment by asking students to complete a worksheet that tests their understanding of the vocabulary and grammar concepts introduced in the lesson. Alternatively, have students participate in a dialogue or role-play activity.

  At the end of the lesson, which may last one or two weeks, have students complete the assessment at the end of the lesson.

R - Reflect (Final Review)

- **Activity:** End the lesson with a reflective activity where students can share their thoughts on what they learned, how they can use it in real-life situations, and any areas where they need further clarification.
- **Objective:** Encourage self-assessment and identify areas for future improvement.
- **Time:** 5-10 minutes

Basic Communication

1

Good morning	Good afternoon	Good evening	Good night
first name	last name	marital status	married
single	divorced	widowed	engaged
age	native country	height	weight
state	live	middle initial	birthday

Student A:

Good morning. My name is John.

Nice to meet you, Anita.

Have a nice day.

Student B:

Good morning, John. My name is Anita.

Nice to meet you too, John.

You have a nice day too.

Pronouns and verbs-to-be go together

Subject Pronouns	Possessive Pronouns	Predicate Pronouns
I	**my**	me
You	**your**	yours
We	**our**	ours
They	**their**	theirs
He	**his**	him
She	**her**	hers
It	**its**	

Verbs to be:
am
is
are
was
were
be

Subject Pronouns	Verb-to-be	Predicate
1. I	am	happy today.
2. You	are	very intelligent.
3. We	are	English students.
4. They	are	my friends.
5. He	is	my brother.
6. She	is	a nice person.
7. It	was	raining yesterday.
8. She	was	sick last week.
9. He	was	working yesterday.

Directions: Complete each sentence with the correct verb-to-be.

Verbs-to-be

Present			Past		future
am	are	is	was	were	be

1. I _____am / was_____ going home at 3:00p.m today.

2. My teacher _____was_____ absent yesterday.

3. The girls _____were_____ playing outside yesterday.

4. Tomorrow, we will _____be_____ traveling.

5. My house _____is_____ being painted now.

6. My mother _____was_____ cooking for two hours yesterday.

7. Your cousin _____is/was_____ very handsome.

8. My shoes _____are/were_____ too small for me.

9. We _____were_____ eating dinner at a restaurant last night.

10. The table _____is/was_____ broken.

11. You _____were_____ very pretty yesterday.

12. We _____are_____ in class now.

13. I _____was_____ sick yesterday.

14. Carla _____is/was_____ my favorite cousin.

15. Next month, I will _____be_____ working 45 hours a week.

STUDY

 **She** (A woman or girl is a "*she*")

 **He** (A boy or man is a "*he*".)

 **She** (A woman or girl is a "**she**".)

 **He** (A boy or man is a "*he*".)

 **They** (More than one person are called "**they**").

 **They** (More than one person are called "**they**".)

 **It** (An "*it*" is something that you can touch and feel.)

 **It** (An "*it*" is something that you can touch and feel.)

Directions: Complete each sentence with the correct pronoun.

He, His, Her, She

1. _____Her_____ name is Brenda Cuevas. _____She_____ is from Venezuela.

2. _____His_____ name is Mario Perez. _____He_____ is from El Salvador.

3. _____Her_____ name is Amy Hernandez. _____She_____ is from Peru.

4. _____His_____ name is Alexander Gutierrez. _____He_____ is from Colombia.

5. What is Amy's last name? _Her last name is Hernandez._

6. What is Brenda's last name? _Brenda's last name is Cuevas._

7. Who is from Colombia? _Alexander is from Colombia._

8. Where is Mario from? _Mario is from El Salvador._

9. Who is from Peru? _Amy is from Peru._

10. Who is from Venezuela? _Brenda is from Venezuela._

Directions. Complete each sentence with the correct **verb-to-be**.

am	is	are	was	were	be

1. Lisa _____is_____ my best friend.
2. The girls _____were_____ singing in music class yesterday.
3. I _____am_____ going to the store today at 3:00p.m.
4. We _____are_____ cold now.
5. Mario _____was_____ late to school yesterday.
6. I _____am_____ learning a lot in my English class.
7. Jose _____is_____ not my brother. He is my cousin.
8. Diana _____is_____ not happy about her new school.
9. The ladies _____were_____ beautiful last night.
10. My dog _____was_____ barking a lot yesterday.

Directions. Use the correct **pronoun** to begin each sentence below.

11. _I, He, She_ was very tired last night.
12. _We, They_ are going to Orlando tomorrow.
13. _____I_____ am going to lunch at 12:00p.m.
14. _____She_____ is wearing a beautiful dress today.
15. _They, We_ are sitting together right now.
16. _You, They_ look very happy today.
17. _She, He_ is taking a test tomorrow.
18. _____I_____ am going to California on Friday.
19. _We, They,_ are having a party on Saturday.
20. _____I_____ am making my mother a cake for her birthday.

Directions: Read the story below and practice the questions and answers.

Hello. My name is Ashley Fuentes. I am 24 years old, and I am from Colombia. I came to the United States three years ago. Now, I live in California. I am a cashier at Family Dollar. In Colombia, I was a secretary in a law office. I am very happy in the United States.

QUESTION	ANSWER
1. What is her name? __a__	a. Her name is Ashley.
2. Where is she from? __b__	b. She is from Colombia.
3. How old is she? __c__	c. She is 24 years old.
4. Where does she live now? __d__	d. She lives in California now.
5. Where does she Work? __e__	e. Ashley works at Family Dollar.
6. What is her last name? __f__	f. Her last name is Fuentes.

Directions: Read the story below and practice answering the questions.

Good morning. My name is Juan-Carlos Hernandez. I am 28 years old and I am from Venezuela. I came to the United States two years ago. Now, I live in Houston, Texas. I am a construction worker at Adams Construction Company. In Venezuela, I was an engineer. I am very happy in the United States.

QUESTION	ANSWER
1. What is his name?	His name is Juan-Carlos
2. Where is he from?	He is from Venezuela. / Juan-Carlos is from Venezuela.
3. How old is Juan-Carlos?	He is 28 years old. / Juan-Carlos is 28 years old.
4. Where does Juan-Carlos live now?	He lives in Houston, Texas now. / Juan-Carlos lives in Houston, Texas now.
5. Where does Juan-Carlos work?	He works at Adams Construction Company. / Juan-Carlos works at Adams Construction Company.
6. What is Juan-Carlos' last name?	His last name is Hernandez. / Juan-Carlos' last name is Hernandez.

YOUR INFORMATION

7. What is your first name?   My first name is _______________________.

8. What is your last name?   My last name is _______________________.

9. Where are you from?   I am from _______________________.

10. Where do you live now?   I live in _______________________ now.

PRONOUNS

1. This is **_Mr. Jackson_**. _____His_____ phone number is 555-1234.

2. **_Dianna and Carlos_** are married. _____Their_____ address is 354 Burns Drive.

3. **_Maria_** is my friend. _____She_____ is a nice person.

4. **_Lisa and I_** are going to the mall. _____We_____ will buy shoes today.

5. **_You_** have a nice car. _____My_____ car looks like my brother's car.

6. **_I_** am so hungry. _____My_____ sandwich is in the refrigerator.

7. My **brothers** are very tall. _____They_____ are also very intelligent.

8. My **parents** are traveling now. _____They_____ are going to Italy.

| Their |
| My |
| His |
| He |
| Her |
| She |
| Your |
| You |
| We |
| They |

9. What's his first name? __b____
10. What's his last name? __f____
11. Where is he from? __h____
12. What's your first name? __i____
13. What's your last name? __e____
14. Where were you born? __a____
15. What's her first name? __c____
16. What's her last name? __g____
17. Where is she from? __d____

a. I was born in Cuba.
b. His first name is Javier.
c. Her first name is Stephanie.
d. She is from China.
e. My last name is Montes.
f. His last name is Rodriquez.
g. Her last name is Cuevas.
h. He is from Russia.
i. My first name is Juan.

Directions: Complete each sentence with **He**, **His**, **Her** or **She**

_____His_____ name is Carlos.

_____He_____ is from Colombia.

_____Her_____ name is Maria.

_____She_____ is from Venezuela.

PRONOUNS

SUBJECT PRONOUNS	POSSESIVE PRONOUNS
I	My
You	Your
We	Our
They	Their
He	His
She	Her
It	Its

Directions: Complete each sentence with the correct **possessive pronoun**.

1. My **_mother_** has a new car. **Her** car is a Toyota.

2. My **_brother_** is upset. **His** cat is sick.

3. **_She_** has a nice house. **Her** house has three bedrooms.

4. **_I_** need a new notebook. **My** notebook is no good.

5. **_We_** are having a party today. **Our** party is at 12:00p.m.

6. **My** car needs new tires. **Its or My** tires are old.

7. **_You_** have beautiful hair. **Your** hair is very long too.

8. **_Carlos_** walks to school now. **His** car is not working.

9. Nidia's **_brother_** works at a car dealership. **His** job is close to his house.

10. **_I_** want a pair of new red shoes. **My** red shoes are old.

Directions: Complete each sentence with the correct **subject pronoun**.

11. **I** am a student at the community school.

12. **He or She** is the new student in class.

13. **We, They, You** are going to the gym after class.

14. **I, He, She** was sick yesterday.

15. **We, They, You** were in Tampa last Tuesday.

16. **I** am going home early. My head hurts.

17. **All pronouns** will be in Orlando tomorrow.

Using Subject Pronouns
Directions: Complete each sentence with the correct pronoun

I	we	us	him	mine	her
she	you	he	me	his	they
he	their	our	your	my	she

1. Hello. **My** name is **student's name.**   **I** am from student's country.

2. **My classmate** is Jennifer. **She** is a very nice person.

3. **Jennifer and I** both have two sisters. **We** love our sisters very much.

4. **Jose** is three years old. **He** is very active.

5. **Leidy** is seven years old. **She** is in the second grade.

6. **Jose and Leidy** like to play. **They** play at the park after school.

7. I am proud of **my family**. **They** are very special to me.

8. My **mother** loves my puppies. **She** likes taking care of them.

9. Both my **children** like the park. The park is **their** favorite place.

10. I love my **family**. **They** make me happy.

Directions: Write all the pronouns that go with the subject pronouns:

11. I	me	my	mine
12. She	her	hers	
13. He	him	his	
14. We	us	our	ours
15. They	them	their	theirs
16. You	your	yours	

REVIEW AND PRACTICE:
is, are, am, was, were

Directions: Complete each sentence with the correct verb to be.

1. She ____is____ my sister's friend.
2. My cousins ____are____ twins.
3. Yesterday, I ____was____ very tired.
4. We ____are____ classmates in the same class.
5. They ____are____ my friends.
6. Tia ____is / was____ my best friend.
7. Last night, my sisters ____were____ dancing at Diana's party.
8. My mother ____was____ in California last month.
9. He ____is / was____ 17 years old.
10. Brenda, Diana, and Jose ____are____ going to the movies on Saturday.
11. You ____are____ going to the store?
12. Marcos and Gloria ____are____ cashiers at the supermarket.
13. My cousins ____were____ taking an English class last year.
14. I ____am____ going to school now.
15. My sister ____is / was____ very intelligent.

USING ARTICLES

Directions: Complete each sentence with an article.

a   an   the

16. I want __a__ new house.
17. __The__ teacher was tardy today.
18. I would like to eat __an__ orange.
19. I live in __an__ apartment.
20. My sister is __a__ nurse.
21. I am going to __the__ doctor at 3:00p.m. today.
22. My mother is __an__ excellent cook!
23. Your jacket is in __the__ classroom.

BIANCA'S FIRST DAY IN ENGLISH CLASS

| interesting | introduced | participated | classmates | dialogues |

My name is Bianca. Today is Monday and I started my first day in my new English class at Collins Community School. It was very **interesting** and I liked it. People from many different countries are in my class. My classmates are from Colombia, Cuba, Argentina, Haiti, Puerto Rico, Mexico, Dominican Republic, India and many other places. A few are from Venezuela, like me. The teacher does not speak Spanish. She is from the United States, and she only speaks English, but the students understand her because she speaks slowly. On the first day of class, we had to speak English. We **introduced** ourselves and said what countries we were from. I was nervous, but when I saw that everyone **participated**, it helped me. We also had to learn new vocabulary words in English. The teacher taught us about pronouns and verbs-to-be. We worked out of a grammar book and we also went to the board to write down some answers. At 10:00a.m., we had a morning break and then we went to lunch at noon. After we returned from lunch, we read short stories called **dialogues**. The teacher is very nice, but she is a little **strict**. She doesn't like it when the students are talking when she is talking. I think I am going to learn a lot in this English class.

Directions: Read the statements below. Put a "**T**" if the statement is **true**. Put an "**F**" if it is **false**.

1. The teacher is telling the story. __F__
2. The first break was at 12:00p.m. __F__
3. The teacher speaks Spanish very well. __F__
4. On the first day, students learned new vocabulary words. __T__
5. The students practiced speaking on the very first day of class. __T__
6. Bianca started her new English class on Wednesday. __F__
7. The students are from different countries. __T__
8. The teacher is also from Venezuela. __F__
9. Before lunch, the students read short stories called dialogues. __F__
10. The teacher is nice, but a little strict. __T__
11. Bianca attends college at Collins Community School. __F__
12. The students went to lunch at 12:00p.m. __T__.
13. The students worked out of a math book on the first day of class. __F__.

BASIC COMMUNICATION

last name	height	signature	night	weight
social security	morning	city	native country	phone number

Directions: Complete each sentence with a vocabulary word from the boxes above.

1. My _____last name_____ is Rodriguez.

2. I live in the _____city_____ of Miami.

3. My _____native country_____ is Peru.

4. Your _____social security_____ number has nine digits.

5. The office needed my _____signature_____ on the paper.

6. This _____morning_____ when I woke up, I heard the birds chirping.

7. We had dinner at a nice restaurant last_____night_____.

8. A _____phone number_____ has seven digits plus a three-digit area code.

9. My _____height_____ is five feet, five inches tall.

10. My _____weight_____ is 145lbs.

Directions: Answer each question in a complete sentence.

11. What is your phone number? My phone number is _____________.

____

12. What city do you live in? I live in _____________.

____

13. What is your complete name? My complete name is _____________.
(first and last name)

____

14. What is your native country? My native country is _____________.

____

AM, IS & ARE

Directions: Circle the correct answer under each question below.

1. **What is your name?**
   a. Her name is Rosa. | b. My name is Rosa. | c. His name is Ricardo.

2. **How old is Lisa?**
   a. Lisa was 23 years old.   b. Lisa has 23 years old. | c. Lisa is 23 years old. |

3. **Are you single, married or divorced?**
   a. I have married. | b. I am married. | c. I are married.

4. **Where are Diana and Ana from?**
   a. They is from Cuba.   b. They am from Cuba.   c. They are from Cuba.

5. **What is your marital status?**
   | a. I am single. | b. I have single.   c. I was single.

6. **How old are you?**
   a. I have 15 years old. | b. I am 15 years old. | c. I was 15 years old.

7. **Where do you live?**
   | a. I live in Miami. | b. I am live in Miami.   c. I lives in Miami.

8. **Where do Pedro and Brenda live?**
   a. They lives in New York. | b. They live in New York. | c. They are live in New York.

9. **How old is your cousin?**
   | a. He is 12 years old. | b. You is 12 years old.   c. She are 12 years old.

10. **Where are the students from?**
   a. The students is from Peru. | b. The students are from Peru. | c. The student is from Cuba.

11. **Where does the teacher live?**
   a. The teacher live in New York. | b. The teacher lives in New York. |
   c. The teacher is live in New York.

12. **How old is your sister?**
   | a. She is 12 years old. | b. She are 12 years old.   c. They are 12 years old.

13. **What color is your hair?**
   a. My color hair black. | b. My hair is black. | c. She color is black.

	Pronoun		Verb-to-be	Contraction
1.	I am	**+**	am =	I'm
2.	You are	**+**	are =	you're
3.	We were	**+**	are =	we're
4.	They	**+**	are =	they're
5.	He	**+**	is =	he's
6.	She	**+**	is =	she's
7.	It	**+**	Is =	it's

STUDY

	PRONOUN + VERB-TO-BE:	**SAME SENTENCE WITH A CONTRACTION:**
1.	**I am** very tired today.	**I'm** very tired today.
2.	**You are** very nice.	**You're** very nice.
3.	**We are** going to the store.	**We're** going to the store.
4.	**They are** playing now.	**They're** playing now.
5.	**She is** my sister.	**She's** my sister.
6.	**He is** washing the car.	**He's** washing the car.
7.	**It is** raining now.	**It's** raining now.

Directions: Rewrite each sentence using a contraction.

1. **We are** reading now. _We're reading now._

2. **You are** very pretty today. _You're very pretty today._

3. **She is** a doctor. _She's a doctor._

4. **It is** going to rain. _It's going to rain._

5. **I am** studying my English now. _I'm studying my English now._

6. **He is** my favorite cousin. _He's my favorite cousin._

7. **They are** going to lunch at 12:00p.m. _They're going back to lunch at 12:00p.m._

Directions: Rewrite each sentence with a contraction from the box. Remember to include your apostrophes.

CONTRACTIONS

I'm	You're	They're	Who's
She's	He's	We're	It's

1. **He is** a student. _He's a student._

2. **She is** from Japan. _She's from Japan._

3. **I am** happy today. _I'm happy today._

4. **They are** my cousins. _They're my cousins._

5. **You are** a nice person. _You're a nice person._

6. **We are** going to a restaurant today. _We're going to a restaurant._

7. **It is** cold outside. _It's cold outside._

8. **Who is** the tall man? _Who's the tall man?_

9. **I am** from Mexico. _I'm from Mexico._

10. **He is** at school. _He's at school._

Directions: Write your own sentences using the following contractions:

11. I'm: _Teacher reviews students' sentences._

12. She's: _______________________________

13. He's: _______________________________

14. You're: _______________________________

15. We're _______________________________

Question Words

Who	What	When	Where	Why	How

1. **What** _______ is your last name?

2. **Where** _______ are you from?

3. **When** _______ is your birthday?

4. **How/Where** _______ are you?

5. Who/Where/How _______ is your teacher?

6. **Why** _______ are you so happy today?

7. **How** _______ much is the microwave?

8. **Who/Where** _______ is the new student?

9. **What** _______ time is your party?

10. **When** _______ is Julio's party?

11. Who/Where/How _______ is your beautiful mother?

Who: The answer is a person or people.	**What**: The answer could be many different things.	**When:** The answer is a timeframe. (date, time, day or year)
Where: The answer is a location.	**Why**: The answer is an explanation usually beginning with "because."	**How:** The answer can be various things.

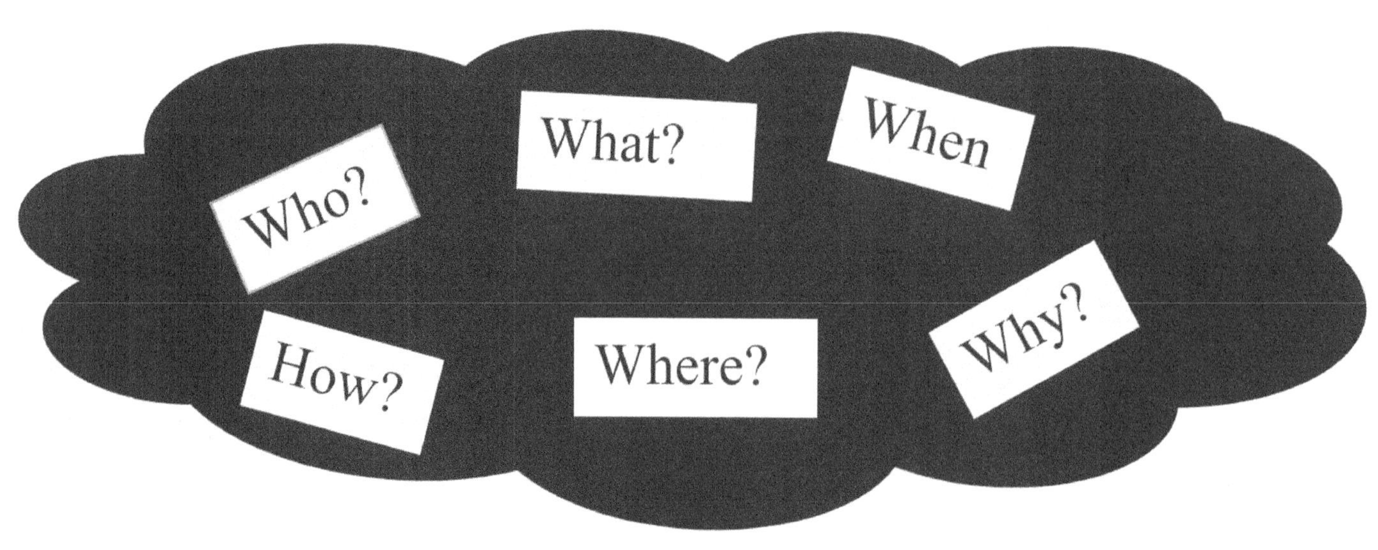

Who's	What's	When's	Where's	Why's	How's

1. **Who's** coming over for dinner?

2. **When's** lunch?

3. **Where's** my bag?

4. **Where's** the store located?

5. **Who's** ready to go?

6. **What's** happening across the street?

7. **Why's** the baby crying?

8. **What's**, **How's** your grandmother doing?

9. **When's**, **How's** breakfast?

10. **How's** the weather in Colombia?

11. **What's** your address?

12. **Where's** my cellphone?

> **Study**
> Contractions with "W" words
>
> Who + is = who's
> What + is = what's
> When + is = when's
> Where + is = where's
> Why + is = why's
> How + is = how's

Directions: Answer the following questions in complete sentences.

13. How's the new teacher? *Example:* The new teacher is very good. ______________________

14. When's your birthday? *Example:* My birthday is on November 3, 2024 ______________________

15. What's your last name? *Example:* My last name is Chu. ______________________

1. Who's your teacher? *Example:* My teacher is Mrs. Sylvia. ______________________

2. Who's your mother? *Example:* Victoria is my mother. ______________________

3. What's your favorite color? *Example:* My favorite color is red. ______________________

<h1 align="center">ARTICLES</h1>
a, an, the

Articles come before nouns. In the English language, there are three articles: **a**, **an** and **the**. "A" is sometimes used for an unfamiliar noun. I need "a" new car. "The" is used for a familiar noun: "The" teacher is absent today. "An" is used before a noun that starts with a vowel (a, e, i, o, u). I need "an" umbrella because it is raining outside.

Vowels: a e i o u

1. My mother is **a** great cook.

2. I have **a** doctor's appointment today.

3. The computer is on **the** desk.

4. You have **a** nice car.

5. My brother is **an** engineer.

6. My brother lives in **an** apartment.

7. I would like **an** orange.

8. We are going to **the** supermarket today.

9. My teacher is **a** nice lady.

10. Lisa needs **a** new car.

11. Ana is having **a** party.

12. We are going to **the** gym later.

A computer

An apple

A doctor

An airplane

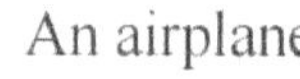

SPEAKING WITH ARTICLES
a, an, the

Directions: Complete each sentence using the correct article for each sentence.

1. I would like __a__ cup of coffee please.

2. Maria has __a__ new car.

3. How much is __the__ shirt?

4. My mother is __an__ assistant at a school.

5. I would like __a__ banana and an orange.

6. Are you going to __the__ supermarket today?

7. Jose is going to __the__ doctor tomorrow.

8. My aunt is __an__ actress.

9. Please turn on __the__ light.

10. I live in __an__ apartment, but my sister lives in __a__ condo.

REVIEW AND PRACTICE

11. I __am__ studying now. (VTB)

12. Lisa needs __a__ new jacket. (article)

13. Angie is my cousin. __She__ is a beautiful person. (subject pronoun)

14. Yesterday, I __was__ in Tampa. (VTB)

15. __My__ sandwich is in my lunchbox. (possessive pronoun)

16. I __am__ going to the supermarket after class. (VTB)

17. Yesterday, we __were__ in Tampa. (VTB)

Directions: Find a partner and ask them the four questions on the left. When you finish, switch and let your partner ask you the questions. When it is time, stand up and read the information on the right to your classmates.

CONVERSATION PRACTICE

What is your first name? _________________	Good morning classmates. My name is__________.
What is your last name?	My last name is ______________. I am from
_____________________	______________, but I live in ___________
	now. This is my partner. His/Her name is
What country are you from?	____________. His/Her last name
_________________	is____________.
	He/she is from the country of ______________,
Where do you live now?	but he/she lives in ______________ now. We are
_____________________	very happy to be here.

Directions: Go home and practice your introduction and be prepared to recite it in class without reading.

INTRODUCTION PRACTICE

Hello classmates,

My name is ______________. My last name is ______________. I am from the country of

______________, but I live in ______________ now. I like to ______________ and

______________. My favorite color is ______________, my favorite food is

______________, and my favorite person is ____________. I have a _________ family. I

have _________brother(s) and ________ sister(s). My first language is ___________, but I

am learning how to speak English now. I am very excited about learning the English

language, and I am happy to be here.

| motivates | practice | reading | writing | speaking |

BIANCA'S FIFTH WEEK IN ENGLISH CLASS

I have been taking an English class for five weeks now and I have learned so much. I have learned about verbs to be, pronouns, regular nouns, proper nouns, articles, verbs and prepositions. In class, we read, write and speak. We also take classroom tests on Fridays. I really like it when we practice speaking because the more I practice my speaking English, the better I become. My reading is better too. I didn't know that I was a good reader, but my teacher tells me that I am. She says that my speaking is clear and I speak naturally. That makes me feel good and motivates me to keep studying. I will be ready to take a CASAS Test soon. This test will determine if I am ready to move to the next level. I must have at least 90 hours before I can test. I think I am ready because I have learned so much. Right now, I am a Level 2. Maybe I can move to a level 3. I am very serious about learning English and I am in the right school with the right teacher! I also have some new friends in my class. I am very happy.

1. What level is Bianca at right now? Bianca /She is a level two now.

2. Name three things that Bianca has learned about in her English class.
Students can choose three things from verbs to be, pronouns, regular nouns, proper nouns, articles, verbs and prepositions.

3. How long has Bianca been taking an English class now? Bianca /She has been taking an English class for five weeks now.

4. Is Bianca serious about learning English? Yes, she is.

5. Who told Bianca that she was a good reader? Bianca's / Her teacher told her that she was a good reader.

6. What test will determine if Bianca is ready to go to the next level? The CASAS test will determine if Bianca goes to the next level.

Directions: Read the questions and answers below. Then, practice your own answers to the same questions.

1. What is your name?   My name is Carmen.

2. Where are you from?   I am from Argentina.

3. Who is your teacher?   My teacher is Mrs. Peters.

4. When did you come to the United States?   I came to the United States in July, 2024.

5. Where is the mall located?   It is located on Riverside Blvd.

6. What is your last name?   My last name is Rodriguez.

7. When is your appointment?   My appointment is tomorrow at 2:30p.m.

8. What is your favorite color?   My favorite color is blue.

9. When is your birthday?   My birthday is August 14th.

10. Where is your notebook?   It is on the table.

11. Why did you cut your hair?   ...because it was damaged.

12. Who is the little baby?   He is my nephew.

13. What time is your appointment?   My appointment is at 3:30p.m.

14. How much was your jacket?   It was $35.00.

15. What time is your lunch break?   It is at 12:00p.m.

16. What is your gender?   I am female.

17. What time did you wake up this morning?   I woke up at 7:00a.m this morning.

18. What time will you go to bed tonight?   I will go to bed at 10:00p.m. tonight.

19. Why are you tardy today?   Because I had an appointment this morning.

20. What do you want for dinner?   I want chicken and rice for dinner.

Working with Partners

Directions: Practice the answers to the questions below. Then, with a partner, ask each other the first five questions, then switch. Do not look at your answers while you are being asked the questions. Then move to the next five questions.

1. What is your name? _______ My name is __________. _______

2. Where are you from? _______ I am from __________. _______

3. Who is your teacher? _______ My teacher is __________. (Ms. Mia) _______

4. When did you come to the United States? _______ I came to the United States in__ / on__ / 3 years ago. _______

5. Where is the mall located? _______ The mall is located on __ / in __________. _______

6. What is your last name? _______ My last name is __________. _______

7. When is your appointment? _______ My appointment is at ___(3:00p.m) / on Tuesday / next month. _______

8. What is your favorite color? _______ My favorite color is ___. / ___ is my favorite color. _______

9. When is your birthday? _______ My birthday is on __________. (May 20th) _______

10. Where is your notebook? _______ My notebook is on / under / next to the table. _______

11. Why did you cut your hair? _______ I cut my hair ___. (yesterday, last week / on Tuesday.) _______

12. Who is the little baby? _______ He/ She is my ___. (brother/sister/cousin,etc.) _______

13. What time is your appointment? _______ My appointment is at __________. (2:00p.m) _______

14. How much was your jacket? _______ My jacket was __________. ($50.00) _______

15. What time is your lunch break? _______ My lunch break is at __________. (12:00p.m.) _______

16. What is your gender? _______ I am __________. (male/female) _______

17. What time did you wake up this morning? _______ I woke up at __________. (6:00a.m) _______

18. What time will you go to bed tonight? _______ I will go to bed at __________. (9:30p.m.) _______

19. Why are you tardy today? _______ Because __________. (I had an appointment) _______

20. What do you want for dinner? _______ I want __________ for dinner. (pasta) _______

Directions: Write the letter of the correct answer next to each question.

1. What is your favorite color? __f__
2. How old are you? __b__
3. Do you go to school? __m__
4. What country do you live in? __h__
5. Do you have a sister? __e__
6. What is your teacher's name? __n__
7. Are you happy today? __c__
8. What is your gender? __j__
9. What is your native country? __a__
10. When is your birthday? __o__
11. What is your favorite food? __f__
12. What is your last name? __k__
13. When is your appointment? __d__
14. How much is the jacket? __i__

a) My native country is Mexico.
b) I am 16 years old.
c) Yes, I am very happy today.
d) My appointment is at 10:30a.m.
e) No. I do not have a sister.
f) My favorite color is blue.
g) My favorite food is pasta.
h) I live in the United States now.
i) It is $30.00.
j) I am male/female.
k) My last name is Gonzalez.
l) No, I do not have a middle initial.
m) Yes, I go to school.
n) My teacher's name is Mrs. Lopez.
o) My birthday is May 20th.

Directions: Answer each question in a complete sentence.

15. What are your favorite colors? _____ My favorite colors are __________. / __ and __ are my favorite colors. _____

16. What is your last name? _____ My last name is __________. / __________ is my last name. _____

17. What do you like to do? _____ I like to __________ and __________. _____

18. What city do you live in? _____ I live in __________. _____

19. What is your native country? _____ My native country is __________. _____

20. What do you like to eat? _____ I like to eat __________ and __________. _____

21. Where do you like to go? _____ I like to go to __________. _____

22. Who is your best friend? _____ My best friend is __________. / __________ is my best friend. _____

23. When is your doctor's appointment? My doctor's appointment is __________. _____

24. When is your birthday? My birthday is __________.

25. What are you learning about in English class? I am learning about __________ in my English class.

MERCY

This is Mercy. She lives in Tampa, Florida, but she is from Venezuela. She is very happy in the United States because she has many opportunities that she did not have before. She is also learning English at a community school in her neighborhood. She has made many friends in her English class, and they hang out sometimes on the weekends. Mercy is more confident about English now because she understands people and she can also speak and ask questions in English. In her English class, she reads, writes, speaks, and practices vocabulary words every day. She is also happy because her cousin Sandra is here in the United States now. Sandra came last week Thursday. Mercy has not seen Sandra for almost two years. Sandra is living with her sister Brenda Cuevas, Brenda's husband, and her two children in Tampa, Florida. Sandra will be here for three months, then she will return to Venezuela. This weekend, Mercy and Sandra will go to the mall, the movies and then they will go to a birthday party for one of Mercy's classmates from English class. Mercy wants to also take Sandra to a new Italian restaurant. Mercy thinks that Sandra should take an English class so she can also learn English. Sandra understands a little English, but not a lot. Mercy is so excited that Sandra is here.

TRUE OR FALSE

1. __T__ Mercy thinks that Sandra should take an English class.

2. __F__ Sandra wants to take Mercy to a new Italian Restaurant.

3. __F__ Mercy does not like living in the United States.

4. __F__ Sandra is happy because Mercy will be here for three months.

5. __T__ Mercy goes to a community school in her area to learn Spanish.

6. __F__ Mercy has not seen Sandra in about three years.

7. __T__ Mercy has friends in her English class.

8. __T__ Mercy and Sandra will go to the mall this weekend.

9. __F__ Sandra does not understand a lot of English.

10. __F__ Mercy will return to Argentina in three months.

11. What is Sandra's sister's name? Sandra's sister is Brenda. / Sandra's sister's name is Brenda.

12. Who is having a birthday party? One of Mercy's classmates is having a birthday party.

S T U D Y

REGULAR NOUNS:

A "**regular noun**" is a person, place, thing or animal. Cities, states and countries are also nouns.

	Person	Place	Thing
1.	teacher	supermarket	book
2.	girl	city	computer
3.	cashier	hospital	pencil
4.	doctor	mall	hat
5.	mother	pharmacy	dress
6.	cousin	park	table
7.	nurse	state	bed
8.	security guard	museum	car
9.	singer	movie theater	chair
10.	father	church	house
11.	secretary	school	shirt
12.	engineer	doctor's office	notebook
13.	boy	university	cell phone
14.	boy scout	gas station	desk
15.	actor	spa	bracelet

PROPER NOUNS:

A **"proper noun"** is the name of a person, place, thing or animal. Proper nouns begin with capital letters.

	REGULAR NOUN	PROPER NOUN
1.	school	Cornerstone Elementary
2.	teacher	Mrs. Merritt
3.	gas station	Chevron
4.	mall	Aventura Mall
5.	hospital	Jackson Memorial Hospital
6.	doctor	Dr. Lopez
7.	month	December
8.	sneakers	Nike
9.	state	Florida
10.	country	Venezuela

Directions: Complete each sentence below with a proper noun or regular noun.

1. I need a new ___computer / house/ car___. (regular noun)

2. We will travel to ___Orlando / Miami___ on Sunday. (proper noun)

3. I am going to the ___supermarket/ mall___ later today. (regular noun)

4. I need to go to ___Aventura Mall / Publix___ on Friday. (proper noun)

5. My ___teacher/ best friend___ is a very nice person. (regular noun)

6. ___Carmen / Julio___ is my best friend. (proper noun)

7. My ___car / jacket___ needs to be washed. (regular noun)

8. My brother lives in ___Tampa / Colombia___. (proper noun)

9. My ___cell phone / notebook___ is on the table. (regular noun)

10. My cousin is going to ___Cuba / California___ next month. (proper noun)

11. I have a black ___car / jacket / cell phone___. (regular noun)

12. ___Sedanos___ is my favorite supermarket. (proper noun)

13. The ___doctor / house/ city___ is very nice. (regular noun)

14. Diana has a beautiful new ___baby / dress / niece___. (regular noun)

15. On ___Saturday / Friday___, I am going to Orlando. (proper noun)

Directions: Write a proper noun next to each word.

REGULAR NOUNS	PROPER NOUN
16. car	Toyota / Honda
17. person	Brenda / Carlos
18. state	Georgia / New York
19. mall	Pembroke Lakes Mall
20. store	Walmart / Publix
21. city	Chicago, Philadelphia
22. country	Argentina / Italy / United States
23. street	Hollywood

Italy	Bogota	Aventura Mall	Hernandez	Fridays
My daughter	Saturdays	May	Las Vegas	Maria
Sheridan Street	Hollywood	Cuba	Diana	December
weekends	February	an apartment	Macys	a house

Directions: Complete each sentence with a **proper noun** from the box above.

1. I am from the country of _Italy / Cuba_.

2. _Decemeber/ May /February_ is my favorite month of the year.

3. My school is on _Sheridan Street_.

4. _Diana_ is my favorite person.

5. I like to go to the beach on _Fridays_.

6. My birthday is in the month of _February / May_.

7. I live in _Bogota / Cuba / Italy_ now.

8. My last name is _Hernandez_.

9. I would like to travel to the country of _Cuba / Italy_ one day.

10. _Aventura Mall_ is my favorite mall.

Directions: Complete each sentence with a **regular noun** from the box above.

Pembroke Lakes Mall	post office	teacher	restaurant	Michael Kors Purse
cell phone	suit	jacket	mall	table
Toyota	Walmart	book	Dolphin Mall	Dr. Rodriquez
bracelet	classmate	school	shoe store	hair

11. I need to buy some sneakers at the _shoe store_.

12. My _suit / jacket_ is in the cleaners.

13. Juan's _bracelet / suit / hair, etc._ is very nice!

14. The _school / teacher / etc._ is in Atlanta.

15. My _teacher_ is a nice person.

16. Your _bracelet, suit, book, etc._ is on the counter.

17. I like to shop at the _mall_.

18. Your _bracelet, cell phone, etc._ is very expensive.

19. You left your _cell phone, bracelet, suit_ in my car.

20. I would like to eat at a _restaurant_.

Directions: Practice speaking the information in the boxes below in complete sentences. Then answer the questions that follow.

Reading and Speaking People Information

Andrea **Last name**: Smith **age**: 27 years old **marital status**: single 1 child **lives**: Miami, FL	Brenda **Last name**: Cuevas **age**: 43 years old **marital status**: married 3 children **lives**: Dallas, TX	David **Last name**: Mitchell **age**: 18 years old **marital status**: single no children **lives**: Queens, NY
Eva **Last name**: Goldman **age**: 56 years old **marital status**: married 4 children **lives**: Hollywood, FL	Fernando **Last name**: Hernandez **age**: 23 years old **marital status**: single no children **lives**: Miami Beach, FL	Gisele **Last name**: Johnson **age**: 39 years old **marital status**: married 4 children **lives**: Ft. Lauderdale, FL
Hannah **Last Name**: Merritt **age**: 32 years old **marital status**: divorced 1 child **lives**: Atlanta, GA	Isabel **Last Name**: Green **age**: 26 years old **marital status**: married 1 child **lives**: Raleigh, NC	Jackie **Last name**: Williams **age**: 35 years old **marital status**: engaged 3 children **lives**: San Francisco, CA

Directions: Answer each question in a complete sentence in the lines provided.

1. What is Fernando's last name? _Fernando's last name is Hernandez. / His last name is Hernandez._

2. What is Andrea's marital status? _She is single / Her marital status is single._

3. How old is Gisele? _Gisele is 39 years old._

4. How many people have one child? _Three people have 1 child._

5. Whose last name is Green? _Isabel's last name is Green._

6. Who lives in San Francisco? _Jackie lives in San Francisco._

7. How many children does David have? _David has no children._

8. Who has three children? _Brenda and Jackie have three children._

9. Who is 56 years old? _Eva is 56 years old._

10. How many people are single? _Three people are single._

DIALOGUE: BASIC COMMUNICATION

Directions: With a partner, practice the dialogues below. Remember to speak as though you are in a "natural" conversation.

1.
Person #1: Good morning. How are you?
Person #2: I am fine. How are you?
Person #1: I'm great. Today is my first week in my new English class. I am excited, but I am a little nervous. I have always wanted to learn English.
Person #2: Why are you nervous? There is no need to be nervous.
Person #1: Because I don't know what to expect, but I am excited to learn.
Person #2: I think if you just listen and pay attention to what the teacher says, you will be fine.
Person #1: I hope so. I really want to learn English.

2.
Person #1: Greetings my friend.
Person #2: Greetings to you too. How are you?
Person #1: I am fine. I am going back to my native country. I will be there for two weeks.
Person #2: That sounds great. What is your native country?
Person #1: My native country is _________________. I am _________________.
Person #2: What city were you born in?
Person #1: I was born in _________________.
Person #2: Oh. Okay. I have an aunt and uncle who live there. Well, have a great time.
Person #1: Thank you. I will. I love visiting my family.

3.
Person #1: Hi. My name is _________________. What is your name please?
Person #2: Hello _______________. My name is _________________. It is very nice to meet you.
Person #1: It is very _________________. to meet you too. Where are you from _________________?
Person #2: I am from El Salvador, but I am living in Atlanta now.
Person #1: Oh. Wow. I am from Haiti, but I am living in Atlanta too. I like living in Atlanta.
Person #2: When did you come to the United States?
Person #1: I came to the United States three months ago. I live with my aunt and uncle.
Person #2: Oh okay. I came to the United States in May, 2024. I live with my daughter.
Person #1: Well, it is nice to meet you. Have a nice day.
Person #2: You have a nice day too!

4.
Person #1: I am so proud of myself. I have been exercising every day.
Person #2: That is wonderful. When do you exercise?
Person #1: I exercise Monday through Friday from 4:00p.m-5:00p.m.
Person #2: Wow! How do you feel?
Person #1: I feel very good.
Person #2: That is great. I am proud of you too.

5.
Person #1: Hello there. I need a little information from you. I have a few questions.
Person #2: Okay. No problem. What do you need to know?
Person #1: Yes. What is your first name and your last name?
Person #2: My first name is _________________. My last name is _________________.
Person #1: What country are you from?
Person #2: I am from _________________. That is my native country.
Person #1: Where do you live now?
Person #2: I live in _________________ now.
Person #1: Great. Thank you for that information.

Person #2: You are very welcome.
Person #1: I had a busy week. I am so tired.
Person #2: What did you do this week? Why are you so tired?

6.

Person #1: Well, on Thursday, I had meetings all day. On Friday, I attended a conference.
Person #2: What did you do on Saturday and Sunday?
Person #1: On Saturday, we went to a carnival and on Sunday, we went to church.
Person #2: Yes, it sounds like you were very busy.
Person #1: Yes, I was.

Person #1: I am learning about months of the year and days of the week in my English class.
Person #2: That is interesting. Do you remember the information that you learn?

7.

Person #1: Yes, I do. I have learned that in the United States, New Years Day is celebrated in January, Valentines Day is celebrated in February, Thanksgiving Day is celebrated in November and Christmas is celebrated in December.
Person #2: Okay. They also celebrate Memorial Day and Mother's Day in May, Father's Day in June and Independence Day in July.
Person #1: Yes. You are right. Some of the holidays are federal holidays and some are not.
Person #2: Yes, that's correct. You have learned a lot about the holidays.
Person #1: Yes. I am excited about learning so much.
Person #2: That is wonderful.

8.

Person #1: Good morning. How are you?
Person #2: I am fine. Thank you, and you?
Person #1: I am wonderful. What did you do yesterday?
Person #2: I went to the supermarket and to the cleaners with my mother.
Person #1: Oh. Okay. I went to the beach, and I also relaxed and listed to music yesterday.
Person #2: I also studied my English when I returned to my house.
Person #1: English is important. I like studying my English too.

9.

Person #1: Good morning. My name is _____________. My last name is _____________.
Person #2: Good morning _________________. Where are you from?
Person #1: I am from_______________ but I live in ______________ now.
Person #2: Oh. Okay. Who do you live with?
Person #1: I live with my _______________.
Person #2: What is your first language?
Person #1: My first language is ______________, but I am learning English now.
Person #2: Do you have a big family?
Person #1: Yes, I do / No, I don't. I have _______ brother(s) and ______ sister(s).
Person #1: What do you like to do?
Person #2: I like to _____coughing_________ and ________________.
Person #1: Well, it was nice to meet you.
Person #2: It was nice to meet you too.

WEEKLY ASSESSMENT:
Basic communication

name	last name	also	country
live	child/children	like	language
learn	am	first name	learning

My _____**name**_____ is _____(your first name)_____. My _____**last name**_____ is _____(last name)_____. I am from the _____**country**_____ of _____(your country)_____, but I _____**live**_____ in _____(your city)_____ now. My first _____**language**_____ is _____(your language)_____, but I am _____**learning**_____ English now. I _**am**_ very happy to be here today.

VERBS-TO-BE

am	**is**	**are**	**was**	**were**	**be**

1. Tomorrow, I will _____**be**_____ traveling all day.
2. My parents _____**are**_____ watching TV at home now.
3. Julio _____**is**_____ my favorite cousin.
4. My sisters _____**were**_____ in California last week.
5. Last night, I _____**was**_____ so tired.
6. I _____**am**_____ listening to my teacher now.
7. Yesterday, I _____**was**_____ very sick.
8. My cousin _____**was**_____ working at Walmart last year.

USING PRONOUNS

it	You	mine	theirs	We
Her	She	I	They	him
They	We	yours	Its	He

9. _____**I**_____ am very tired today.
10. _____**We**_____ are going to a party on Saturday night.
11. My mother has a new car. _____**Her**_____ car is very nice.
12. Julia and Dave are very nice people. _____**They**_____ are my neighbors.
13. Alexandra is my sister. _____**She**_____ lives in Colombia.

14.   Jorge is my favorite cousin. _____**He**_____ is in college now.

15.   There are three cars in the parking lot. The red one is _**mine, yours**_.

16.   My children love to eat seafood. _**They**_____ eat seafood on weekends.

ARTICLES: a, an, the
Directions: Answer the question below using the correct article.

17.   Your computer is on _____**the**_____ desk.

18.   I am going to _____**the**_____ doctor at 2:30p.m. today.

19.   Diana lives in _____**a**_____ beautiful house.

20.   I sent you _____**an**_____ email at 12:00 today.

21.   I would like _____**a**_____ cup of coffee please.

22.   Please give this paper to _____**the**_____ teacher.

23.   I would like _____**an**_____ orange please.

24.   My mother is _____**an**_____ excellent cook.

REGULAR AND PROPER NOUNS

Directions: Write the correct regular or proper noun in the sentences below:

25.   Next year, I am moving to _____**Chicago**_____. (proper)

26.   _____**Saturday**_____ is my favorite day of the week. (proper)

27.   I need a new _____**notebook**_____ for school. (regular)

28.   I like your lovely _____**bag**_____. (regular)

29.   _____**Bianca**_____ is my best friend. (proper)

30.   Maria drives a red _____**Toyota**_____. (proper)

Directions: Write the contraction for each of the words below:

31.   who   +   is =   _____**who's**_____

32.   she   +   is =   _____**she's**_____

33.   it   +   is   _____**it's**_____

34.   what   +   is =   _____**what's**_____

Lesson 2: Family

Dear ESL Teacher,

As you prepare to guide your students through Lesson 2 on the Family, you have a structured framework aimed at enhancing their understanding of family-related vocabulary and communication skills in English. Through engaging activities such as vocabulary introduction, sentence practice, grammar drills, and conversation exercises, students will explore the dynamics of family relationships and roles. The instructional procedures outlined, include direct instruction to introduce new concepts, guided practice to support application, and independent practice to reinforce learning. These strategies ensure a comprehensive approach that accommodates diverse learning styles and abilities. Our commitment to differentiation and adaptations equips you with strategies to support English language learners through visual aids and simplified instructions, while providing an assessment at the end of the lesson to meet the needs of all learners. Use this guide as a resource to cultivate a supportive classroom environment where every ESL student can confidently navigate the nuances of family-related language and communication.

OBJECTIVES:

1. Students will identify and use vocabulary related to family relationships and roles.

2. Students will construct and practice sentences using targeted vocabulary and grammar concepts.

3. Students will demonstrate understanding of basic grammar concepts including verbs to be, pronouns, contractions, and articles.

4. Students will engage in conversations using learned vocabulary and grammar related to family topics.

5. Students will comprehend and respond to simple reading passages about family life.

6. Students will participate in dialogues to practice communication skills related to family scenarios.

7. Students will demonstrate their learning through a comprehensive assessment covering vocabulary, grammar, reading comprehension, and dialogue creation.

INSTRUCTIONAL PROCEDURES

Direct Instruction:

- **Objective:** Present new vocabulary and grammar concepts clearly and explicitly.
- **Details:** Begin by introducing vocabulary related to family relationships and roles. Use visual aids such as family trees or photographs to illustrate different family members. Explain the meanings

of vocabulary words using contextual examples and encourage students to repeat and practice pronouncing the words aloud for better retention. Have students read each practice sentence using the vocabulary words for this lesson.

Guided Practice:

- **Objective:** Help students apply new knowledge in a supportive environment.
- **Details:** Facilitate activities where students practice constructing sentences about family using the vocabulary and grammar structures introduced. Provide sentence frames or prompts to guide their practice. Walk around the classroom, offering guidance and feedback as students work in pairs to complete tasks, ensuring active participation and understanding.

Independent Practice:

- **Objective:** Reinforce learning through individual or paired activities.
- **Details:** Assign tasks that require students to independently apply their understanding of family-related vocabulary and grammar. This includes completing activities from the book with exercises on family roles, writing short paragraphs about their own families, or creating presentations about family traditions. Encourage self-assessment by asking students to review their work for accuracy and clarity before sharing it with peers.

Differentiation/Adaptations:

Provide visual aids and simplified instructions for English language learners:

- **Objective:** Support comprehension for students with varying English proficiency levels.
- **Details:** Use visual aids such as family diagrams, simplified family trees, or pictorial representations of family members to aid understanding. Provide bilingual dictionaries or glossaries for students needing additional language support. Adjust the pace of instruction to accommodate slower processing speeds, allowing extra time for practice and comprehension.

Offer additional practice or alternative assessments for students with diverse learning needs:

- **Objective:** Address individual learning needs and preferences.
- **Details:** Offer differentiated assignments such as role-playing family scenarios, creating multimedia presentations about diverse family structures, or conducting interviews with family members. Provide alternative assessment options such as oral presentations or digital projects that demonstrate comprehension of family-related vocabulary and concepts. Use flexible grouping strategies to support social and emotional needs, ensuring all students feel valued and included.

ACTIVITIES:

Vocabulary Introduction:

- **Objective:** Introduce key vocabulary words essential for discussing family relationships.
- **Details:** Use visuals like family photos or illustrations to introduce and explain vocabulary related to family roles and relationships. Provide examples of sentences using each vocabulary word in context to enhance understanding.

Sentence Practice:

- **Objective:** Help students construct meaningful sentences using family-related vocabulary and grammar concepts.
- **Details:** Guide students in forming sentences that describe family members, their relationships, and activities they do together. Begin with simple sentence structures and progress to more complex ones as students gain confidence.

Grammar Drill:

- **Objective:** Reinforce understanding of grammar rules related to verbs to be, pronouns, contractions, and articles in the context of family communication.
- **Details:** Conduct exercises where students practice using these grammar elements correctly in sentences about family life. Provide opportunities for them to identify and correct errors in sentences.

Conversation Practice:

- **Objective:** Develop students' ability to engage in spoken communication using family-related vocabulary and grammar.
- **Details:** Pair students for conversational activities where they discuss family traditions, roles, and experiences. Provide prompts or scenarios that encourage meaningful exchanges about their own families or fictional scenarios.

Reading Comprehension:

- **Objective:** Enhance students' ability to understand written English through reading passages about family topics.
- **Details:** Select age-appropriate reading materials or stories that explore different aspects of family life. After reading, ask comprehension questions that require students to recall details, make predictions, or discuss the main ideas.

Dialogue Creation:

- **Objective:** Encourage students to apply learned vocabulary and grammar by creating dialogues about family situations.

- **Details:** Guide students in pairs to read the dialogues at the end of the lesson that demonstrate natural conversations.

Assessment:

- **Objective:** Evaluate students' comprehension and application of lesson content related to family vocabulary, grammar, and communication skills.
- **Details:** The assessment is found at the end of the lesson.

Materials and Resources:

- It's Time to Learn English book
- Vocabulary cards
- Family photos or illustrations
- Whiteboard and markers
- Textbooks or reading materials about family life
- Worksheets for grammar exercises
- Audio recordings for listening activities

Technology Needed:

- Projector or screen for displaying visuals
- Computer or tablet for accessing digital resources such as online family stories or multimedia presentations

Lesson 2: Family 1 week

T - Think Back (Review)

Activity: Begin the lesson by reviewing key concepts and vocabulary from the previous lesson. Use a brief warm-up activity to engage students and assess their understanding of any family-related terms they might already know.

Time: 5-10 minutes

E – Entry (Introduction/Beginning)

Activity: Introduce new vocabulary words related to family relationships and roles using visual aids such as family trees, photos, or illustrations. Provide clear definitions, pronunciation examples, and use each word in sentences to demonstrate usage.

Time: 15 minutes

A - Application (Teaching/Presentation/Delivery)

- **Activity:** Present new grammar concepts clearly and explicitly. Use direct instruction to introduce verbs to be, pronouns, contractions, and articles. Provide examples and demonstrate their usage in sentences.
- **Time:** 20 minutes

C - Collaborative Practice (Student Practice)

Activity: Facilitate guided practice by having students work in pairs or small groups to complete structured activities using sentence frames or prompts. Walk around the classroom to offer support and feedback. Encourage students to engage in conversations about family traditions, roles, and experiences. Assign activity pages from the book for students to complete independently.

Time: 25 minutes

H - Highlight (Wrap-up/Closing)

Activity: Summarize the key points of the lesson, highlighting the new vocabulary and grammar rules learned. Assign a reading comprehension activity using a passage about family life. Discuss the main ideas and ask comprehension questions.

Objective: Reinforce the lesson's content and ensure students understand the material.

Time: 10 minutes

E - Evaluate (Assessment/Evaluation)

- **Activity:** Administer a comprehensive assessment found at the end of the lesson. Assess students on vocabulary, grammar, reading comprehension, and dialogue creation.
- **Time:** 20 minutes

R - Reflect (Final Review)

- **Activity:** End the lesson with a reflective activity where students can share their thoughts on what they learned, how they can use it in real-life situations, and any areas where they need further clarification. Encourage students to share their thoughts on their progress and areas they want to improve.
- **Time:** 5-10 minutes

Family

2

Vocabulary

FAMILY MEMBERS	FAMILY MEMBERS	VOCABULARY WORDS
1. mother	13. grandmother	height
2. father	14. grandfather	weight
3. sister	15. granddaughter	feet
4. brother	16. grandson	inches
5. husband	17. sister-in-law	English
6. wife	18. brother-in-law	relatives
7. son	19. daughter-in-law	area code
8. daughter	20. son-in-law	address
9. aunt	21. mother-in-law	zip code
10. uncle	22. father-in-law	divorced
11. niece	23. cousin	widowed
12. nephew	24. family friend	single

FAMILY MEMBERS
Practice Sentences

1. I am learning the **English** language in my ESOL class.

2. My daughter's **height** is 5'1' tall.

3. My **grandmother** is widowed. My **grandfather** died six years ago.

4. My **mother** and **father** were **divorced** in 2021.

5. I have a big family. I have three **sisters**, three **brothers**, 11 **cousins**, five **aunts** and three **uncles**.

6. I have a big **family**. My **relatives** are all over the United States.

7. Your **area code** is the first three numbers of your phone number.

8. I need your **address** to complete the application.

9. My **brother** is very tall. His height is 6'8" tall.

10. My **weight** is going down. I loss eight pounds.

11. My mother has two **nieces**. One lives in California and one lives in New York.

12. The **United States** is a beautiful and rich country.

13. Maria is **single,** but she has a boyfriend.

14. Our **grandmother** keeps her two **grandchildren** during the day.

15. Maria's **niece** is in college at the local university.

16. Carlos' father is a pilot. He flies big airplanes.

17. I have three **sisters** and two **brothers**. Do you have brothers and sisters?

18. My brother's wife Julia is my **sister-in-law**.

19. Mia's **mother-in-law** is helping her with the new baby.

20. My **grandfather** worked at the bank before he retired.

21. Diana's **nephew** Mauricio has a new job at a law office.

22. My **relatives** are fun people. They love to have a good time.

Study the family relationships below:

mother	father	son	daughter	Husband
sister	brother	grandmother	grandfather	wife
niece	nephew	aunt	uncle	son-in-law

Susan   Natalie Jennifer David Nicolas Brian Grandma Nancy

Family Relationships:

Brian/Susan	Husband & wife
Susan/Natalie	Mother & daughter
Susan/David	Mother & son
Natalie/Jennifer	Sisters
Natalie/David	Sister & brother
David/Nicholas	Brothers
Grandma/Natalie	Grandmother & granddaughter
Grandma/David/Nicholas	Grandmother & grandsons
Brian/Natalie	Father & daughter
Brian/Nicolas/David	Father & sons

1. What is the father's name in this family? _____ Brian is the father. _____

2. Who are the youngest two children? _____ Natalie is the youngest. _____

3. How many children are in this family? _____ Four children are in this family. _____

4. What is the husband's name? _____ The husband is Brian. _____

5. What is the relationship between David and Nicolas? _____ They are brothers. _____

6. Who made sandwiches for the family? _____ Grandma Nancy made the sandwiches. _____

7. Who is wearing a suit? _____ Brian is wearing a suit. _____

8. Who is the oldest in this family? _____ Grandma Nancy is the oldest. _____

9. How many members are in this family? _____ Seven members are in this family. _____

10. Who is the tallest child? _____ Jennifer is the tallest child. _____

11. Who is the oldest daughter? _____ Jennifer is the oldest daughter. _____

12. What is the name of the youngest son? _____ Nicolas is the youngest son. _____

13. How many children does Susan have? _____ Susan has four child. _____

14. What is the relationship between Susan and David? _____ They are mother and son. _____

EMMA AND TOM HAMILTON
"Happy Grandparents"

Emma and Tom Hamilton are retired grandparents. They are very happy. They live in Pt. St. Lucie, Florida. In 2024, they moved to Pt. St. Lucie from Chicago after they retired. Emma was a schoolteacher and she retired in 2022. Tom continued to work after Emma retired. He was a bus driver. He finally retired in June, 2023. Emma and Tom have three children - one son and two daughters: Heather, Kimberly, and Bobby. Their oldest daughter Heather has one son, Chris. Chris is the oldest grandchild. He is 21 years old and is in college at the local university. Kimberly has one daughter Amy, and one son Robert. Amy is 7 years old, and Robert is 4 years old. Emma and Tom's son Bobby is the youngest and only son. He is single and has no children. He is a physical education (PE) teacher at a local high school. Each of Emma and Tom's children live in different cities. Heather lives in New York. Kimberly lives in Chicago and Bobby lives in Atlanta. Heather, Kimberly and Bobby visit their parents every holiday. They go to Pt. St. Lucie for Christmas, Mother's Day, Father's Day, Thanksgiving Day and Christmas. Emma and Tom are always happy when their children come to visit because they get to see their grandchildren. Emma and Tom are enjoying their retired lives, and they are very happy.

Directions: Answer the questions below from the story above. Write answers only.

1. Where does Kimberly live? _____ She lives in Chicago. _____

2. What is the name of Emma and Tom's oldest grandchild? _____ His name is Chris. _____

3. What is Bobby's occupation? _____ He is a PE teacher. _____

4. Who is the mother of Amy and Robert? _____ Kimberly is their mother. _____

5. Who is Chris' mother? _____ Heather is Chris' mother. _____

6. What was Emma's occupation before she retired? _____ She was a school teacher. _____

7. When did Emma and Tom move to Pt. St. Lucie? _____ They moved to Pt. St. Lucie in 2024. _____

8. Where do Emma and Tom live now? _____ They live in Pt. St. Lucie now. _____

9. Where did Emma and Tom move from? _____ They moved from Chicago. _____

10. What was Tom's occupation? _____ He was a bus driver. _____

11. How many children do Emma and Tom have? _____ They have three children. _____

12. When did Tom retire? _____ He retired in 2023. _____

13. Who is the youngest of Emma and Tom's children? _____ Bobby is the youngest. _____

14. Which one of Emma and Tom's children live in New York? _____ Heather lives in New York. _____

15. Who lives in Atlanta? _____ Bobby lives in Atlanta. _____

Directions: Answer the questions regarding the family below.

The Family Tree

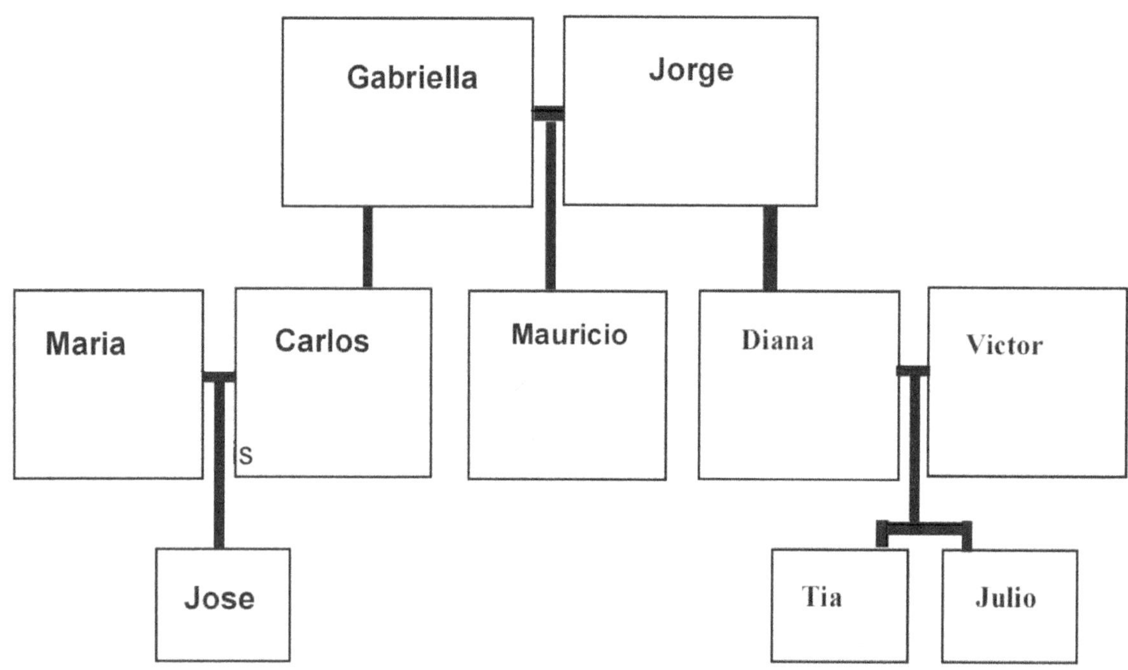

1. How many children do Gabriella and Jorge have? _They have three children._

2. Who is Victor married to? _He is married to Diana._

3. What is Diana's daughter's name? _Her daughter is Tia._

4. Who is Jose's mother? _Maria is Jose's mother. / Jose's mother is Maria._

5. Who is Mauricio's father? _Mauricio's father is Jorge. / Jorge is Mauricio's father._

6. How many children do Maria and Carlos have? _They have one child. / Maria and Carlos have one child._

7. How many people are in this family? _Ten people are in this family. / There are 10 people in this family._

8. How many grandchildren are in this family? _Three grandchildren are in this family. / There are three grandchildren_

Directions: Answer the questions below about relationships between family members.

mother	father	son	daughter	Husband	wife
sister	brother	grandmother	grandfather	aunt	uncle
niece	nephew	aunt	uncle	mother-in-law	father-in-law
sister-in-law	brother-in-law	Son-in-law	Daughter in-law	cousin	

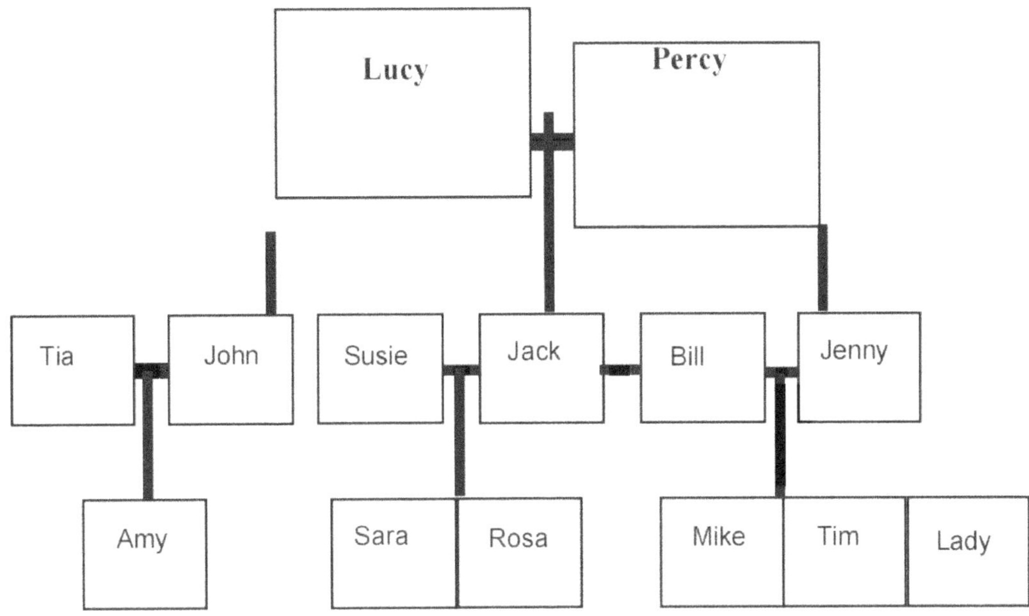

Example: What is the relationship between Lucy and Percy? **Husband and wife.**

1. What is the relationship between Mike and Tim? _______ brothers _______
2. What is the relationship between Lucy and Rosa? ___ Grandmother and granddaughter
3. What is the relationship between Bill and Amy? _______ uncle and niece _______
4. What is the relationship between Amy and Mike? _______ cousins _______
5. What is the relationship between Sara and Rosa? _______ sisters _______
6. What is the relationship between John and Jenny? _______ brother and sister _______
7. What is the relationship between Bill and Rosa? _______ Uncle and niece _______
8. What is the relationship between Tia and John? _______ husband and wife _______
9. What is the relationship between Percy and Bill? _______ father-in-law and son-in-law
10. What is the relationship between Tia and Jenny? _______ sisters-in-law _______

Directions: Circle the correct answer to each question below.

1. **What is your name?**
   a. Name is John.   b. Your name is John.   c. My name is John.

2. **What is your native country?**
   a. My native country Peru.   b. My native country is Peru.   c. Native Country Peru.

3. **Are you a student?**
   a. Yes, I am.   b. Yes, I do.   c. Yes, I is.

4. **Do you have a social security number?**
   a. no, I don't.   b. no, I didn't.   c. no, I am.

5. **Are you taking an English class?**
   a. yes, I do.   b. yes, I am.   c. yes, I didn't.

6. **How many brothers and sisters do you have?**
   a. I one brother only   b. I has two sisters   c. I have one brother and one sister.

7. **Are you cold?**
   a. No, I'm not cold.   b. No, I don't cold.   c. No, I am.

8. **What is your last name?**
   a. My last name is Jose.   b. My last name is J.   c. It is Hernandez.

9. **How old are you?**
   a. I have 27 years old.   b. I 27 years old.   c. I am 27 years old.

10. **Where do you live now?**
   a. I lives in the United States now.
   b. I live in the United States now.
   c. I live on the United States now.

11. **How are you?**
   a. I am 23 years old.   b. I am fine. Thank you.   c. I doing fine.

12. **What color are your eyes?**
   a. My color eyes brown.   b. They are brown.   c. My eyes the color
      brown.

13. **When is your birthday?**
   a. It is May 20th.   b. It is in May 20th.   c. It May 20th.

Verbs & Gerunds

Verb: A verb is a word that shows action in a sentence. It can also show inaction (such as sleep, look, stand, think, etc.)

Gerund: A gerund is a verb that ends in "ing".

VERB	GERUND
work	working
learn	learning
play	playing
jump	jumping
sleep	sleeping
learn	learning
dance	dancing
walk	walking
type	typing
hear	hearing
drive	driving
count	counting

RULES:

❖ When your subject is "**he**", "**she**", or "**it**", your verb needs an "**s**". (Bianca works…)

❖ When your subject is "**I**", "**you**", "**we**" or "**they**", you need a simple verb, **no "s"** (We read…)

❖ When there is a **subject** + a **verb-to-be** in the subject, a **gerund** follows. (We are learning…)

1. We are _____ going _____ to lunch at 12:00p.m. today. (go/going)

2. I am _____ driving _____ now. (drive/driving)

3. Lisa _____ cooks _____ dinner everyday. (cook/cooks/cooking)

4. My cousins _____ play _____ football after school. (play/plays/playing)

5. My microwave _____ works _____ only sometimes. (work/works/working)

6. Julia and Ana are _____ leaving _____ at 3:00p.m. (leave/leaves/leaving)

7. Rosa is _____ sleeping _____ now. (sleep/sleeps/sleeping).

8. My brother _____ works _____ overtime on Fridays. (work/works/working)

9. Carlos and David _____ listen _____ to music after school. (listen/listens/listening)

RULE FOR SUBJECT/VERB AGREEMENT

❖ When the subject in a sentence is: **He** (Carlos), **She** (Diana), or **it** (the microwave) there is an "**s**" on the verb.

❖ When the subject in a sentence is **I**, **You**, **We** (Tina and I), or **They** (my sisters), there is **no "s"** on the verb.

1. Lisa _____cooks_____ on Sundays. (cook/cooks)

2. Maria _____exercises_____ on weekends. (exercise/exercises)

3. My house _____needs_____ to be painted. (need/needs)

4. We _____read_____ in my English class every day. (read/reads)

5. Diana _____sings_____ beautifully. (sing/sings)

6. I _____eat_____ my lunch at 12:00p.m every day. (eat/eats)

7. Luis and I _____celebrate_____ our birthdays in June. (celebrate/celebrates)

8. My puppy _____barks_____ at strangers. (bark/barks)

9. Tina _____lives_____ in Tampa now. (live/lives)

10. My mother _____bakes_____ cakes on holidays and special occasions. (bake/bakes)

RULE FOR GERUNDS

❖ When there is a subject + verb to be, you need a gerund:
Example: I am *cleaning*.   Mary is *sleeping*.

11. Victor is _____sleeping / reading_____ now.

12. Yesterday, I was _____studying / cleannig_____.

13. Bianca and Rosa are _____writing_____.

14. Tomorrow, I am _____going/driving_____ to the supermarket.

15. My teacher is _____speaking_____ now.

16. You are _____cooking_____ now?

17. Right now, my mother is _____sleeping / praying_____.

Directions: Answer each question using the correct **verb** or **gerund**.

answer	opens	like	liking	practicing
paints	practice	moving	answering	dance
prepare	going	kiss	exercising	dancing

1. I usually _____ practice _____ my English at home.
2. Lisa is _____ going _____ to travel to Colombia next month.
3. Marcos _____ opens _____ the door for me every morning.
4. We are _____ practicing _____ our reading and writing in class now.
5. You _____ answer _____ your questions very well.
6. My father _____ paints _____ big buildings.
7. We are _____ moving _____ to Tampa next week.
8. Michael and Tony _____ like _____ to eat pasta.
9. You love to _____ dance _____ to fast music?
10. Mary and Luis are _____ exercising _____.

GERUNDS AND THE INFINITVE "TO"

work	reading	read	study	dancing
learning	travel	eat	speaking	sleeping
jump	singing	eating	driving	drive

11. The children are _____ sleeping _____ now.
12. My brother needs to _____ eat _____.
13. Kristina was _____ reading _____ yesterday.
14. Maria needs to _____ work _____.
15. I am _____ eating _____.
16. My daughter wants to _____ drive _____.
17. My husband loves to _____ travel _____.
18. We were _____ singing _____ yesterday.
19. The children were _____ dancing _____ last night.
20. I like to _____ study _____ on Sundays.

Skill: Subject Verb Agreement

play	We	The baby	My wife and I	The boys
drive	My neighbors	worked	playing	went
My daughter	jumped	reading	My mother	traveled

Directions: Choose a word from the box above to complete each sentence correctly.

1. The baby _______________ needs her bottle.
2. My daughter _______________ wants a long dress for her prom.
3. The children are _______ playing _______ in the park right now.
4. My wife and I _______________ like to go to church twice on Sundays.
5. Last week I _______ worked _______ three hours overtime.
6. We _______________ drive to the beach every weekend.
7. I am _______ reading _______ a good book right now.
8. The boys _______________ jump the fence every day.
9. My mother _______________ cooks every day.
10. Yesterday, we _______ went _______ to the bookstore.

Directions: Complete each sentence with a part of speech in the parenthesis.

11. Please put the book _______ on _______ the bookshelf . (preposition)
12. I really like your _______ nice _______ car. (adjective)
13. I need to go to _______ Walmart _______ today. (proper Noun)
14. In my English class, we _______ read _______ a lot. (verb)
15. My classmate is wearing _______ a _______ pair of blue jeans today. (article)
16. We _______ are _______ going to New York next year. (VTB)
17. I would like a new _______ watch _______ (regular noun)
18. Last year, I _______ studied _______ a lot. (past tense verb)
19. _______ My _______ mother is cooking a big dinner on Sunday. (pronoun)
20. The girls need three _______ dollars _______ each. (plural noun)

ADJECTIVES

An adjective describes a noun. Example: **red** car, **fast** computer, **expensive** restaurant, **short** man, **pretty** lady, **beautiful** woman, **cold** classroom, **red** jacket, **ugly** dress, **fast** car, etc.

short	tall	upset	Martha	skinny	happy
serious	Jason	big	older	pretty	black

Directions: Complete the sentences below with an answer from the box above.

Nicolas   Marilyn   Bobby   Kimberly   John   Martha

1. Nicolas has a __________ big __________ stomach.

2. Martha is an __________ old __________ lady.

3. Bobby has __________ brown __________ hair.

4. John is very __________ tall __________.

5. Marilyn is __________ happy __________.

6. John is tall and __________ skinny __________.

7. Kimberly looks __________ upset __________ today.

8. Kimberly has __________ curly __________ hair.

9. Martha looks very __________ serious __________.

Directions: Complete each sentence with an **adjective**.

1. I have a _______ leather _______ jacket.
2. My mother has a _____ new _______ car.
3. I like your _______ black _______ hair.
4. Your mother is a ______ great _______ cook.
5. My grandmother is _____ sick _______ today.
6. Your father is a ______ tall _______ man.
7. You are an _____ intelligent _______ person.
8. Diana is wearing a _____ long _______ dress.
9. We had a _____ wonderful _______ time at the party.
10. I love _____ spicy / Cuban _____ food.

Reminder: An adjective describes a noun.

REVIEW AND PRACTICE

Directions: Rewrite each sentence and capitalize every **proper noun** in each sentence.

11. Let's play soccer on saturday at hollywood park. __Saturday, Hollywood Park__

12. My best friend is maria. She lives in tampa florida. __Maria, Tampa, Florida__

13. I went to cuba to visit my family last year. ____Cuba____

14. I love to celebrate christmas with my family every december. __Christmas, December__

15. My favorite two months are december and january. __December, January__

CHRISTINA

My name is Christina. I am from Guatemala. I came to the United States in July of 2024, and I live in Tampa with my Aunt Rita. I began taking an English class in August because I need to learn the English language. I was afraid to learn English at first because I thought it was a hard language to learn. It was difficult for me on my first day of class. I cried a few times, but I continued to go to class every day and I have learned so much. My teacher makes us practice speaking English every day in class. We are not allowed to speak in our native languages while in class. I have learned about pronouns, verbs to be, regular nouns, proper nouns, adjectives, prepositions, articles, past tense verbs, singular and plural nouns, contractions and so much more. I am so proud of myself. I understand a lot of English now. When I learn enough English, I will be able to get a job. Everyday in class, we practice reading, writing, speaking and listening. I have also made some new friends. They are wonderful people. When I go home, I complete my homework, practice my vocabulary words, and study my grammar. Sometimes my Aunt Rita helps me. My teacher Mrs. Johnson says that if I continue to improve, I may test out of her class and go to the advanced class. I am excited about my future in the United States.

Directions: Read each sentence below. If the statement is true, put a "**T**" next to it. If the sentence is not true, put an "**F**" next to the sentence.

True or False

1. Christina came to the United States in July 2022. __F__
2. Christina doesn't need English to get a good job. __F__
3. When Christina gets home, she does her homework and plays video games. __F__
4. Christina is from Guatemala. __T__
5. Christina came to the United States with her Aunt Rita. __F__
6. Christina understands a lot of English now. __T__
7. Christina has made some friends in her English class. __T__
8. It was easy for Christina on the first day of class. __F__
9. Christina's Aunt says that if she continues to improve, she may test out. __F__
10. What is Christina's teacher's name? ____Her teacher is Mrs. Johnson.____

____

11. Name three skills that Christina has learned in her English class. ____Any 3 skills____

____

____

Study

I have a small/<u>medium</u>/large family. I have 3 brother<u>s</u> and 2 sister<u>s</u>. I also have 7 cousin/<u>cousins</u>. My family is from Mexico, but I live in the United States now.

This is my partner <u>Diana</u>. She has a <u>large</u> family. She has <u>5</u> sisters and <u>4</u> brothers. She also has <u>12</u> cousins. Her family is from <u>Peru</u>, but she lives in the United States now too.

Practice

You:

I have a small/medium/large family. I have _____ brother(s) and _____ sister(s). I also have _____ cousin(s). My family is from the country of ______________, but I live in ________________ now.

Your partner:

This is my partner __________. She/He has a __________ family. She/He has

_____ Sister(s) and _____ brother(s). She/He also has _____ cousin(s). Her family is from the country of ______________, but she/he lives in ______________ now.

SINGULAR AND PLURAL NOUNS

STUDY

	Singular	Plural
1.	boy	boy**s**
2.	nurse	nurse**s**
3.	school	school**s**
4.	cell phone	cell phone**s**
5.	shirt	shirt**s**
6.	car	car**s**
7.	school	school**s**
8.	teacher	teacher**s**
9.	shirt	shirt**s**
10.	office	office**s**

RULES:

- A regular noun finishes with an "s"   ***Example:*** paper, papers
- When the noun ends in **x**, **s**, **ch**, **sh**, add "**es**"   ***Example***: church = churches
- When the noun ends with a **vowel + y**, add "s"   ***Example:*** turkey = turkeys
- When the noun ends with a **consonant + y**, add "***ies***" (no y)

   Example: family = families

	Singular	Plural
1.	beach	beach**es**
2.	brush	brush**es**
3.	box	box**es**
4.	kiss	kiss**es**
5.	baby	bab**ies**
6.	family	famil**ies**
7.	chair	chair**s**
8.	turkey	turkey**s**
9.	birthday	birthday**s**
10.	car	car**s**

MAKING PLURAL NOUNS

Directions: Complete each sentence using the correct plural noun for each.

regular noun: s	x, s, ch, sh: es	v+y: s	con +y: ies (no y)

1. I bought three ______shirts______ from Walmart today. (shirt)

2. Lisa has two little ______babies______ . (baby)

3. I found my ______brushes______ under the cabinet. (brush)

4. We had two ______turkeys______ for Thanksgiving. (turkey)

5. My mother gave me many ______kisses______ when I came home from college. (kiss)

6. There were many ______families______ at Disney this weekend. (family)

7. We have two ______cars______ in the garage. (car)

8. I need two ______computers______ for my job. (computer)

9. Leslie needs four ______copies______. (copy)

10. I found my ______brushes______ under the bathroom cabinet. (brush)

11. My son is 5 feet 2 ______inches______ tall. (inch)

12. Will you please help me with the ______boxes______? (box)

13. Both of Hannah's siblings are ______attorneys______. (attorney)

14. Daniel had five ______cookies______ with his lunch today. (cookie)

Directions: Complete each sentence with an **adjective**.

15. The movie was very ______good______.

16. I cannot find my ______blue______ dress.

17. The new restaurant on the corner is very ______nice______.

18. My supervisor is a(n) ______intelligent______ person.

19. Linda is a(n) ______steak______ and ______kind______ person.

20. The baby is ______crying______.

21. Sandra has a(n) ______amazing______ job.

22. My mother's house is ______old______.

23. David has a(n) ______expensive______ car.

Directions: Circle the correct **plural noun** on the right for the words below:

1. **family**   familys   families
2. **monkey**   monkies   monkeys
3. **computer**   computer   computers
4. **birthday**   birthdays   birthdayes
5. **brush**   brushes   brushs
6. **kiss**   kisses   kissies
7. **paper**   paperies   papers
8. **girl**   girls   girles
9. **turkey**   turkies   turkeys
10. **lady**   ladys   ladies
11. **circus**   circuses   circusies

Directions: Complete the sentences below with the correct word from the box.

restaurants	teachers	babies	dollars	pencils
tables	churches	windows	shirts	stores

12. There are many ______restaurants______ to eat at in South Beach.
13. Please open the ______window______ because it is very hot in here.
14. We need more ______tables______ in the room for all of the guests.
15. Raquel has two beautiful little ______babies______.
16. I need three ______pencils______ for class.
17. There are 18 ______teachers______ working at the school.
18. Daniel needs 30 ______dollars______ for the fieldtrip.
19. There are several ______churches______ to go to in Miami.
20. I bought my brother five new ______shirts______ today.

IRREGULAR PLURAL NOUNS

SINGULAR	PLURAL
child	children
person	people
foot	feet
man	men
woman	women
tooth	teeth
mouse	mice
knife	knives
child	children
life	lives
sheep	sheep (no change)
fish	fish (no change)
deer	deer (no change)
shrimp	shrimp (no change)
fireman	firemen
goose	geese
leaf	leaves
potato	potatoes
tomato	tomatoes
half	halves
wife	wives
thief	thieves
self	selves

Directions: Complete each sentence with the correct **plural form** of the noun below:

1. My sister has three _______children_______. (child)
2. We have three _______fish_______ in the aquarium. (fish)
3. In my class, there are three _______birthdays_______ in the month of September. (birthday)
4. There were so many _______people_______ in line today. (person)
5. Two of my daughter's _______teeth_______ came out. (tooth)
6. I have two _______computers_______, one at home and one at work. (computer)
7. There were two _______witnesses_______ in the trial. (witness)
8. I hurt both of my _______feet_______ while running yesterday. (foot)
9. There were many _______families_______ at the beach this weekend. (family)
10. Our _______lives_______ must be lived through God. (life)
11. Please put all of the _______knives_______ in the kitchen drawer. (knife)

REVIEW AND PRACTICE

Directions: Using English grammar rules, answer each question using the correct part of speech.

12. I would like a_______straw_______ for my drink. (noun)
13. You always look so _______nice_______ when you go to work. (adjective)
14. We love going to _______Hollywood Beach_______ on Saturdays. (proper noun)
15. Miriam _______needs_______ $100.00 to buy some clothes. (verbs)
16. They _______don't_______ like to eat too much fried food. (negative contraction)
17. My mom _______cooks_______ every day. (verb)
18. My sister is _______an_______ accountant. (article)
19. I _______am_______ learning English now. (VTB)
20. My mother has three _______cars_______. (irregular plural noun)
21. We need three more _______chairs_______. for the classroom (plural noun)

Directions: Practice the conversations below with a partner.

CONVERSATION PRACTICE

<table>
<tr><td>

Conversation #1:

Person #1: Hello.
Person #2: Hello. How are you?
Person #1: I am fine. Thank you, and you.
Person #2: I am doing well.
Person #1: Do you have a small, medium or large family?
Person #2: I have a ___________ family, and you?
Person #1: OK. I have a ___________ family.
Person #2: How many brothers and sisters do you have?
Person #1: I have ________ brothers and ________ sister(s). You?
Person #2: Oh. Okay. I have ________ brothers and ________ sister(s).
Person #2: Oh, that is interesting.
Person #1: Yes, it is.

</td><td>

Conversation #2:

Person #1: Greetings my friend.
Person #2: Greetings to you too. How are you?
Person #1: I am fine. Thank you and you?
Person #2: I am well. How is your family?
Person #1: My family is good. My brother lives in Chicago. He is a mechanic and my sister lives in Florida. She is a teacher.
Person #2: That is great. …and your parents?
Person #1: My mother and father are well. They are old, but they are well. And you? How is your family?
Person #2: Everyone is doing good. My sister is married now and my brother is still single.
Person #1: Wow. I am glad to hear that everyone is doing well. Say hello to your family for me.
Person #2: I will and you say hello to your family for me.
Person #1: Yes. I will.

</td></tr>
</table>

Directions: Practice your personal introduction.

Good morning classmates. My name is __________________. My last name is __________________. I am from __________________, but I live in __________________ now. I speak __________________, but I am learning English at ______________. I am __________________ and I have ________(pet(s). I like to __________________ and I also like to __________________. My favorite color is __________________, my favorite food is __________________ and my favorite person/people is/are my __________________. I am very happy to be here.

Directions: Now, practice introducing yourself to a partner.

BROTHERS AND SISTERS

My name is Sherry. I have four siblings: three sisters and one brother. I love them very much, but we live in different cities. We visit our parents every year for Thanksgiving. My sister Carmen lives in a big, beautiful house in Texas. Her house has four bedrooms and three bathrooms. She also lives on a golf course. My sister Kimberly lives in an apartment in New York City. Her apartment has a balcony that overlooks a beautiful lake. She also has two large closets. My younger sister Miriam lives in a condo on the west side of Chicago. Her condo has two bedrooms and two bathrooms. She has a big closet and a home office in her condo. She also has a beautiful dining room. My brother John lives in a big, beautiful home in Miami Beach. His house has six bedrooms and four bathrooms. He has a three-car garage, and he also lives on a lake. I live in a nice apartment in Hollywood, Florida. My apartment only has two bedrooms and one bathroom, but I really like it. It is on the 3rd floor and it is quiet and clean, but one day in the future, I would like to buy a house after I get married. For now, I am happy with my apartment.

1. How many siblings does Sherry have? _Shery has 4 siblings._

2. Who lives in New York? _Kimberly lives in New York._

3. Whose house has four bedrooms and three bathrooms? _Carmen's house._

4. Who is Sherry's youngest sister? _Miriam is the youngest sister._

5. Who lives in Miami Beach? _John lives in Miami Beach._

6. Who lives on a golf course? _Carmen lives on a golf course._

7. When do the siblings visit their parents? _Every year on Thanksgiving_

8. What does Miriam live in? _She lives in a condo._

9. What floor does Sherry live on? _Sherry lives on the 3rd floor._

10. Who has two large closets? _Kimberly has two large closets._

11. Who has a beautiful dining room? _It is Miriam._

12. Who has a three-car garage? _John has a three-car garage._

SUBJECT VERB AGREEMENT

1. I ______ **am** ______ going to the movies on Saturday. (am/is)

2. Odessa ______ **works** ______ at the shoe store on weekends. (work/works)

3. Mary ______ **plays** ______ the piano at church on Sundays. (play, plays)

4. The house ______ **is** ______ leaking water from the roof. (is/are)

5. My shoes ______ **are** ______ too big for my feet. (is/are)

6. We ______ **are** ______ having a party on Thursday. (is/are)

7. Martha and Robin ______ **take** ______ the bus to school every day. (take/takes)

8. My dog ______ **barks** ______ all night long when he can't sleep. (bark/barks)

9. My sister ______ **is** ______ 16 years old. (is, are, have, has)

10. My brother and I ______ **work** ______ at Starbucks. (work/works)

11. My cousin and his sister ______ **like** ______ to listen to jazz music. (like/likes)

12. I ______ **type** ______ 65 words per minute on my computer. (type/types)

13. Olga's class ______ **is** ______ at lunch now. (are/is)

14. Derrick ______ **has** ______ 200 for new clothes. (is/are/have/has)

15. Isha and Ivan ______ **are** ______ twins. (are/is)

Directions: Practice answering the questions below in a complete sentence.

16. Where does Marvin work? ______ Marvin works at ______.

17. Where did you go yesterday? ______ I went to ______ yesterday.

18. How many siblings do you have? ______ I have ______ siblings.

19. Where are you living now? ______ I am living in ______ now.

READING AND SPEAKING PEOPLE INFORMATION

Name: Robin **Last name:** Castro **native country:** India **city:** Miami Gardens **marital status:** divorced **family members:** 2 children, 3 brothers, 2 sisters, 5 cousins	**Name:** Diana **Last name:** Hernandez **native country:** Mexico **city:** Houston **marital status:** single **family members:** 1 child, 2 brothers, 1 sister, 6 cousins, 2 aunts, 3 uncles	**Name:** Thomas **Last name:** Perez **native country:** Venezuela **city:** Chicago **marital status:** married **family members:** 4 children, 7 grandchildren, 6 brothers, 3 sisters, 5 nieces, 3 nephews
Name: John **Last name:** Rodriquez **native country:** Puerto Rico **city:** Pembroke Pines **marital status:** married **family members:** 2 children, 3 sisters, no brothers, 7 cousins, 2 aunts, 3 uncles	**Name:** Elsa **Last name:** Russo **native country:** Panama **city:** Hollywood **marital status:** engaged **family members:** no children, 3 sisters, 1 brother, 2 nieces, 1 nephew, 4 cousins	**Name:** Jennifer **Last name:** Arrieta **native country:** Colombia **city:** New York **marital status:** divorced **family members:** 1 child, 1 brother, 1 sister, 2 cousins, 2 aunts, 3 uncles

Directions: Answer the questions below using the information above.

1. How many cousins does Elsa have? _____ Elsa /She has 4 cousins.

2. How many brothers does John have? _____ He has no brothers.

3. What is Thomas' marital status? _____ Thomas / He is married.

4. How many siblings does John have? _____ John / He has 3 siblings.

5. Who lives in Chicago? _____ Thomas lives in Chicago.

6. What is Elsa's native country? _____ Elsa's / Her native country is Panama.

7. Who is from India? _____ Robin is from India.

8. Whose last name is Hernandez? _____ Diana's last name is Hernandez.

9. How many grandchildren does Thomas have? _____ Thomas / He has seven grandchildren.

10. Who is divorced? _____ Robin and Jennifer are divorced.

<h1 style="text-align:center">Dialogue: FAMILY MEMBERS</h1>

1.
Person #1: I have a very big family. They are here visiting for the Mother's Day weekend.
Person #2: How nice. Which of your relatives are here?
Person #1: Two of my sisters, three of my brothers, two of my aunts and my one uncle are here. Some of my cousins are here too.
Person #2: Wow, that is a lot of people. They must like it here.
Person #1: Yes, they love my grandmother, and they also love the Florida weather.
Person #2: What do you have planned for your grandmother?
Person #1: We are taking her to a nice restaurant on Sunday, and then give her some gifts. We will also celebrate other mothers in our family.
Person #2: That sounds like a great idea. Have fun and enjoy your family.
Person #1: Thank you!

2.
Person #1: Good morning my friend.
Person #2: Good morning to you too.
Person #1: Are you still taking an English class at the community school?
Person #2: Yes, I have learned so much. I really like it. My English is getting better.
Person #1: Really? What have you learned about so far?
Person #2: Well, we have learned about pronouns, verbs to be, regular nouns, proper nouns, articles, prepositions and many other parts of speech. The lesson this week is "Family Members".
Person #1: It sounds like you have learned lots of information. How do you remember everything?
Person #2: Sometimes I forget, but I go home and practice because I really want to learn English.
Person #1: Yes, practicing at home is very important.

3.
Person #1: I heard you talking about proper nouns the other day. What is a proper noun? I don't know the difference between a regular noun and a proper noun.
Person #2: A proper noun is "the name" of a person, place or thing. Proper nouns are capitalized.
Person #1: Oh. That is interesting. You mean like a person's last name? Is that a proper noun?
Person #2: Yes, or their first name or middle name. They all are proper nouns.
Person #1: What about days of the week and months of the year?
Person #2: Yes, they are proper nouns too. Cities, states, names of stores, countries and the names of streets are also proper nouns. They all require a capital letter when writing them in sentences.
Person #1: Okay. I think I understand now.

4.
Person #1: My aunt and uncle are here visiting from Peru. They came with their two children, my cousins. I picked them up from the airport yesterday at 1:45p.m.
Person #2: That is very nice. How long will they be here?
Person #1: They are going to be here for one month, then they will go back to Peru. I am very happy that they are here. They are returning on June 8, 2024.
Person #2: That is wonderful. I hope you have a nice time with your family.
Person #1: Thank you so much. I am going to show them this beautiful city. I am also taking them to the beach; the movies and to some nice restaurants.
Person #2: Awesome! That is very nice of you. I hope they enjoy themselves while they are here.
Person #1: Thank you. I am sure they will.

5. **Person #1:** I am so excited about my grandmother's birthday party! She is turning 92 years old and we are having a big party for her. Some of my family members are coming from other states to celebrate.
Person #2: Wow! 92 years old. That is wonderful! Does she know about the party?
Person #1: No. It is a surprise. She thinks that we are taking her to church on Saturday evening. My grandfather and my uncle are helping to plan it.
Person #2: She is going to be so surprised. I think she will also be very happy.
Person #1: I think so too. I will tell you all about it since you will be out of town.
Person #2: Yes. Please do. I hate that I am going to miss it.

6. **Person #1:** Who is picking you up from English school today?
Person #2: My cousin is picking me up at 1:30p.m. She is coming with her son after she picks him up from school. He wasn't feeling good, so she is picking him up early.
Person #1: That is very nice of your cousin. Is this the one who works at Walmart?
Person #2: Yes, she gets off work at 1:00p.m., so she will come by my school to get me when she gets off work. Her son's school is close to her job, so she'll pick me up after she gets him.
Person #1: Oh. Okay. When will your car be fixed? It has been at the mechanic for a while.
Person #2: Yes, I have not had transportation for two weeks now. The mechanic said it will be ready on Wednesday after 3:00p.m. I am so glad because I do not like not having a car.
Person #1: Okay. Well at least you don't have to wait too much longer.
Person #2: No. I don't. I am happy about that.

7. **Person #1:** My sister and my brother both have birthdays in December.
Person #2: Oh really? When are their birthdays?
Person #1: My sister's birthday is December 3rd and my brother's birthday is December 22nd.
Person #2: That means you have to buy Christmas gifts and birthday gifts in the same month correct?
Person #1: Yes, that is correct, but sometimes I say, "Here is one gift. It is for your birthday AND Christmas."
Person #2: Oh no! You get only one gift for two occasions? That does not seem fair.
Person #1: Oh well. I sure do. It saves me money that way.

8. **Person #1:** Every Sunday, my family gets together to eat dinner. Everyone brings something. We have meat, starches, vegetables, dessert and different beverages.
Person #2: That sounds very nice. Does everyone in the family come?
Person #1: Yes, mostly everyone comes: my mother and father, my sisters and brothers, my aunts and uncles, my cousins and my grandmother and grandfather all come. There is about 37 of us.
Person #2: Wow! You have a big family!
Person #1: Yes, I do. We have lots of fun together and we are very close.
Person #2: That is wonderful. I have a small family because my mother and father have no sisters or brothers. They were the only children of their parents.
Person #1: Well, you can come to my house and meet my family whenever you want to.
Person #2: Oh. Thank you so much! I would love to come.

Family Members: **ASSESSMENT**

Directions: Complete each sentence with the correct word:

is, am, are, was, were

1. Lisa ___was___ sick yesterday.
2. I ___am / was___ very tired today.
3. Julio ___is___ going to Cuba for three weeks.
4. Carlos ___is___ 28 years old.
5. You ___are___ my best friend.
6. Ana, Maria, and Kimberly ___are___ going to New York tomorrow.
7. Yesterday, I ___was___ in Orlando.
8. I ___am___ going to the supermarket later today.
9. We ___were___ dancing at the party on Saturday.
10. We ___were___ exercising at the park yesterday.

Directions: Circle the correct plural noun on the right for the words below:

11. **house**	housies	(houses)
12. **woman**	(women)	woman
13. **computer**	computer	(computers)
14. **birthday**	(birthdays)	birthdayes
15. **brush**	(brushes)	brushs
16. **fish**	fishes	(fish)
17. **paper**	paperies	(papers)
18. **girl**	(girls)	girles
19. **dog**	doges	(dogs)
20. **turkey**	(turkeys)	turkies
21. **circus**	(circuses)	circusies

Directions: Complete each sentence with an **article** that makes sense in the sentence.

22. Lisa has _____ a _____ new job.

23. I need to go to _____ the _____ doctor today.

24. My sister is _____ an _____ accountant.

25. I ate _____ an _____ apple for a snack today.

26. We saw _____ an _____ elephant at the zoo yesterday.

Directions: Complete each sentence with an **adjective** that makes sense in the sentence.

27. I am wearing a _____ red _____ shirt today.

28. The new restaurant is very _____ expensive _____.

29. Sometimes, it is _____ cold _____ in the classroom.

30. The man is very _____ thin _____.

31. Rocio has a _____ beautiful _____ baby.

Directions: Answer each question below in a complete sentence.

32. How many brothers and sisters do you have? _____ I have _____ brother(s) and _____ sister(s).

33. Do you have a small family or a large family? I have a _____ family.

34. Who is your favorite cousin? _____ is my favorite cousin. (My favorite cousin is _____.)

35. Where is your family from? My family is from _____.

36. Where do you live now? I live in _____ now.

Lesson 3: Housing

Dear ESL Teacher,

As you prepare to guide your students through Lesson 3 on Housing, you are equipped with a meticulously designed plan to enhance their proficiency in English language skills related to housing and accommodation. This lesson integrates vocabulary building, grammar exercises, reading comprehension, and practical conversation activities to foster a comprehensive understanding of housing-related concepts. The instructional procedures outlined, which includes direct instruction for clear concept presentation, guided practice to scaffold learning, and independent practice to reinforce skills ensure a balanced approach that accommodates diverse learning styles and abilities.

Emphasizing our commitment to differentiation and adaptations, this guide provides tools such as visual aids and alternative assessments to support English language learners and students with diverse needs. Utilize these resources to create an engaging and supportive learning environment where students can confidently explore and apply language skills essential to understanding housing.

OBJECTIVES:

1. Students will identify and use vocabulary related to housing and accommodation.

2. Students will construct and practice sentences using targeted vocabulary and grammar concepts.

3. Students will demonstrate understanding of basic grammar concepts (subject-verb agreement, prepositions, using have/has).

4. Students will engage in conversations using learned vocabulary and grammar.

5. Students will comprehend and respond to simple reading passages about housing.

6. Students will participate in dialogues to practice communication skills related to housing.

7. Students will demonstrate their learning through a comprehensive assessment.

INSTRUCTIONAL PROCEDURES:

Direct Instruction:
- **Objective:** Present new vocabulary and grammar concepts clearly and explicitly.

- **Details:** Begin the lesson by introducing new housing-related vocabulary words and sentences explaining their meanings with visuals and contextual examples. Use the whiteboard or projector to display images or diagrams illustrating housing terms and their usage in sentences. Provide clear definitions, pronunciation guides, and encourage students to practice pronouncing the words aloud.

Guided Practice:

- **Objective:** Help students apply new knowledge in a supportive environment.

- **Details:** Facilitate structured activities where students practice using housing vocabulary and grammar concepts with teacher guidance. Provide sentence frames or prompts that incorporate the new vocabulary and grammar structures. Encourage peer collaboration by having students work in pairs or small groups to complete tasks, ensuring active participation and providing feedback as needed.

ACTIVITIES:

Vocabulary Introduction:

- **Objective:** Introduce key housing-related vocabulary words.
- **Details:** Use visual aids such as flashcards, images, or charts to illustrate each vocabulary word related to housing and accommodation. Provide contextual examples in sentences or short paragraphs to demonstrate how each word is used in different contexts. Encourage students to repeat and practice saying the words aloud to enhance retention.

Sentence Practice:

- **Objective:** Help students construct meaningful sentences using new vocabulary and grammar concepts.
- **Details:** Guide students step-by-step in forming sentences that incorporate housing vocabulary and different areas of the house and target grammar structures (e.g., subject-verb agreement, prepositions, have/has). Begin with simple sentence structures and gradually increase complexity as students become more proficient. Provide scaffolded support with sentence starters or frames if needed.

Grammar Drill:

- **Objective:** Reinforce understanding of grammar rules related to subject-verb agreement, prepositions, and using have/has.
- **Details:** Conduct focused exercises where students practice using these grammar elements correctly in the context of housing. This can include fill-in-the-blank activities, matching exercises, or creating sentences that demonstrate proper usage. Provide explanations and examples to clarify any misunderstandings as they arise.

Conversation Practice:

- **Objective:** Develop students' ability to engage in spoken communication using housing-related vocabulary and grammar.
- **Details:** Pair students or organize small groups for conversational activities focused on housing topics. Provide prompts or scenarios that require the use of targeted vocabulary and grammar structures in a meaningful context, such as discussing different types of houses, describing a dream home, or talking about neighborhood amenities. Encourage students to take turns speaking and actively listen to their peers, fostering both speaking and listening skills.

Reading Comprehension:

- **Objective:** Enhance students' ability to understand written English through housing-related reading passages.

- **Details:** Select age-appropriate reading materials or passages that align with the lesson's vocabulary and grammar focus on housing. After reading, ask comprehension questions that require students to recall details, make inferences, or summarize key points related to housing concepts. Encourage students to read aloud to practice pronunciation and fluency.

Dialogue Creation:

- **Objective:** Encourage students to apply learned vocabulary and grammar by creating dialogues about housing scenarios.
- **Details:** Guide students in pairs or small groups to develop dialogues that incorporate the lesson's housing-related vocabulary and grammar concepts. Provide scenarios or contexts (e.g., discussing renting an apartment, negotiating house rules with roommates) and encourage creativity in dialogue creation. Emphasize natural conversational flow and appropriate language use.

Puzzle Activity:

- **Objective:** Reinforce housing-related vocabulary and concepts through a fun and engaging puzzle activity.
- **Details:** Have students complete the word search in the lesson from their books using key housing vocabulary words and related terms. Students may work individually or in pairs to complete it. This activity helps reinforce vocabulary retention and encourages students to think critically about housing-related language.

Independent Practice:

- **Objective:** Reinforce learning through individual or paired activities.

- **Details:** Assign tasks that require students to independently apply housing vocabulary and grammar rules. This could include completing worksheets from the book with sentence completion exercises, where students practice using subject-verb agreement, prepositions, and have/has correctly in context. Monitor progress and provide assistance as students work through the tasks.

Differentiation/Adaptations:
- Provide visual aids such as charts and diagrams alongside verbal explanations to enhance understanding for English language learners.

- Break down complex grammar concepts into smaller steps and offer bilingual dictionaries or picture dictionaries for additional language support.

- Offer alternative assessments such as oral presentations or digital projects to accommodate diverse learning needs and preferences.

Assessment:
- **Objective:** Evaluate students' comprehension and application of housing-related language and concepts.
- **Details:** The assessment is located at the end of the lesson and includes a written component covering vocabulary usage, grammar rules (subject-verb agreement, prepositions, have/has), reading comprehension questions related to housing passages, and a dialogue creation task.

Materials and Resources:
- Book: It's Time to Learn English
- Vocabulary cards with housing terms
- Whiteboard and markers for visual aids
- Textbooks or reading materials about housing
- Worksheets for grammar exercises
- Audio recordings for listening comprehension activities

Technology Needed:
- Projector or screen for displaying visuals
- Computer or tablet for accessing digital resources

Lesson 3: Housing

T - Think Back (Review)

Activity: Begin the lesson by reviewing key concepts and vocabulary from the previous lesson. Use a brief warm-up activity to engage students and assess their current understanding of any housing-related terms they might already know.

Time: 5-10 minutes

E – Entry (Introduction/Beginning)

Activity: Introduce new vocabulary words related to housing and accommodations using visual aids such as flashcards, images, or charts. Explain the meanings, provide clear definitions, model pronunciations, and use each word in sentences to demonstrate usage.

Time: 15 minutes

A - Application (Teaching/Presentation/Delivery)

Activity: Present new grammar concepts clearly and explicitly. Use direct instruction to introduce subject-verb agreement, prepositions, and using have/has. Provide examples and demonstrate their usage in sentences.

Time: 20 minutes

C - Collaborative Practice (Student Practice)

Activity: Facilitate guided practice by having students work in pairs or small groups to complete structured activities from the book using sentence frames or prompts. Assign exercises from the book for students to complete. Walk around the classroom to offer support and feedback. Encourage students to engage in conversations about housing topics, such as different types of houses or describing their dream home.

Time: 25 minutes

H - Highlight (Wrap-up/Closing)

Activity: Summarize the key points of the lesson, highlighting the new vocabulary and grammar rules learned. Assign a reading comprehension activity from the book using a passage about housing. Discuss the main ideas and ask comprehension questions.

Time: 10 minutes

E - Evaluate (Assessment/Evaluation)

Activity: Upon completion of the lesson, administer the comprehensive assessment found at the end of the lesson. Assess students on vocabulary, grammar, reading comprehension, and dialogue creation.

- **Time:** 15 minutes

R - Reflect (Final Review)

- **Activity:** End the lesson with a reflective activity where students can share their thoughts on what they learned, how they can use it in real-life situations, and any areas where they need further clarification. Encourage students to share their thoughts on their progress and areas they want to improve.

Time: 5-10 minutes

Housing

3

VOCABULARY

house

apartment

mobile home

hotel

HOUSING	ROOMS	FURNITURE
1. house	living room	sofa/couch
2. apartment	family room	chair
3. mobile home	dining room	coffee table
4. condominium	home office	television (TV)
5. duplex	kitchen	table
6. efficiency	bedroom	sink
7. hotel	bathroom	refrigerator
8. motel	closet	stove
9. townhouse	utility room	microwave
10. mansion	laundry room	dresser
11. cottage	sitting room	bed
12. villa	movie room	picture
13. dormitory	guest room	nightstand
14. houseboat	playroom	toilet
15. studio	attic	shower
16. cabin	basement	bathtub
17. front yard	houseboat	love seat
18. back yard	dormitory	headboard

HOUSING SENTENCES

1. I live in an **apartment** in Geogia.

2. My sister lives in a big **house** in New Jersey.

3. My brother pays a lot of money each month for rent.

4. Lisa has a new **condominium** on Miami Beach.

5. Our new **house** has four **bedrooms** and three **bathrooms**.

6. We have large **closets** in our **house**.

7. Do you have a small or large **microwave**?

8. The small garbage can go in the **bathroom**.

9. My parents have a big **backyard**.

10. Bianca has a beautiful garden in her **front yard**.

11. I have a friend who lives in a nice **mobile home**.

12. Tomorrow we will find an **apartment** for you.

13. We pay $1,800 in **mortgage** each month.

14. The **landlord** repaired the broken **sink** for us.

15. We eat dinner at the **dining** room **table** every evening.

16. We watch movies in the **family room**.

17. Do you have a **television** (TV) in your **bedroom**?

18. I baked a cake in my new **stove**.

19. The cold food goes into the **refrigerator**.

20. My cousin just bought a big **house**. It has six **bedrooms** and five **bathrooms**.

Study

house

hotel

apartment

motel

mobile Home

mansion

duplex

efficiency

villa

Study

 sofa/couch

 microwave

 chair

 Refrigerator

 table

 dresser

 TV

 lamp

 toilet

Directions: Complete the sentences below with the correct word from the box.

living room	bedroom	kitchen	dining room	bathroom
closet	home office	family room	utility room	bed
microwave	refrigerator	shoes	pictures	chair
lamp	toilet	computer	printer	table

1. The ___refrigerator___ goes in the kitchen.

2. The ___bed___ goes in the bedroom.

3. The ___toilet___ goes in the bathroom.

4. Shoes go in the ___closet___.

5. The computer goes in the ___home office___.

6. The ___lamp___ goes on the nightstand.

7. The ___pictures___ go on the wall.

8. The ___printer___ goes in the home office.

9. You sleep in your ___bed___.

10. You wash clothes in the ___utility room___.

11. You take a shower in the ___bathroom___.

12. We watch TV in the ___living room___.

13. Clothes go in the ___closet___.

14. Food goes in the ___kitchen___.

15. We eat dinner in the ___dining table___.

Directions: Complete each sentence with the correct form of the verb "**live**"

lives   live   living

1. I ______live______ in a house.
2. You ______live______ in a beautiful condo.
3. We are ______living______ in Houston, TX now.
4. Robert ______lives______ in my neighborhood.
5. We ______live______ near the mall.
6. Lisa is ______living______ in an apartment.
7. Diana ______lives______ in a mobile home.
8. We ______live______ in a small community.
9. They are ______living______ close to their children.
10. Ana is______living______ in Texas now.
11. Mary and Victor ______live______ in Colombia now.
12. My aunt ______lives______ near my teacher.
13. We are ______living______ in a condo now.
14. They ______live______ in a beautiful apartment.

REVIEW AND PRACTICE: ARTICLES

a, an, the

*"**an**" is only used before a noun that begins with a vowel: **a e i o u***

15. Lisa found her cell phone in ___the___ car.

16. I am going to ___the___ doctor at 2:30p.m. today.

17. Diana lives in ___a___ beautiful house.

18. I sent you ___an___ email at 12:00 today.

19. I would like ___a___ cup of coffee please.

20. Please give this paper to ___the___ teacher.

21. I would like ___an___ orange please.

22. My mother is ___an___ excellent cook.

MOVING INTO OUR NEW HOUSE!

My name is Alexandra. I am very excited today because we are moving into our new house. My husband Juan Carlos and my two children, Mary and Jose came to the United States from Colombia ten years ago. My husband found a construction job right away and we have been living in a two-bedroom apartment. My husband is also a security guard at a school at night. I am a cashier at Sedanos' Supermarket. I make $16.00 an hour. I have been working there for five years. We saved our money, and we were able to put $6,000 down on a house. Our new house has three bedrooms, two bathrooms and a big backyard for the children to run around and play in. It also has a beautiful garden in the front yard. Jose and Mary are happy to have their own rooms. Jose wants a green room and Mary wants a pink room. We do not have a garage, but we do have a driveway. We will move our things into the house on Saturday. We have many things to move out of the apartment. We need to put things into the bedrooms, bathrooms, kitchen, closets, dining room and family room. We will be finished moving out of the apartment by the end of July and we will move into the new house by August 1st. Mary's 10th birthday is August 23rd and I want to have a bar-b-que birthday party for her in the backyard of our new house. Hopefully, everything will be ready by then.

Directions: Answer the questions below in complete sentences.

1. What are the names of Alexandra's children? _Mary and Jose are their names._

2. How old is Mary now? _She is nine years old (She will be 10 on Aug. 23rd)_

3. What does this family live in now? _They live in an apartment._

4. Where is the garden located? _The garden is located in the front yard._

5. What is Alexandra's husband's name? _Juan-Carlos is his name._

6. Where is this family from? _They are from Colombia._

7. Where does Alexandra work? _She works at Sedanos Supermarket._

8. What color does Jose want his room to be? _He wants a green room._

9. Who is telling the story? _Alexandra is telling the story._

CONVERSATION PRACTICE

Directions: Complete the information below about what you have in your house.

Example: I live in an apartment. My apartment has two bedrooms and one bathroom. My apartment also has a living room, a large closet and a dining room. In my apartment, I also have a microwave, a table, and pictures.

I live in a(n) _________________. My _________________ has _____ bedroom(s) and _____

bathroom(s). My _________________ also has a(n) _________________, a(n) _________________

and a(n) _________________. In my _________________, I also have a(n) _________________,

a(n) _________________ and _________________.

This is my partner _________________. He/She lives in a(n) _________________. His/Her

_________________ has _____ bedroom(s) and _____ bathroom(s). His/Her _________________

also has a(n) _____________, a(n) _________________ and a(n) _________________. In His/Her

_________________, He/She also has a(n) _________________, a(n) _________________ and

_________________.

1. Where is your microwave located? It is located in the _____________.

2. Where are your shoes located? They are in the _____________.

3. Do you have a garden? Yes, I have a garden. / No, I don't have a garden.

4. Where is your TV? It is in the _____________.

PEOPLE INFORMATION: HOUSING

Name: Bianca **Last name:** Palacios **From:** Honduras **Lives:** Tampa **Residence:** house **bedrooms:** 4 **bathrooms:** 3 * large closets, beautiful garden family room	**Name:** Julio **Last name:** Rodriguez **From:** Colombia **Lives:** The United States **Residence:** apartment **bedrooms:** 1 **bathrooms:** 1 *office, dining room, utility room	**Name:** Victor **Last name:** Oquendo **From:** Venezuela **Lives:** California **Residence:** Condominium **bedrooms:** 3 **bathrooms:** 2 *large kitchen, balcony, lake in the back
Name: Pierre **Last name:** Joseph **From:** Haiti **Lives:** Tampa **Residence:** Mobile Home **bedrooms:** 2 **bathrooms:** 1 utility room, small kitchen	**Name:** Carla **Last name:** Brown **From:** Argentina **Lives:** Georgia **Residence:** apartment **bedrooms:** 3 **bathrooms:** 2 patio, connected garage, office	**Name:** Dor **Last name:** Collins **From:** Brazil **Lives:** Weston **Residence:** house **bedrooms:** 7 **bathrooms:** 5 3-car garage, beautiful garden, pool, big backyard

Directions: Answer each question in a complete sentence.

1. Who has a connected garage? __Carla has a connected garage.__
2. How many people live in a house? __2 people live in a house.__
3. Who lives in California? __Victor lives in California.__
4. Who is from Haiti? __Pierre is from Haiti.__
5. Where is Victor from? __Victor is from Venezuela__
6. How many bathrooms does Carla have? __Carla has one bathroom.__
7. Who is from Argentina? __Carla is from Argentina.__
8. How many bedrooms does Bianca have? __Bianca has 4 bedrooms.__
9. Who lives in a big house? __Dor has a big house.__
10. Who lives in a small apartment? __Julio lives in an apartment.__
11. What do YOU live in? __I live in a(n) __________.__
12. How many bedrooms and bathrooms do you have? __I have ____ bedrooms a ___ bathrooms.__

PREPOSITIONS

A preposition is a word that expresses relation to another word.

above	across	after
against	along	among
around	at	before
behind	below	beneath
beside	in-between	beyond
by	down	outside
over	through	throughout
in	out	to
on	off	under
toward	into	from
within	underneath	upon
in front of	in back of	across from
nearby	next to	together

Directions: Complete each sentence with a **preposition** that makes sense in the sentence.

1.   I am going to the party ________ with ________ my cousin.

2.   Julio is sitting ________ next to ________ me.

3.   Lisa's computer is ________ on ________ the desk.

4.   The bathroom is ________ around ________ the corner.

5.   Walmart is ________ on ________ Miramar Parkway.

6.   Amy lives ________ at ________ 4785 Lakewood Drive.

7.   I am ________ in / from ________ Germany.

8.   Lisa is ________ in front of ________ Rosa and Carlos.

9.   Rosalita is sitting ________ behind ________ Milena.

10.   I work ________ at / in ________ a hospital.

11.   The cell phone is ________ on ________ the table.

12.   Your socks are ________ under / on / next to ________ the bed.

13.   My birthday is ________ in ________ October.

14.   Bank of America is ________ at ________ 3645 Filmore Street.

15.   I came to the United States ________ in ________ July.

PREPOSITIONS

- I live **at** 4855 Gardenhill Road.
- I live **on** Gardenhill Road.
- I live **in** New York.
- My birthday is **on** May 20th.
- I work **at** a hospital.

Directions: Complete each sentence with a preposition.

1. Roberto works ______ at / in ______ Home Depot.
2. My cousin lives ______ in ______ California.
3. Lisa is ______ from / in ______ Cuba.
4. Lisa works ______ in / at ______ Walmart.
5. Theresa is a teller ______ in / at ______ a bank.
6. Please put the baby ______ in / on ______ the bed.
7. My school is ______ on ______ Taft Street.
8. Daniel works ______ in / at/ next to ______ Walmart.
9. I came to the United States ______ in ______ December.
10. Your notebook is ______ on / next to / beside ______ the desk.
11. The teacher is ______ in / in front of / next to ______ the classroom.
12. My birthday is ______ on ______ June 2nd.
13. The party is ______ in ______ May.
14. Please turn the light ______ on / off ______ .
15. I live ______ at ______ 2847 Simmons Street.
16. The children are ______ in ______ the house.
17. Please put the cell phone ______ on ______ the table.
18. My brother works ______ at / in ______ a bank.
19. The store is ______ at ______ 2648 Jefferson Street.
20. I came to the United States ______ on ______ August 17th.

Directions: Find the words in the puzzle below.

living room	bedroom	kitchen	house	bathroom
closet	home Office	family Room	shower	bed
microwave	refrigerator	shoes	picture	chair
lamp	toilet	computer	printer	table

f	a	m	i	l	y	r	o	o	m	q	e	p	k	l	a	m	p
a	s	d	f	g	h	j	k	l	c	v	b	i	z	c	t	d	c
r	e	f	r	i	g	e	r	a	t	o	r	c	c	h	a	i	r
m	i	c	r	o	w	a	v	e	d	c	b	t	q	w	b	p	l
z	x	c	v	b	b	n	m	b	h	c	a	u	s	s	l	o	p
a	s	h	o	u	s	e	w	e	q	w	t	r	h	h	e	r	i
b	e	d	r	o	o	m	n	d	x	z	h	e	o	o	d	t	y
z	x	c	r	e	t	n	i	r	p	a	r	e	e	w	e	q	h
q	r	h	j	e	p	t	r	e	c	s	o	d	s	e	w	a	j
a	d	c	s	h	t	o	i	l	e	t	o	q	w	r	q	a	p
s	d	o	q	m	n	v	a	q	y	t	m	r	e	a	w	s	f
x	l	m	l	i	v	i	n	g	r	o	o	m	t	o	p	l	m
c	c	p	q	a	s	d	f	g	h	j	k	l	m	z	x	c	v
q	r	u	t	h	o	m	e	o	f	f	i	c	e	c	v	b	n
a	e	t	g	y	m	o	u	q	w	e	r	t	y	u	i	o	p
z	d	e	b	u	i	p	q	a	z	s	d	f	g	h	j	k	l
x	c	r	h	j	k	l	k	i	t	c	h	e	n	q	j	f	f

Directions: Answer the questions below in complete sentences.

1. Where does the bed go? **Example**: <u>The bed goes in the bedroom.</u>
2. Where does the computer go? <u>The computer goes in the home office.</u>
3. Where do you eat? <u>I eat at the dining room table.</u>
4. Where do the shoes go? <u>The shoes go in the closet.</u>
5. Where does the microwave go? <u>The microwave goes in the kitchen.</u>
6. Where does the chair go? <u>The chair goes in the living room (bedroom, dining room).</u>
7. What room do you sleep in? <u>I sleep in my bedroom.</u>

HEATHER'S NEW FRIEND

Heather Greenberg is a 13 year-old 7th grade student. She attends Lawrenceville Middle School in Tampa, Florida. Heather lived in Houston, TX all her life, but in 2024, her family moved to Tampa because her father got a really good job in Tampa. Heather was sad because she had to leave all of the friends that she has known all of her life. In Tampa, she will have to make new friends, learn a new city and attend a new school. She is sad about moving. She didn't want to go to Tampa, but she had to go. Her little brother is only 3 years old, so he doesn't understand what is happening. On Heather's first day in her new class, her teacher Mr. Richardson welcomed her and introduced her to the students in her homeroom class. When Heather told the teacher that she was from Texas, the teacher introduced her to Kimberly Campbell, who is also from Texas. Heather and Kimberly started talking and they discovered that they both lived in Houston. They both attended the same elementary school and they both shopped at the same mall. They even know some of the same people. Heather and Kimberly became friends really fast. Now, they talk every day and they eat lunch together too. On Saturday, they plan on going to the movies at the local mall in Tampa. Heather feels a lot better about her new school now.

1. _____F_____ Heather's little sister is 3 years old.

2. _____T_____ Heather is in the 7th grade.

3. _____F_____ Heather and Kimberly were friends in Houston.

4. _____T_____ Heather's family moved to Houston in 2024.

5. _____T_____ Heather was sad because she had to leave her friends in Houston.

6. _____F_____ Heather was excited about going to Tampa.

7. _____T_____ Heather lives in Florida now.

8. _____F_____ Heather and Kimberly are going to a concert this coming Saturday.

9. _____T_____ Heather has one sibling.

Directions: Answer each question below in a complete sentence.

10. What is Heather's teacher's name? Her teacher's name is Mr. Richardson (or) Richardson is Heather's teacher's name.

11. Where is Heather from? Heather is from Houston, TX.

12. Why did Heather move to Tampa? Because she got a really good job in Tampa.

ANSWERING QUESTIONS:

1. **Do you live in a house or an apartment?**
    a. I live in an apartment   b. I live on the house   c. We live at the mobile home

    a. My house have 3 bedrooms   b. It has 3 bedrooms   c. It have 3 bedrooms

2. **Does your house have a laundry room?**
    a. Yes, it does   b. Yes, it do   c. yes, it doesn't

3. **What state is your house in?**
    a. My house is in Georgia   b. My house is in Atlanta   c. My house is in Miami

4. **What is your native country?**
    a. My native country is California   b. It is Colombia   c. It has Colombia

5. **What is your marital Status?**
    a. We is single   b. We is married   c. I am single

6. **Do you have a TV in your house?**
    a. Yes, I do   b. Yes, I did   c. Yes, it doesn't

7. **Where does the microwave go?**
    a. The microwave going in the kitchen   b. It goes in the kitchen   c. It in the kitchen

8. **Where does the toilet go?**
    a. The toilet goes in the bathroom   b. It going in the bathroom   c. It in the bathroom

9. **Do you live near a Walmart store?**
    a. Yes, I do   b. Yes, I did   c. Yes, I will

10. **Where is Julio sitting?**
    a. Julio sitting next to Ana   b. He sitting next to Irene   c. He is sitting next to Ana

11. **What is your teacher's first name?**
    a. Her name is Rodriguez   b. It is Maria   c. My teacher first name is Maria

1. **What street do you live on?**
    a. I live at 56th Street   b. I live on 56th Street   c. I live in 56th Street

2. **Is there a supermarket in yoiur neighborhood?**

    a. Yes, there isn't.   b. Yes, there is.   c. No, they are not.

Directions: Practice speaking the information in each box in complete sentences. Then, complete the sentences below with either "true" or "false."

READING AND SPEAKING PEOPLE INFORMATION

Name: Angela **Last name:** Mendez **From:** Havana, Cuba **Dwelling**: house **Lives:** Bronx, NY 4 bedrooms, 3 bathrooms, dining room, balcony, 2-car garage, swimming pool **mortgage:** $1,850	**Name:** Kimberly **Last name:** Castro **From:** Venice, Italy **Dwelling:** condominium **Lives:** Houston, TX 3 bedrooms, 3 bathrooms, dining room, balcony, family room, utility room, large closets **mortgage:** $2,300	**Name:** Zelda **Last name:** Perkins **From:** Lima, Peru **Dwelling:** apartment 8766 Greenville Lane **Lives:** Miami, FL 2 bedrooms, 1 bathroom, dining room, balcony **rent:** $1,400 **lease:** 1 year
Name: Eduardo **Last name:** Rodriquez **From:** Colombia **Dwelling:** mobile home 9007 Brown Lake Drive **Lives:** Hialeah, FL 2 bedrooms, 1 bathroom, dining room, 2 large closets **rent:** $1,300	**Name:** Bianca **Last name:** Montes **From:** Atlanta, GA **Dwelling:** house **Lives:** Colombia, SC 7 bedrooms, 5 bathrooms, dining room, balcony **rent:** $6,300	**Name:** Juan Carlos **Last name:** Hernandez **From:** Venezuela **Dwelling:** apartment **Lives:** Hollywood, FL 4 bedrooms, 2 bathrooms, 2-car garage, swimming pool, patio, large closets **rent:** $2,300 **lease:** 1 year

TRUE OR FALSE

1. ___F___ Eduardo lives in Atlanta, GA.

2. ___F___ Zelda Perkins pays in $2,300 in rent.

3. ___T___ Bianca Montes is from Atlanta, GA.

4. ___F___ Kimberly Castro lives in Venice, Italy

5. ___T___ Juan Carlos pays $2,300 in rent

6. ___T___ Eduardo Rodriquez has two large closets in his mobile home

7. ___F___ Kimberly Castro's condominium is $3,300 a month.

8. ___T___ Zelda Perkins lives on Greenville Lane.

9. ___T___ Angela Mendez lives in a 4 bedroom, 3 bathroom apartment

microwave	dining room table	bed	sofa
lamp	picture	stove	refridgerator

stove

lamp

couch

picture

microwave

dining room table

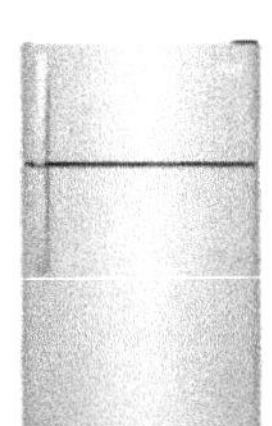

refrigerator

bed

have / has

Rules: ❖ When the subject is "*he*", "*she*", or "*it*", your verb is <u>has</u>.
 ❖ When the subject is "*I*", "*you*", "*we*", or "*they*" your verb is <u>have</u>.

Directions: Complete each sentence with the correct form of "**have**" or "**has**".

1. I ___have___ large closets in my bedroom.
2. We ___have___ three bedrooms in our apartment.
3. Lisa ___has___ a beautiful garden.
4. My brother ___has___ a swimming pool in his backyard.
5. My mother and father ___have___ a big house.
6. Your house ___has___ two floors.
7. Julio's backyard ___has___ a swing for the children.
8. Our new house ___has___ a home office.

HOUSE	APARTMENT	MOBILE HOME	CONDOMINIUM
for sale	for rent	For rent	For sale
4 bdrms, 3 bath	2 bdrms, 1 bath	3 bdrms, 2 bath	2 bdrms, 2
Swimming pool	overlooks the lake	beautiful garden in	bathrooms
Big kitchen	gated community	front yard	near the beach
new washer/dryer	$2,300.00 monthly	near the mall	family room
$296,000	Call: 813-968-4562	$1,500.00 monthly	on a golf course
Call: 505-965-7852		Call: 305-968-7841	$3,965.00
			Call: 796-845-9300

9. The ___condo___ is on a golf course.
10. The ___apartment___ and the ___condo___ have two bedrooms.
11. The ___condo___ is more than $3,000 a month.
12. The ___apartment___ is located in a gated community.
13. The ___house___ has a new washer and dryer.
14. The ___mobile home___ has three bedrooms.
15. The ___mobile home___ is near the mall.
16. The ___house___ has a big kitchen.

REVIEW AND PRACTICE

Directions: Answer the questions below with the correct answer.

1. **How old are you?**
   a. I have 27 years old   b. I was 37 years age   c. I am 37 years old.

2. **Are you going to Walmart today?**
   a. Yes, I do   b. Yes, I was   c. Yes, I am

3. **Do you have a large family?**
   a. Yes, I do   b. Yes, I am   c. Yes, I will

4. **Is that your sister?**
   a. No, she is   b. no, she isn't   c. no, she are

5. **Will they sing on Sunday?**
   a. No, they will   b. no, they won't   c. no, they do

6. **Is Maria your sister?**
   a. Yes, he isn't   b. yes, she are   c. yes, she is.

7. **Are you single?**
   a. No, I'm not   b. no, I don't   c. no, I do

8. **Do you take an English class at Hispanic Unity?**
   a. Yes, I don't   b. yes, I am   c. yes, I do

9. **Are you going to the concert on Saturday?**
   a. Yes, I do   b. Yes, I am   c. Yes, I was

10. **Do you have my cell phone?**
    a. No, I do   b. no, I don't   c. no, I won't

11. **Is your lunch at 12:00p.m?**
    a. Yes, I do   b. Yes, it is   c. yes, they are

12. **Is your birthday on September 5th?**
    a. Yes, it isn't   b. yes, it is   c. yes, I do

13. **Are you happy today?**
    a. Yes, I am   b. Yes, he is   c. No, I isn't

Hello. My name is Mercedes Gomez. I am 38 years old and I live in Atlanta, GA with my two daughters, Lisa and Ashley. Lisa is 16 years old and Ashley is 10 years old. My husband Felipe died in a motorcycle accident last year. I am a widower now. It was very difficult for us when Felipe died. I was devastated and my daughters were very sad. They loved their father. He was very good to them. Felipe worked for a construction company, and they paid for his funeral. I am a secretary at a furniture store, and I make good money, but we still had to move because I could not afford the house that we were living in after Felipe died. We live in an apartment now. It has two bedrooms and one bathroom, and it is nice and clean. It is in a good neighborhood. The girls and I are doing better. We are in a happy place. We spend lots of time together. We go to the beach, the mall and we love to watch movies together. Ashley likes to wash and style my hair. Lisa likes to sing and dance. Lisa works at Publix. She makes $11.00 an hour and she works four days a week. She does not work on Mondays and Tuesdays. She helps me with the bills, and I am very thankful for that. I am proud of both of both my daughters.

1. Where does Lisa work? _____ Lisa works at Publix. _____

2. What is Mercedes' occupation? _____ Mercedes is a secretary. _____

3. Who was Felipe? _____ Felipe was Mercedes husband / Lisa and Ashley's father. _____

4. How did Felipe die? _____ In a motorcycle accident. _____

5. How much does Lisa make on her job? _____ She makes $11.00 an hour. _____

6. What does Ashley like to do? _____ She likes to wash and style Mercedes' hair. _____

7. What does Mercedes like to do with her girls? _____ watch movies _____

8. Who likes to sing and dance? _____ Lisa likes to sing and dance. _____

9. What do they live in now? _____ They live in an apartment. _____

10. Where did Felipe work? _____ He worked at for a construction company. _____

11. How old are Lisa and Ashley? _____ Lisa is 16 and Ashley is 10. _____

12. Where does Mercedes work? _____ She works at a furniture company. _____

TRUE OR FALSE

13. __T__ They were very sad when Felipe died.

14. __F__ Mercedes makes $12.00 an hour on her job.

15. __F__ Their apartment has 2 bathrooms and 1 bedroom.

16. __F__ They live in Chicago, IL

17. __T__ Lisa is 16 years old.

18. __T__ They had to move because Mercedes could not afford to pay the bills in their house.

HOUSE	APARTMENT	MOBILE HOME	CONDOMINIUM
for sale 4 bdrms, 3 bath Swimming pool Big kitchen new washer/dryer $296,000 Call: 505-965-7852	for rent 2 bdrms, 1 bath overlooks the lake gated community $2,300.00 monthly Call: 813-968-4562	For rent 3 bdrms, 2 bath beautiful garden in front yard near the mall $1,500.00 monthly Call: 305-968-7841	For sale 2 bdrms, 2 bathrooms near the beach family room on a golf course $3,965.00 Call: 796-845-9300

Directions: Answer the questions below using **do**, **does**, **don't doesn't**

Example: Does the apartment have a gated community? <u>Yes it does.</u>

1. Does the mobile home have 4 bedrooms? <u>No it doesn't</u>

2. Does the house have a swimming pool? <u>Yes, it does</u>

3. Do the apartment and condo have two bedrooms? <u>Yes, they do</u>

4. Does the apartment have one bathroom? <u>Yes, it does</u>

5. Does the apartment have a garden? <u>No, it doesn't</u>

6. Do the apartment and the mobile home have three bedrooms? <u>No, they don't</u>

7. Does the condo have a family room? <u>Yes, it does</u>

8. Does the mobile home have a garden? <u>Yes, it does.</u>

9. Is the condo for rent? <u>No, it isn't (It is for sale)</u>

10. Is the apartment for rent? <u>Yes, it is.</u>

11. Are the house and the condo for sale? <u>Yes, they are.</u>

ANSWERING QUESTIONS

12. How many bathrooms does the condo have? <u>The Condo / It has two bathrooms.</u>

13. Which one has a swimming pool? <u>The house has a swimming pool.</u>

14. Which ones are for sale? <u>The house and condo are for sale.</u>

15. How much is the rent on the apartment? <u>The apartment is / It is $2,300 a month.</u>

16. How many places are for rent? <u>Two places are for rent.</u>

REVIEW & PRACTICE

Directions: Complete each sentence with the correct form of **have** or **has**.

1. My new house ____has____ three bedrooms.
2. Does your house ____have____ a utility room?
3. My parents ____have____ a big backyard.
4. My sisters ____have____ new beds for their bedrooms.
5. Lisa's house ____has____ large closets.
6. My puppy ____has____ fleas.
7. Luis' house ____has____ a very big kitchen.
8. Carol's condominium ____has____ a balcony.
9. Rosa and I ____have____ a new teacher.
10. Do you ____have____ a pool?

Directions: Complete the sentences with the correct **parts of speech**.

11. Dianna is my good friend. ____She____ is coming over for dinner on Friday night. (pronoun)
12. I ____am / was____ so tired today. (verb to be)
13. That is a ____pretty____ blouse that you are wearing. (adjective)
14. ____Gucci____ is my favorite store. (proper noun)
15. ____I / We / They____ ate all of the chocolate cake. (pronoun)
16. Rosa ____is / was____ singing at church on Sunday. (verb to be)
17. The basketball player is very ____tall____. (adjective)
18. Ana's ____new____ car is very nice. (adjective)
19. We ____are____ going to the supermarket later. (VTB)
20. Please put the cup ____on / next to____ the table. (preposition)

21. Do you live in a house, apartment, mobile home, condominium or other? __I live in a(n) ________.

____

22. How many bedrooms and bathrooms do you have? __I have 2 bedrooms and 2 bathrooms.

____

HOUSING DIALOGUES

1.
Person #1: My neighbor just sold their house.
Person #2: Really? Why did they sell their house?
Person #1: Because they retired and moved back to their home state.
Person #2: What is their home state?
Person #1: They are originally from New York, so they moved back there.
Person #2: Will you miss them? It sounds like you really like them.
Person #1: Yes, I am going to miss them. They were good neighbors, and they are very nice people. Their daughter Mimi and I went shopping many times before she went away to college. I ate dinner at their house sometimes too. One year, I went on vacation with them to Orlando.
Person #2: They sound like very nice people.
Person #1: Yes, they are. They lived next door to me for 15 years. they are like my family. They told me to come visit them in New York. New York is a beautiful state. I am excited to go.
Person #2: When will you go to visit them?
Person #1: Maybe in the summers.
Person #2: I think you will like New York.

2.
Person #1: Good evening.
Person #2: Good evening to you too.
Person #1: I like your new house.
Person #2: Thank you. It has 3 bedrooms and 3 bathrooms. It has big closets and a large family room. It also has a home office.
Person #1: That is very nice. Do you like it?
Person #2: Yes, I love it. Thank you.

3.
Person #1: My three sisters and I have our own places.
Person #2: Really, are you living in the same area?
Person #1: No, my younger sister bought a house in Virginia. My other sister purchased a townhouse in Miami and my oldest sister got a house in Tampa.
Person #2: What is the difference between buying and renting?
Person #1: Well, when you rent, you pay to live there every month. The place is not yours, but when you buy a house, you are paying a mortgage and one day the house will be yours.
Person #2: Okay. I understand. My mother and father own their house, but my brother lives in an apartment and he rents it. He likes his apartment, but one day he wants to buy a house.
Person #1: Yes, you are correct.
Person #2: Well, I want a house. I want to pay a mortgage so one day the house will be mine.
Person #1: Yes, it is nice to own your own house.

4.
Person #1: Hi **(name here)** ___________. Do you still live in a condominium on the west side of town?
Person #2: Yes, I am still living there. Why do you ask?
Person #1: Because my brother just bought a condo in the same community that you live in.
Person #2: That's nice. I really like my condo. It is quiet and clean. I think your brother will like it too.
Person #1: Yes, my brother says he likes it. He says the landscaping is beautiful.
Person #2: Yes, it is. I don't want to move anytime soon.
Person #1: I like your new apartment. It is really nice. The kitchen is big and your bathroom is big too. How many bedrooms does it have?

5. **Person #2:** My apartment has two bedrooms and two bathrooms. It also has a balcony that overlooks the lake. Sometimes I go on my balcony to read and sometimes to look at the lake.
Person #1: Wow! That is nice. How much rent do you pay?
Person #2: I pay $1,400 per month in rent. That includes utilities and maintenance.
Person #1: Oh, okay. That is a little expensive for me. I cannot afford to pay that.
Person #2: Yes, it is a little expensive, but I got a promotion on my job and I am making more money now. I can afford it.
Person #1: That's good. Congratulations on your promotion.

6. **Person #1:** Hello friend. How are you?
Person #2: I am fine and you? How is your family? Where is everyone living now?
Person #1: We are doing fine. Lisa is living in California. My brother Pedro lives in Chicago. My younger sister lives in Texas and my oldest sister lives in Florida with me.
Person #1: Wow, your brothers and sisters are all over the country.
Person #2: Yes, I know, but we come together during the holidays. We were just together last month. Everyone came to Florida for my mother's birthday party.
Person #2: That's nice. Well, say hello to everyone for me.
Person #1: Thank you. I sure will.

7. **Person #1:** My cousin just bought a new house. It is a beautiful home in Orlando. It has 3 bedrooms and 2 bathrooms. It also has a garage and a pool.
Person #2: Wow! That is nice. Congratulations to him. The last time I talked to him, he told me that he was saving his money to buy a house. I am glad he did it.
Person #1: Yes, he really wanted to buy a house. He saved his money for three years.
Person #2: Will he have a housewarming party? He can get many things for the house if he has a housewarming party.
Person #1: Yes, it is going to be in two weeks. I will give you the information later.
Person #2: Perfect. Thank you. I will buy him some things for the kitchen.
Person #1: That's nice. I am going to buy him some things for the bathrooms.

8. **Person #1:** I found a beautiful apartment in the city. I signed the lease yesterday.
Person #2: Congratulations! Do you like it? How many bedrooms does it have?
Person #1: Yes, I love it. It has 2 bedrooms and 2 bathrooms. It also has a beautiful dining room and large closets. I will move in on Saturday. I have so many things to move, but I am happy to have my own place!
Person #2: I can help you move some of your things. What time do you want me to come help?
Person #1: You can come to my mother's house at 10:00a.m and help me pack some things.
Person #2: Okay. I will meet you there. I will bring my brother to help also.
Person #1: Thank you so much. I can use all the help I can get!

WEEKLY ASSESSMENT:
Housing

dining table	couch/sofa	bed	trash can	bathtub
refrigerator	kitchen	picture	microwave	chair

1. The __________ bed __________ goes in the bedroom.
2. The __________ bathtub __________ goes in the bathroom.
3. The __________ chair __________ goes in the living room.
4. Please put the __________ picture __________ on the wall
5. We wash the dishes in the __________ kitchen __________.
6. We eat dinner at the __________ dining table __________.
7. We keep cold food in the __________ refrigerator __________.
8. We sit on the __________ couch / sofa __________ and watch TV.
9. We take a bath in the __________ bathtub __________.

Directions: On the lines below, write the correct **preposition** to complete each sentence.

in	on	at	under	in between
in front of	in back off	behind	with	next to

10. Marcos is sitting __________ in back of __________ Maria and he is pulling her hair.
11. I am going to the doctor __________ at __________ 2:30p.m. today.
12. Carmen is sitting __________ next to __________ Maria and is looking at her paper.
13. Are you going to the wedding __________ with __________ your husband?
14. Jerry is sitting __________ in front of __________ Charlie and Jose.
15. Please put the juice __________ in __________ the refrigerator.
16. Did you turn the light __________ on __________ ?

Directions: Complete each sentence with the correct **verb to be**.

was	were	is	am	are

17. I __________ am __________ very tired and want to go to sleep no.
18. What __________ are __________ your favorite two colors?
19. You __________ are/were __________ very pretty today.
20. Miriam __________ is __________ going to New Jersey for two weeks.

Directions: Complete each sentence with either **have** or **has**.

21. I _______have_______ a beautiful new coat.
22. You _______have_______ long beautiful hair.
23. Lisa _______has_______ a small new puppy.
24. We _______have_______ two hours to go shopping.
25. My teacher _______has_______ a new computer.
26. They _______have_______ a new teacher today.
27. He _______has_______ a beautiful family.
28. The dog _______has_______ fleas.

Directions: Answer the following questions in complete sentences:

29. How many bedrooms and bathrooms do you have? _I have 3 bedrooms and two bathrooms._

30. Do you live in a house, apartment, or other? _______I live in an apartment._______

31. What state do you live in? _______I live in _______._______

32. What do you have in your living room? _I have a couch, a chair, a coffee table and a rug._

Lesson 4: Food

Dear ESL Teacher,

Welcome to Lesson 4: Exploring Food! This lesson dives deep into the world of culinary vocabulary and grammar, aimed at enriching your students' language skills through engaging activities. Divided into essential food categories such as fruit, vegetables, beverages, meat, and desserts, students will not only learn to identify and describe these items but also practice using them in context.

One of the highlights of this lesson is the interactive skit, where students assume different roles while ordering food at a restaurant. This activity not only enhances their speaking and listening abilities but also reinforces the practical application of the vocabulary and grammar structures learned.

In addition to hands-on activities, students will explore their preferences and similarities using a Venn Diagram. They will identify what one person likes on the left side, what another person likes on the right side, and discover shared preferences in the middle. This visual tool encourages critical thinking and collaborative learning among students.

As you guide your class through Lesson 4, you will find a structured approach that includes direct instruction, guided practice, and independent practice. These methods ensure a comprehensive learning experience that accommodates various learning styles and abilities. Our commitment to differentiation and adaptations further supports every student's journey towards language proficiency, offering tailored support where needed.

We encourage you to utilize this lesson plan as a foundation for engaging and effective teaching, empowering your students to confidently navigate the language of food and communicate fluently in English.

OBJECTIVES:

1. Students will identify and use vocabulary related to food and food categories (fruit, vegetables, beverages, meat, desserts).
2. Students will construct and practice sentences using subject-verb agreement and negative forms (don't, doesn't, no, not).
3. Students will demonstrate understanding of past tense verbs and plural nouns using the letter "s".
4. Students will engage in conversations using learned vocabulary and grammar.
5. Students will comprehend and respond to reading comprehension passages related to food.
6. Students will create dialogues to practice communication skills.
7. Students will demonstrate their learning through a comprehensive assessment on food.

INSTRUCTIONAL PROCEDURES:

Direct Instruction:
- **Objective:** Present new vocabulary and grammar concepts clearly and explicitly.

- **Details:** Introduce vocabulary words related to food categories (fruit, vegetables, etc.) with visuals and contextual examples. Explain grammar concepts such as subject-verb agreement, negative forms (don't, doesn't, no), past tense verbs, and plural nouns using "s". Use visuals and examples on a whiteboard or projector for clarity.

Guided Practice:
- **Objective:** Help students apply new knowledge in a supportive environment.

- **Details:** Have students work on activities from the book where they practice using food vocabulary and grammar structures in guided exercises. Provide sentence frames and prompts for structured practice. Encourage peer collaboration in pairs or small groups to reinforce learning.

Independent Practice:
- **Objective:** Reinforce learning through individual or paired activities.

- **Details:** Assign worksheet pages from the book focusing on food vocabulary usage, grammar rules (subject-verb agreement, past tense verbs, plural nouns), and conversational skills. Provide clear instructions and examples. Monitor progress and offer support as needed.

Differentiation/Adaptations:
- **Support for English Language Learners:** Use visual aids and simplified instructions. Break down complex concepts and provide bilingual dictionaries if necessary.

- **Accommodations for Diverse Learners:** Offer alternative assessments or activities. Provide extensions for advanced learners and adjust pacing for slower learners. Use flexible grouping to support social and emotional needs.

ACTIVITIES:

1. **Vocabulary Introduction:**

Objective: Introduce food categories through visual aids and practice pronunciation.

Details: Use flashcards with images of various foods (fruit, vegetables, beverages, meat, desserts). Display each flashcard, pronounce the word, and ask students to repeat. Provide examples of sentences using each food item to demonstrate usage.

2. **Grammar Drill:**

Objective: Reinforce grammar concepts including subject-verb agreement, negative forms, past tense verbs, and plural nouns.

Details: Conduct exercises such as:
Subject-Verb Agreement: Provide sentences with missing verbs and ask students to fill in the correct form (e.g., She ___ apples every day).

Negative Forms: Create sentences using negatives (e.g., I don't like seafood, Lisa has no lunch money today).

Past Tense Verbs: Give sentences in present tense and ask students to rewrite them in past tense.

Plural Nouns: Provide singular nouns and have students write their plural forms (e.g., apple → apples).

3. Conversation Practice:
Objective: Develop speaking skills through dialogues about food-related scenarios.

Details: Assign characters from the skit provided in the lesson on 'Natasha's Birthday Dinner' which emphasizes ordering food. Have certain students act out their parts in the skit.

4. Reading Comprehension
Objective: Have students read the story found in the lesson. Enhance reading skills with passages about food found in the story.

Details: Ask comprehension questions such as:

- What is the main idea of the passage?
- What foods are mentioned in the text?
- How do the characters in the story feel about the food?

5. Natasha's Birthday Dinner Skit

Objective: Practice reading a skit using food vocabulary and grammar structures in a social context.

Details:
Distribute prompt sheets

- *Preparation:*
Introduce the scenario to students: Natasha is celebrating her birthday at a restaurant with her friends. Each student will play a different character.

- *Character Assignments:*
Assign roles to students (e.g., Natasha, friends named Alex, Maria, and James). Each character will have specific preferences and roles in the dialogue.

- *Role-Play:*
Allow students time to practice their lines and interactions in pairs or small groups. Encourage natural conversation flow and pronunciation practice.

- *Performance:*
Have groups perform their dialogues in front of the class or record them for later feedback. Encourage students to use gestures and expressions to enhance their presentations.

- *Reflection:*
Discuss the experience: What did they learn about ordering food in a restaurant? How did they use the vocabulary and grammar structures in their dialogue?

6. **Dialogues:**
Objective: Foster creativity and application of vocabulary and grammar in context through reading short dialogues in conversational tone.

Details: Students will get into pairs. Teacher will assign students a dialogue number to read. Students will take five minutes to practice their dialogue silently, then the teacher will call on each dialogue number and the pair of students who were given that number will read.

7. **Venn Diagram on Food**
Objective: Compare and contrast different types of food categories using a Venn diagram.

Details: Give students a Venn diagram with circles. Have them identify similarities, differences and same using the dialogues provided.

8. **Speaking with Negatives:**
Objective: Practice using negatives (don't, doesn't, no, not) in spoken language.

Details: Provide sentence prompts where students express preferences or situations using negatives:

" I like pasta, but I <u>don't</u> like seafood.
"Lisa has lunch, but she has <u>no</u> money today."

9. **Assessment:**
Objective: Evaluate comprehension and application of lesson content.

Details: The assessment is located at the back of the lesson.

Materials and Resources:
- Book: It's Time to Learn English
- Vocabulary cards
- Whiteboard and markers
- Textbooks or reading materials
- Worksheets for grammar exercises
- Audio recordings for listening activities

Technology Needed:
- Projector or screen for displaying visuals
- Computer or tablet for accessing digital resources

Lesson 4: Food

T - Think Back (Review)

Activity: Begin the lesson by reviewing key concepts and vocabulary from the previous lesson. Use a brief warm-up activity to engage students and assess their understanding of any food-related terms they might already know.

Time: 5-10 minutes

E – Entry (Introduction/Beginning)

Activity: Introduce new vocabulary words related to food categories (fruit, vegetables, beverages, meat, desserts) using flashcards, images, or charts. Explain the meanings, provide clear definitions, pronunciation examples, and have students read the sentences in the book to demonstrate usage.

Time: 15 minutes

A - Application (Teaching/Presentation/Delivery)

Activity: Present new grammar concepts clearly and explicitly. Use direct instruction to introduce subject-verb agreement, negative forms (don't, doesn't, no), past tense verbs, and plural nouns using "s". Provide examples and demonstrate their usage in sentences.

- **Time:** 20 minutes

C - Collaborative Practice (Student Practice)

Activity: Facilitate guided practice by having students work in pairs or small groups to complete structured activities using sentence frames or prompts. Walk around the classroom to offer support and feedback. Encourage students to engage in conversations about food-related scenarios, such as ordering food at a restaurant or discussing their favorite foods. Assign pages from the book for students to complete to practice their understanding.

- **Time:** 25 minutes

H - Highlight (Wrap-up/Closing)

Activity: Summarize the key points of the lesson, highlighting the new vocabulary and grammar rules learned. Assign a reading comprehension activity using a passage about food. Discuss the main ideas and ask comprehension questions.

Time: 10 minutes

E - Evaluate (Assessment/Evaluation)

Activity: Administer the comprehensive assessment found at the end of the lesson. Assess students on vocabulary, grammar, reading comprehension, and dialogue creation.

Time: 15 minutes

R - Reflect (Final Review)

Activity: End the lesson with a reflective activity where students can share their thoughts on what they learned, how they can use it in real-life situations, and any areas where they need further clarification. Encourage students to share their thoughts on their progress and areas they want to improve.

Time: 5-10 minutes

Food

4

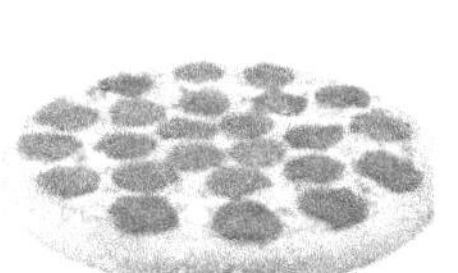

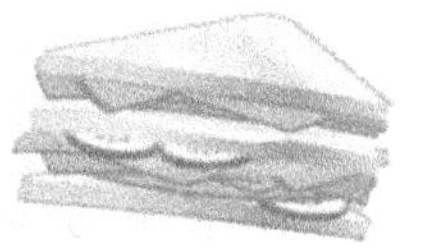

FRUIT	VEGETABLES	BEVERAGES	MEAT	DESSERTS
apples	asparagus	coffee	chicken	chocolate cake
bananas	broccoli	milk	turkey	cheesecake
oranges	corn	water	fish	flan
peaches	celery	juice	pork	ice-cream
pears	carrots	tea	beef	apple pie

VOCABULARY WORDS:

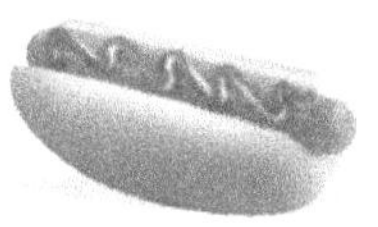

eat	breakfast
drink	lunch
hungry	dinner
beverage	meal
taste	spoon
soup	knife
salad	fork
appetizer	cheap
entrée	expensive
dessert	seafood
pie	juice

Vocabulary Sentences

Food

1. I am so **hungry**. What do you have to eat?

2. I want to **eat** seafood and salad for **dinner** tonight.

3. Cheesecake is my favorite **dessert**.

4. Fruit punch is my favorite **juice**.

5. For my **appetizer**, I would like buffalo wings.

6. You need a **knife** to cut your steak.

7. I will have a steak, a potato, and green **vegetables** for my **entrée** please.

8. I would like a lemonade for my **beverage**.

9. You must use a salad **fork** to eat your salad.

10. **Dinner** is my favorite **meal** of the day.

11. My mother **baked** my brother a cake for his birthday.

12. I love to eat pancakes for **breakfast**.

13. My mother made me chicken **soup** when I was sick.

14. We are going to a restaurant for **dinner** tonight.

15. You must eat ice-cream with a **spoon**.

16. My coffee **cup** is in the cabinet.

17. My mother's food **tastes** very good.

18. My mother had red **wine** with her dinner tonight.

19. I like **fried** chicken, but fried food is not good for you.

20. Walmart is **cheaper** than Trader Joe's Supermarket.

21. I bought an apple **pie** from Sweethouse Bakery today.

22. Would you like a **slice** of chocolate cake?

Study

1. 

Fork
We eat food with a <u>fork</u>.

2. 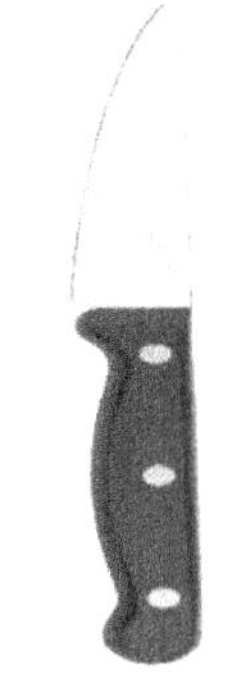

knife
You cut meat with a <u>knife</u>.

3. 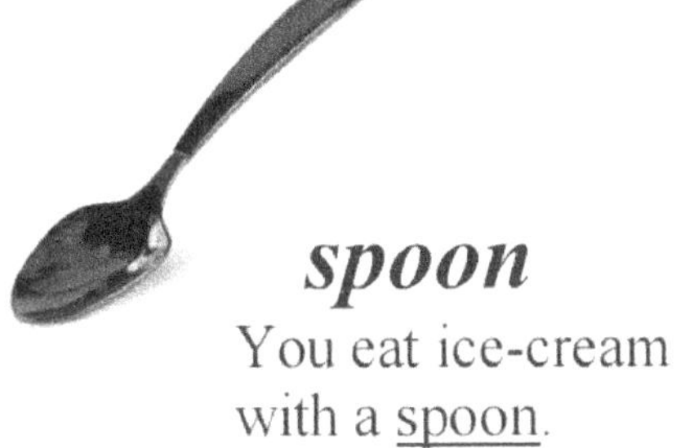

spoon
You eat ice-cream with a <u>spoon</u>.

4. 

bowl
You eat cereal in a <u>bowl</u>.

5. 

cup
You drink water from a <u>cup</u>.

6. 

coffee cup
You drink coffee from a <u>coffee cup</u>.

FRUIT	VEGETABLES	BEVERAGES	MEAT	DESSERTS
apples	asparagus	coffee	chicken	chocolate cake
bananas	broccoli	milk	turkey	cheesecake
oranges	corn	water	fish	flan
peaches	celery	juice	pork	ice-cream
pears	carrots	tea	beef	apple pie

SPEAKING WITH LIKE AND DISLIKE

Directions: Complete the sentences with what you like and what you don't like from the above chart.

I like celery .   I don't like pears .
I like oranges .   I don't like tea .
I like beef .   I don't like pork .

SUBJECT/VERB AGREEMENT GRAMMAR RULE:

❖ When the subject is <u>he</u>, <u>she</u>, or <u>it</u>, there is an **"s"** on the verb.

❖ When the subject is <u>I</u>, <u>you</u>, <u>we</u>, or <u>they</u> there is **no "s"** on the verb.

Example:

HE, SHE, IT:	I, YOU, WE, THEY:
He likes chicken.	I like celery.
She likes turkey.	You like corn.
It (the dog) likes beef.	We like carrots. They like broccoli.

Example:

1.	Maria likes oranges.
2.	I like flan.
3.	Jorge likes coffee.
4.	We like juice.
5.	You like bananas.

Directions: Choose the correct answer to complete each sentence below.

SUBJECT/VERB AGREEMENT GRAMMAR RULE:

❖ When the subject is <u>he</u>, <u>she</u>, or <u>it</u>, you say "doesn't." (negative)

❖ When the subject is <u>I</u>, <u>you</u>, <u>we</u>, or <u>they</u> you say "don't." (negative)

Example:

1. Maria ___likes___ eggs. ○ like ○ likes ○ don't like
2. Roberto ___likes___ toast. ○ doesn't likes ○ likes ○ don't like
3. I ___don't like___ spaghetti. ○ likes ○ doesn't like ○ don't like
4. You ___like___ beef. ○ likes ○ doesn't like ○ like
5. He ___likes___ garlic bread. ○ likes ○ doesn't likes ○ like
6. We ___don't like___ pasta. ○ don't like ○ doesn't like ○ likes
7. Diana ___doesn't like___ beans. ○ don't like ○ doesn't like ○ like
8. They ___don't like___ seafood. ○ likes ○ don't like ○ doesn't like

CONVERSATION PRACTICE

Example: Hello. My name is Mia. Breakfast is my favorite meal of the day. For breakfast, I usually eat bacon, eggs and toast. This is my partner Rosa. Dinner is her favorite meal of the day. For dinner, she usually likes to eat chicken, rice and vegetables.

Now, you practice:

My name is ___________________. My favorite meal of the day is ___________________. I

usually like to eat ___________________ , ___________________ , and ___________________ .

This is my partner ___________________ . His/Her favorite meal of the day is

___________________. He/She usually likes to eat ___________________ for

___________________.

Directions: Review the chart below and answer the questions below.

RULE:

He, She: **doesn't**   I you, we, they: **don't**

Question: Does Tina like coffee?   *Answer*: Yes, she does or No she doesn't.

"does"   "don't"   "does"   "doesn't"

	Flan	Chocolate cake	Lemonade	coffee
David	yes	no	yes	no
Christian	yes	yes	yes	no
Jenny	yes	yes	no	no
Tina	yes	no	no	yes
Mary	no	yes	yes	yes
Victor	no	no	yes	yes

1. Does Christian drink lemonade? _____Yes, he does._____
2. Does Mary like flan? _____No, she doesn't._____
3. Do David and Tina like flan? _____Yes, they do._____
4. Does Victor like coffee? _____Yes, he does._____
5. Do David and Tina like chocolate cake? _____No, they don't._____
6. Does Victor like flan? _____No, he doesn't._____
7. Does Tina like to drink lemonade? _____No, she doesn't._____
8. Does David like chocolate cake? _____No, he doesn't._____
9. Does Mary like coffee? _____Yes, she does._____
10. What does Victor not like? _____Victor doesn't like flan and chocolate cake._____
11. What do David and Christian not like? _____They don't like coffee._____
12. What does Victor like? _____Victor likes lemonade and coffee._____
13. Do Mary and Victor like coffee? _____Yes, they do._____

Directions: Answer the questions about yourself below.

14. What foods do you like? _____I like _____________ and _____________._____
15. What foods do you **not** like? _____I don't like like _____________ and _____________._____
16. What do you like to drink? _____I like to drink like _____________ and _____________._____
17. What is your favorite dessert? _____My favorite dessert is _____________._____

Directions: Complete the sentences below with a word from the chart below:

FRUIT	VEGETABLES	BEVERAGES	MEAT	DESSERTS
apples	asparagus	coffee	chicken	chocolate cake
bananas	broccoli	milk	turkey	cheesecake
oranges	corn	water	fish	flan
peaches	celery	juice	pork	ice-cream
pears	carrots	tea	beef	apple pie

1. My favorite fruits are (answers may vary) and (answers may vary).

2. We had ice-cream and cake for Rachel's birthday.

3. My favorite dessert is dessert may vary).

4. My favorite vegetables are (vegetables may vary) and vegetables may vary).

5. I like to eat (answer may vary) with rice and vegetables for dinner.

6. Sometimes, I eat (answer may vary) for dessert after my dinner.

7. I love to drink (beverage may vary) for breakfast. I also like to drink (beverage may vary).

8. Lisa drinks low-fat milk with her cereal.

9. My mother baked me a chocolate or cheese (cake) for my birthday last week.

10. Lisa's favorite meat is (meat may vary).

11. I like to eat (answers may vary) with (answers may vary) for dinner sometimes.

Directions: Complete the sentences below:

12. For breakfast, I like to eat (answers may vary) and (answers may vary).

13. For lunch, I like to eat (answers may vary) and (answers may vary).

14. For dinner, I like to eat (answers may vary) and (answers may vary).

15. My favorite beverages are (answers may vary) and (answers may vary).

16. My favorite meal of the day is one: breakfast, lunch, or dinner.

Directions: Complete the sentences below from the information in the Venn Diagram.

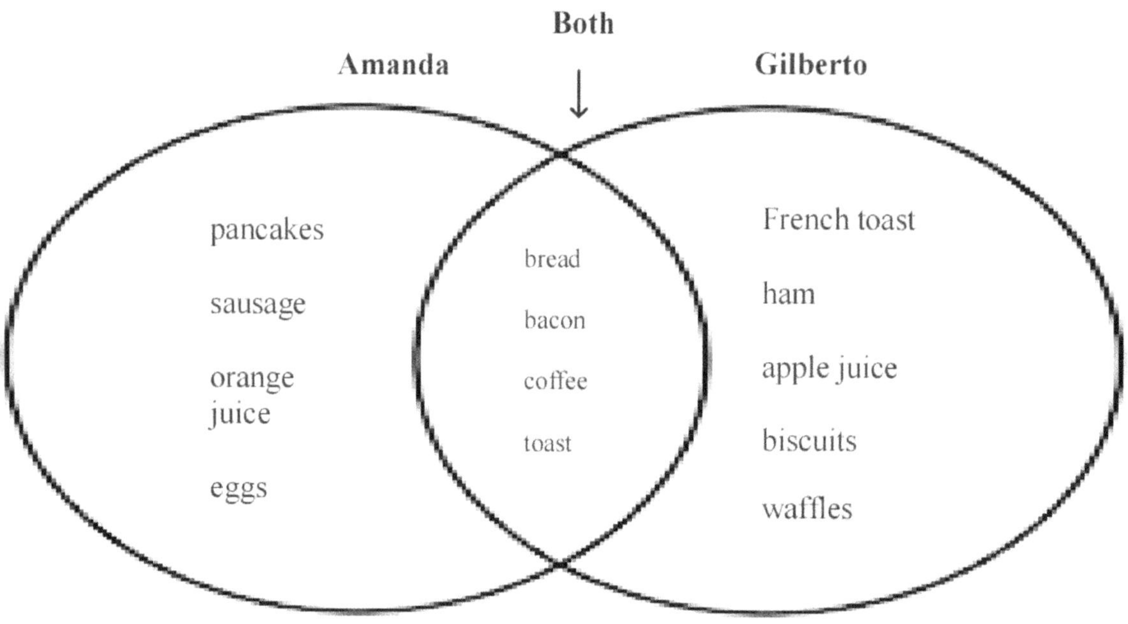

1. Amanda doesn't like (answer may vary) .

2. Gilberto likes (answer may vary) .

3. Gilberto doesn't like (answer may vary) .

4. Amanda likes (answer may vary) .

5. Amanda and Gilberto both like bacon, bread and coffee or toast .

6. Amanda likes to drink orange juice or coffee .

7. Gilberto likes to drink apple juice or coffee .

8. Amanda doesn't like to drink apple juice .

9. Amanda doesn't like (answer may vary) and Gilberto doesn't like (answer may vary) .

10. Amanda likes (answer may vary) but Gilberto doesn't like (answer may vary) .

11. Gilberto likes biscuits, but Amanda doesn't like biscuits.

Directions: Complete each sentence with a simple verb or an **infinitive** from the chart below. With an infinitive the word "to" goes immediately after a simple verb. Ex. I need "to" sleep.

eat	drink	to	taste	leave	learn
prepare	make	cook	go	move	sleep

1. I want _____ to _____ go to dinner at 7:00p.m.

2. We want _____ to _____ go to the mall on Saturday.

3. I like to _____ cook _____ for my family every day.

4. My mother likes to _____ make _____ a big Thanksgiving dinner each year.

6. We will _____ prepare _____ to leave in one hour.

7. My friend wants to _____ make _____ me a cake for my birthday.

8. I would like to _____ learn _____ to speak English.

9. What would you like to _____ drink _____ with your meal?

10. Would you like to _____ taste _____ my soup? It is delicious.

CONVERSATION PRACTICE

Hello classmates. For breakfast this morning, I had a/**some pancakes**, a/**some eggs** and a/**some bacon**. For my beverage, I drank some **coffee**. This is my friend **Leslie**. For breakfast this morning, he/**she** had some **yogurt**, a/some **fruit** and a/some **oatmeal**. For his/**her** beverage, he/she drank **orange juice**.

Hello classmates. For breakfast this morning, I had a/an/some _____________ a/an/some, _____________ and a/an/some _____________. For my beverage, I drank some _____________. This is my friend _____________. For breakfast this morning, he/she had some _____________, a/some _____________ and a/some _____________. For his/her beverage, he/she drank some _____________.

Directions: Complete each sentence with the past tense form of the verb.

regular = ed	cons + y = (no y) ied	vowel + y = ed	ends with e = d only

1. My friends ______played______ in the park yesterday. (play)
2. I ______exercised______ for three hours yesterday. (exercise)
3. We ______moved______ to Pembroke Pines last year. (move)
4. My family ______celebrated______ my mother's birthday yesterday. (celebrate)
5. My father ______worked______ three hours overtime last night. (work)
6. Last week, we ______learned______ many things in our English class. (learn)
7. We ______danced______ for hours at the party last night. (dance)
8. I ______practiced______ my vocabulary words yesterday. (practice)
9. The nice boy ______smiled______ at me 10 minutes ago. (smile)
10. We ______disagreed______ a lot 1 year ago, but now we get along. (disagree)

Directions: Complete each sentence with the plural form of the noun provided.

regular = s	cons + y = ies (no y)	vowel + y = s only	ends with: x,s,ch,sh = es

11. The three ______ladies______ at the door are my sisters. (lady)
12. We have three ______birthdays______ in my class this month. (birthday)
13. My brother grew two ______inches______ since last year. (inch)
14. There were two ______witnesses______ in the case. (witness)
15. I ate two ______sandwiches______ for lunch today. (sandwich)
16. The teacher read us three ______stories______ today. (story)
17. We saw many ______monkeys______ at the zoo today. (monkey)
18. I bought two ______jackets______ at the mall today. (jacket)
19. I need three ______notebooks______ for class. (notebook)
20. The ______boxes______ are very heavy. (box)

Directions: Complete the sentences below with the correct verb that agrees with the subject.

SUBJECT/VERB AGREEMENT GRAMMAR RULE:

❖ **VERB**: A "verb" is a word that shows action in a sentence. The verb tells what the subject is doing in the sentence. Example: My daughter **sleeps** late on Saturdays.

1. Maria _____sleeps_____ three times a week.   (sleep/sleeps)

2. Jose _____lives_____ in Houston now.   (live/lives)

3. We _____play_____ outside every day.   (play/plays)

4. My car _____drives_____ very fast.   (drive/drives)

5. You _____sing_____ beautifully.   (sing/sings)

6. I _____run_____ in the park after work.   (run/runs)

7. We _____read_____ in my English class in the afternoons.   (read/reads)

8. My cousin _____makes_____ seafood on Fridays.   (make/makes)

9. My father _____works_____ 50 hours a week.   (work/works)

10. The baby _____sleeps_____ eight hours a day.   (sleep/sleeps)

SUBJECT/VERB AGREEMENT GRAMMAR RULE:

❖ *Infinitive*: "to" An infinitive word "to" in front of it. It can be used in many ways including as the subject of a sentence.

Example:

1. Mary wants **to go** to the store.   *The infinitive is "to" and the verb is* go.

2. You need **to stop** smoking.   *The infinitive is "to" and the verb is* stop.

3. My father loves **to eat** at Pollo Tropical.   *The infinitive is "to" and the verb is* eat.

4. The baby needs **to sleep**.   *The infinitive is "to" and the verb is* sleep.

5. The teacher likes **to sing** in class.   *The infinitive is "to" and the verb is* sing.

6. Diana's son wants **to work** at the mall.   *The infinitive is "to" and the verb is* work.

RULE:
A **simple verb** (no s) is written after an infinitive.

Directions: Complete the sentences below with either an infinitive **or** with a simple verb from the box below.

sit	stop	continue	listen	study
eat	wash	invite	ask	know

1. I like to _____eat_____ seafood on weekends.
2. You need to _____study_____ your English words every day.
3. I like to _____sit_____ next to my friends in class.
4. I want _____to_____ see a movie on Saturday.
5. You need _____to_____ stop smoking.
6. My mother likes to _____wash_____ clothes on weekends.
7. I would like _____to_____ order takeout tonight.
8. My son wants _____to_____ celebrate his birthday in Tampa.
9. We want to _____continue_____ taking an English class next term.
10. John wants to _____invite_____ 100 people to his party.
11. I would like to _____ask_____ you a question.
12. We want _____to_____ stay in California on vacation.
13. You need to _____listen_____ to me when I am speaking.
14. We would like to _____know_____ what time the movie starts.
15. Bobby wants _____to_____ work at a hospital.

SUBJECT VERB AGREEMENT:

He, she, it: Requires an "s" on the verb. **I, you, we, they**: There is "no s" on the verb.

16. My daughter loves to _____sing_____. She is _____singing_____ now. (sing)
17. My husband _____eats_____ around 6:00p.m. He is _____Bogota / Cuba / Italy_____ now. (eat)
18. Brian and Tony _____play_____ football. Tony _____plays_____ on Saturdays and Brian _____plays_____ on Fridays. (play)
19. My classmates _____read_____ in class every day. They are _____reading_____ now. (read)

LISSETTE'S BIRTHDAY CELEBRATION

Last night, my family went to La Carreta's Restaurant to celebrate my sister Lissette's 22nd birthday. La Carreta's Restaurant is located on Miami Beach and we sat outside on the balcony to eat. There were 11 of us and we had a wonderful time. The birthday girl ordered lobster soup for her appetizer. She had chicken and shrimp pasta for her main entrée with a side salad. She had red wine for her beverage. After the restaurant, we went to my mother's house and sang happy birthday to Lissette. We gave her some birthday gifts and had a wonderful time. One of her gifts was a beautiful two-carat diamond necklace from her boyfriend Juan-Carlos. She was so happy to receive such a beautiful gift. She also received a pretty black dress, a nice handbag, a blouse and over $200 in cash. I gave her a $50 gift card from Macys. She said to me, *"Thank you David. I love Macy's."* That made me happy. I am glad that she liked my gift card. On Friday night, she will go on a weekend vacation to Palm Beach with Juan-Carlos, and she will return on Sunday night. She was very happy to celebrate her birthday with all of the people she loves and who loves her. Her sisters, brothers and parents were also happy for her. Happy birthday to Lissette!

1. How old is Lissette now? _Lissette is 22 years old now. / She is 22 years old now._

2. What was Lisette's beverage? _Lissette had red wine._

3. What was David's gift to Lissette? _He gave her a diamond necklace._

4. What is Lissette's boyfriend's name? _His name is Juan-Carlos._

5. Where is Lissette going for the weekend? _She is going to Palm Beach._

6. Does Lissette have sisters and brothers? _Yes, she does._

7. Where is La Carreta's Restaurant located? _It is in on Miami Beach._

8. How many people celebrated Lissette's birthday at the restaurant? _There were 11 people._

9. Who gave Lissette the diamond necklace? _It was Juan-Carlos._

10. What was Lissette's main entrée? _She had chicken and shrimp pasta._

11. Did Lissette order an appetizer? _Yes, she ordered lobster soup._

12. When is Lissette going to Palm Beach? _She will leave on Friday night._

13. Who was telling the story? _David is telling the story. (Lissette's brother)_

Tony's Lunch Receipt

Server: Bianca   Table #11

LUNCH RECEIPT

cheese sticks	$6.40
cheeseburger	$7.70
French Fries	$4.35
pink lemonade	$2.75
1 slice of cheesecake	$5.30
	$26.50
Tax:	$1.59
Total:	$28.09

Tip: 10%: $2.80   15%: $4.21   20%: $5.61

1. What was Tony's beverage? _It was a pink lemonade._

2. Did Tony order an appetizer? _Yes, he ordered cheese sticks._

3. What was the total cost of the bill without tax? _The bill without tax was $26.50._

4. What was Tony's dessert? _His dessert was a slice of cheesecake._

5. What is the total cost of the bill with 15% tip? _It was $32.30 with a 15% tip._

6. What table did Tony sit at? _Tony sat a table #11._

7. What was Tony's main entrée? _His main entree was a cheeseburger with fries._

8. How much was the tax? _The tax was $1.59._

9. Who was Tony's server? _Bianca was Tony's server._

1. **What would you like for breakfast?**
    a.   I would like roast beef, vegetables and a baked potato.
    b.   I would like a cheeseburger and fries.
    c.   I would like a bacon and egg sandwich.

2. **What are your favorite beverages?**
    a.   My favorite beverages is coffee, tea and mango juice.
    b.   My favorite beverage is coffee, tea and mango juice.
    c.   My favorite beverages are coffee, tea and mango juice.

3. **What would you like for your dessert?**
    a.   I would like some flan for dessert.
    b.   I like flan for dessert.
    c.   For dessert, I make flan.

4. **What is your favorite color?**
    a.   My favorite colors are black and white.
    b.   My favorite color is blue.
    c.   My favorite blue is color.

5. **What meats will you buy?**
    a.   I will buy turkey.
    b.   I will buy fish and roast beef.
    c.   I buy pork.

6. **How much are the chips and the bread?**
    a.   The chips are $2.00 and the bread are $1.79.
    b.   The chips is $2.00 and the bread is $1.79.
    c.   The chips are $2.00 and the bread is $1.79.

7. **How much is the ice-ream and the cookies?**
    a.   The ice-cream $3.49 and the cookies is $2.29.
    b.   The ice-cream is $3.49 and the cookies are $2.29.
    c.   The ice-cream are $3.49 and the cookies are $2.29.

8. **What time are you going to the restaurant?**
    a.   I going to the restaurant at 6:00p.m. this evening.
    b.   I am going to the restaurant at 6:00p.m. this evening.
    c.   I go to the restaurant at 6:00p.m. this evening.

9. **Where are you going?**
    a.   I am going fine thank you.
    b.   I am doing to my house.
    c.   I am going to my house.

10. **What are you eating?**
    a.   I am making chicken and rice.
    b.   I am eating seafood now.
    c.   I am cooking chicken and rice for dinner tonight.

READING AND SPEAKING PEOPLE INFORMATION

Directions: Practice speaking the information in each box in complete sentences. ***For example:*** Her name is Katrina. Her last name is Cuevas. She is 27 years old. She is from Honduras, but she lives in Miami Gardens now. Her favorite foods are pasta and seafood. Her favorite dessert is flan. She likes to drink water and lemonade.

Name: Katrina **Last name**: Cuevas **age**: 12 **From**: Honduras **Lives**: Miami Gardens **Favorite food**: Pasta, seafood **Dessert**: flan **Beverage(s)**: water, lemonade	**Name**: John **Last name**: Rodriguez **From**: Cuba **Lives**: Hollywood **Favorite food**: Pork, Chicken, black beans, vegetables **Dessert**: chocolate cake **Beverage(s)**: mango juice, coca cola, water	**Name**: Moses **Last name**: Greenberg **From**: Africa **age**: 23 **Lives**: West Palm Beach **Favorite food**: fish, turkey, broccoli, salads **Dessert**: cheesecake **Beverage(s)**: water
Name: Joseph **Last name**: Williams **From**: Colombia **age**: 16 **Lives**: Plantation **Favorite food**: pasta, steak, baked potatoes, fried chicken **Dessert**: apple pie, cheesecake **Beverage(s)**: coffee, tea, apple juice, pineapple juice	**Name**: Jennifer **Last name**: Hernandez **From**: Puerto Rico **Lives**: Ft. Lauderdale **Favorite food**: fish, pork, corn, black beans, carrots and fried chicken **Dessert**: flan **Beverage(s)**: wine, beer, coffee, tea, lemonade and Pepsi	**Name**: Mia **Last name**: Merritt **From**: The United States **Lives**: Pembroke Pines **Favorite food**: Caesar Salad, chicken/shrimp pasta, fried shrimp **Dessert**: cheesecake **Beverage(s)**: lemonade

Directions: Answer the questions below with the information above.

1. Who lives in Hollywood? John lives in Hollywood.

2. Who is 16 years old? Joseph is 16 years old.

3. Whose favorite dessert is flan? Flan is Katrina ad Jennifer's favorite dessert.

4. What is Mia's favorite beverage? Mia's favorite beverage is lemonade.

5. Where is Moses from? Moses is from Africa.

6. Where does John live? John lives in Hollywood.

7. How old is Katrina? Katrina is 12 years old.

8. Who likes to eat broccoli and salads? Moses likes to eat broccoli and salads.

9. Who is from Colombia? Joseph is from Colombia.

NATASHA'S BIRTHDAY DINNER

Characters: Lisa, Dianna, Mia, Michael, David,
Mom, Natasha, Greeter, Tracy (waitress)

Lisa: Hello family
Everyone: Hello
Lisa: How was your day today?
Dianna: I had a good day.
Michael: My day was fine.
David: Fine. Thank you.
Mia: I had a long day. I'm tired.
Mom: I had a good day. Thank you … And you?
Lisa: I had a great day. I wanted to talk to you about taking Natasha to dinner tonight to celebrate her birthday. She turned 24 years old today.
Dianna: Okay. What did you want to talk about?
Lisa: What restaurant do you want to take her to and what time should we leave?
Mom: Let's go to the new restaurant on Johnson Street. It's called Antonio's. She gets home around 5:30p.m, so let's give her time to get home and freshen up before we leave.
David: Yes, I saw that restaurant. I always wanted to go there. I wonder what kind of food they have. Let's take her there. It looks like a nice restaurant.
Dianna: I think it is an Italian restaurant. I agree. Let's plan to leave around 7:00p.m.
Michael: Yes, I think 7:00p.m. is a good time to leave.
David: Yes, that's a good time. I agree.
Lisa: Perfect. So everyone needs to be ready at 7:00p.m.
Michael: I will be ready.
Mom: I'll be ready too.
David: Me too.

*** Natasha comes home. ***

Natasha: Good evening everyone.
Everyone: Happy Birthday! How was your day today?
Natasha: Thank you. I had a good day at work. My coworkers sang happy birthday to me and they had a cake and balloons. I had a great day! I am very happy.
Lisa: That is great. We want to take you to dinner tonight. Can you be ready to leave at 7:00p.m.?
Natasha: Yes, I will be ready at 7:00p.m.
Lisa: Perfect.

**7:00p.m. **

Lisa: Okay everyone. It's time to go. Is everyone ready?
Natasha: Yes, I am ready.
Mia: Ready!
Michael: I'm ready.
Dianna: I am ready too.
Mom: Me too.
Lisa: Alright let's go.

*** At Antonio's Restaurant ***

Greeter: Welcome to Antonio's Restaurant. How many are in your party please?
Lisa: Yes, can we have a table for seven please?
Greeter: Sure, come right this way. Your server will be with you soon.
Michael: Thank you.

*** Server Comes to the Table***

Waitress: Good evening. My name is Tracy. I will be your server today. May I start you off with some beverages?
Lisa: Yes, I would like a strawberry lemonade.
Dianna: I would like a diet coke.
David: I would like a diet coke too.
Mia: I would like a sprite.
Natasha: I would like an iced tea please. Mom what would you like?
Mom: I would like an iced tea too.
Michael: Can you please bring me a regular lemonade?
Waitress: Sure, so I have one diet coke, one sprite, an iced tea, a strawberry lemonade and a regular lemonade?
Lisa: Yes, that is correct.
Waitress: Perfect. Would you like any appetizers?
David: Yes, can we please have some nachos and buffalo wings?
Waitress: Sure. I will be right back with your appetizers. Here are the menus. The soup for the day is New England Clam Chowder soup. I will be right back with your drinks.

***

Mia: So Natasha. How does it feel turning 24 years old? Do you feel older?
Natasha: No. I feel the same. I'm just glad to be alive.
Lisa: That is wonderful. Did you receive some gifts at work?
Natasha: Well, someone gave me a beautiful necklace. I also received a bracelet, a picture frame, and a beautiful blue blouse.
Dianna: Those are some nice presents. That was nice.
Natasha: Yes, I work with some wonderful people on my job.
Michael: How is your supervisor?
Natasha: My supervisor is well. He is a nice man. I really like him.
David: That is good. It is important to like your supervisor.
Natasha: Yes, I am happy on my job.

*** Waitress returns with drinks and appetizers ***

Waitress: Okay. Here are your appetizers and your drinks. Have you decided what you would like to order for your entrees?
Lisa: Yes, I would like to order the spaghetti with garlic bread.
Dianna: I would like the baked chicken with vegetables and mashed potatoes. Please add butter on my mashed potatoes.
Mia: May I please have the shrimp and steak with a baked potato and a side salad?
Waitress: Yes, absolutely. What kind of salad dressing would you like?
Mia: I would like ranch dressing with my salad please.
Waitress: Yes, got it. Anything else?

Mia: Yes, may I have extra butter for my baked potato?
Waitress: Absolutely. And you sir. What would you like?
Michael: I would also like the shrimp and steak with a baked potato and a side salad.
Waitress: Okay. …and what kind of salad dressing would you like?
Michael: I would like Italian dressing with my salad.
Waitress: Perfect. And you, what would you like?
Natasha: I would like a chicken Caesar salad with Caesar dressing, but I do not want any onions or cheese on my salad.
Waitress: We don't put onions on our salads.
Natasha: Great. Thank you.
Michael: Natasha, is that all you want? This is your birthday. You can have whatever you want.
Natasha: Awww. Thank you, but I am on a diet. I am trying to lose some pounds.
David: You look great. You don't need to lose any weight.
Natasha: Thank you guys, but I'm fine. I will keep the salad.
Mom: Well, I would like the fettucine pasta with chicken.
Waitress: Yes, I have it. Would you like anything else with that?
Mom: No. Thank you.
David: I would like the turkey meat with vegetables and white rice.
Waitress: Okay Perfect. Got it. I will be right back with everyone's entrees.

*** Waitress Leaves ***

Lisa: These nachos are sooooo good!
Natasha: I love these buffalo wings! They are delicious too!
Mia: Yes, the nachos are good. I don't want to eat them all because I need to be able to eat my food when it comes.
Michael: My lemonade is perfect.
David: Mom, how is your iced tea?
Mom: It's actually pretty good.

*** Waitress returns ***

Waitress: Okay. Here is the spaghetti with garlic bread.
Lisa: Thank you. That's mine.
Waitress: …and here is the baked chicken with vegetables.
Dianna: That's mine.
Waitress: …and the two shrimp and steak.
Mia: One of them is mine. Thank you.
Michael: …and the other one is mine.
Waitress: … and here is the Caesar dressing.
Michael: That's mine too. Thank you.
Waitress: …and the turkey meat with vegetables and white rice
David: Yes, that is mine. Thank you.
Waitress: … and last but not least, the fettucine pasta with chicken.
Mom: That is mine. Thank you very much.
Waitress: Okay. Great. Does anyone need anything else?
Dianna: Yes, may I have a refill on my diet coke?
Waitress: Yes, you may.
David: May I have a refill too?
Waitress: Yes absolutely. I'll be right back.

Lisa: Oh my goodness. This food is so good!
Dianna: Yes, it is! …and the place is so nice.
Waitress: Here is the refill on your diet coke ma'am and here is yours, sir.
Dianna: Thank you.
David: Thank you.
Waitress: You're welcome.
Lisa: I didn't know this restaurant would be so nice inside.
Natasha: Yes! …and I love the soft music.
Mom: I am coming back here. I love the environment here and they are so nice to the customers.
Lisa: Yes, I am so happy we came here. Natasha, how do you like this restaurant?
Natasha: I love it here. I drive by here all the time, but I never knew it was so nice.
Mom: Me neither.
Lisa: And I cannot believe how good this food is. It is delicious!
Dianna: Yes, the food is really good. I am so happy we came here.
Waitress: Is everything okay? Do you need anything? Would you like some dessert?
Mia: I am full. I don't want any dessert today.
David: I don't want any dessert either.
Michael: Neither do I.
Mom: Natasha, it's your birthday. Would you like some dessert?
Natasha: No, but thank you. I told you that I am on my diet. I don't want to eat anything fattening.
Lisa: Can we please have some napkins and the bill please?
Waitress: Sure, here you go.
Lisa: Thank you. Here is my credit card.
Waitress: Thank you. I will be right back.

*** **Waitress leaves** **

Waitress: Here is your receipt. Have a nice day and please come again.
Lisa: Oh yes, we will come again. We really enjoyed this restaurant. Here is your tip. You were a wonderful waitress.
Waitress: Wow! Thank you so much!
Lisa: You're welcome.
Natasha: Thank you everyone for a wonderful birthday dinner. I had a great time. I love you.
Everyone: We love you too and happy birthday Natasha! (Everyone gives Natasha a hug).

NATASHA'S BIRTHDAY DINNER

1.   Who called the family together to talk about Natashas birthday?

    a.   Mom
    b.   Lisa
    c.   Diana

2.   Where did Natasha go for her birthday?

    a.   to a restaurant
    b.   to the spa
    c.   to the beach

3.   What time did the family leave to go to the birthday dinner?

    a.   at 6:30p.m
    b.   at 7:00a.m
    c.   at 7:00p.m.

4.   What is the name of the restaurant that the family went to?

    a.   Italian restaurant
    b.   Antonio's restaurant
    c.   Natasha's restaurant

5.   How many people were in Natasha's family went to the restaurant?

    a.   11 people
    b.   seven people
    c.   five people

6.   What was the name of the server?

    a.   Mia
    b.   Tracy
    c.   Natasha

7.   What beverage did Diana order?

    a.   diet coke
    b.   regular lemonade
    c.   strawberry lemonade

8.   What beverage did Lisa order?

     d.   Coca cola
     e.   lemonade
     f.   strawberry lemonade

9.   What was the soup of the day?

     a.   chicken soup
     b.   New England Clam Chowder
     c.   turkey beef soup

10.   What did Natasha NOT get as a gift?

     a.   a gold watch
     b.   a necklace
     c.   a bracelet

11.   Does Natasha like her supervisor?

     a.   Yes, she does
     b.   No, she doesn't

12.   Who ordered a chicken Caesar Salad as an entrée?

     a.   Natasha
     b.   David
     c.   Lisa

13.   Who ordered shrimp and steak?

     a.   Natasha
     b.   David
     c.   Mia

14.   Who ordered Italian dressing with their salad?

     a.   Michael
     b.   David
     c.   Natasha

15.   Who ordered iced tea?

     a.   Mia
     b.   David
     c.   Mom

16.   Who ordered spaghetti with garlic bread?

        a. Diana
        b. Natasha
        c. Lisa

17.   What did Natasha order for dessert?

        a.   chocolate cake
        b.   cheesecake
        c.   nothing

18.   Who was on a diet?

        a.   Mom
        b.   Diana
        c.   Natasha

19.   Did they like the restaurant?

        a.   No, they didn't
        b.   Yes, they did

20.   Who paid for the bill with their credit card?

        a.   Natasha
        b.   Lisa
        c.   Michael

21.   What was your favorite part about this skit?   Answers will vary.

____

____

22.   How do you think Natasha felt after her birthday dinner? Answers will vary.

____

____

FOOD: VOCABULARY

hungry	dessert	eat	meal	eating
drink	breakfast	pork	cooks	beverage
dinner	salad	ate	beverages	popcorn

1. ___Pork___ is my favorite meat.

2. Chicken with rice is my favorite ___stomachache___.

3. What would you like to ___drink___ for your beverage?

4. I had coffee, eggs and bacon for my ___breakfast___ this morning.

5. Chocolate cake is my favorite ___backache___.

6. What is your favorite food to ___cold___?

7. My mother ___cooks___ a big dinner every Sunday.

8. ___Dinner___ will be ready at 7:30p.m. tonight.

9. I had a side ___salad___ with my food at the restaurant today.

10. I am very ___hungry.___. I want to eat.

11. Water and wine are my favorite ___beverages___ to drink.

Directions: Read the questions below and circle the letter of the correct answer.

12. What time is your cooking class?
    a. It at 6:00p.m.   b. It starts at 6:00p.m.   c. It cooking class 6:00p.m.

13. What is your favorite beverage?
    a. Favorite beverage water   b. My favorite beverage water.   c. Water is my favorite beverage.

14. What is your favorite food?
    a. Pasta is my favorite food.   b. Favorite food pasta.   c. Pasta me food favorite.

15. What is your favorite meal of the day?
    a. My favorite meal of the day is lunch.   b. Me favorite lunch is meal   c. It is lunch.

16. What time is your appointment?
    a. It appointment 3:00a.m.   b. It is at 3:00a.m.   c. It is at 3:00p.m.

17. How much is the hamburger?
    a. They are $5.27   b. It is 5.47   c. It $5.47

Example: Bread at Gonzalo's: **$2.49**   Bread at Luana's: **$2.79**

Bread is **cheaper** at Gonzalo's.   Bread is **more expensive** at Luana's.

Gonzalo's Supermarket		Luana's Supermarket	
bread $2.49	bacon $3.99	bread $2.79	bacon $3.89
milk $3.19	bananas $.69 lb	milk $3.09	bananas $.79 lb
cheese $4.69	apples $.69 lb	cheese $4.59	apples $.79 lb
turkey $2.13 lb	ketchup $4.19	turkey $1.13 lb	ketchup $4.39
eggs $2.89	jelly $2.49	eggs $2.79	jelly $2.39
mayonnaise $4.39	chips $2.89	mayonnaise $4.59	chips $2.69
juice $3.29	ice-cream $4.79	juice $3.19	ice-cream $4.49

Directions: Complete the sentences below with the words "**cheaper**" or "**more expensive**."

1. Juice is _____more expensive_____ at Gonzalo's.

2. Bread is _____cheaper_____ at Gonzalo's.

3. Bacon is _____cheaper_____ at Luana's.

4. Chips are _____cheaper_____ at Luana's.

5. Turkey is _____more expensive_____ at Gonzalo's.

6. Apples are _____more expensive_____ at Luana's.

7. Cheese is _____cheaper_____ at Luana's.

8. Ice-cream is _____more expensive_____ at Gonzalo's.

9. Bread is _____more expensive_____ at Luana's.

10. Mayonnaise is _____cheaper_____ at Gonzalo's.

Directions: Answer the following questions in a complete sentence using:
"They are" or "It is"

Example: JUICE: It is $3.29/They are $3.45 each.

11. Apples: _____They are $.79 a pound._____(Luana's)

12. Juice: _____It is $3.19._____ (Gonzalo's)

13. Bread: _____It is $2.79._____ (Luana's)

14. Bacon: _____It is $3.99._____ (Gonzalo's)

15. Chips _____They are $2.69._____ (Luana's)

Directions: Complete the sentences below from the information in the Venn Diagram.

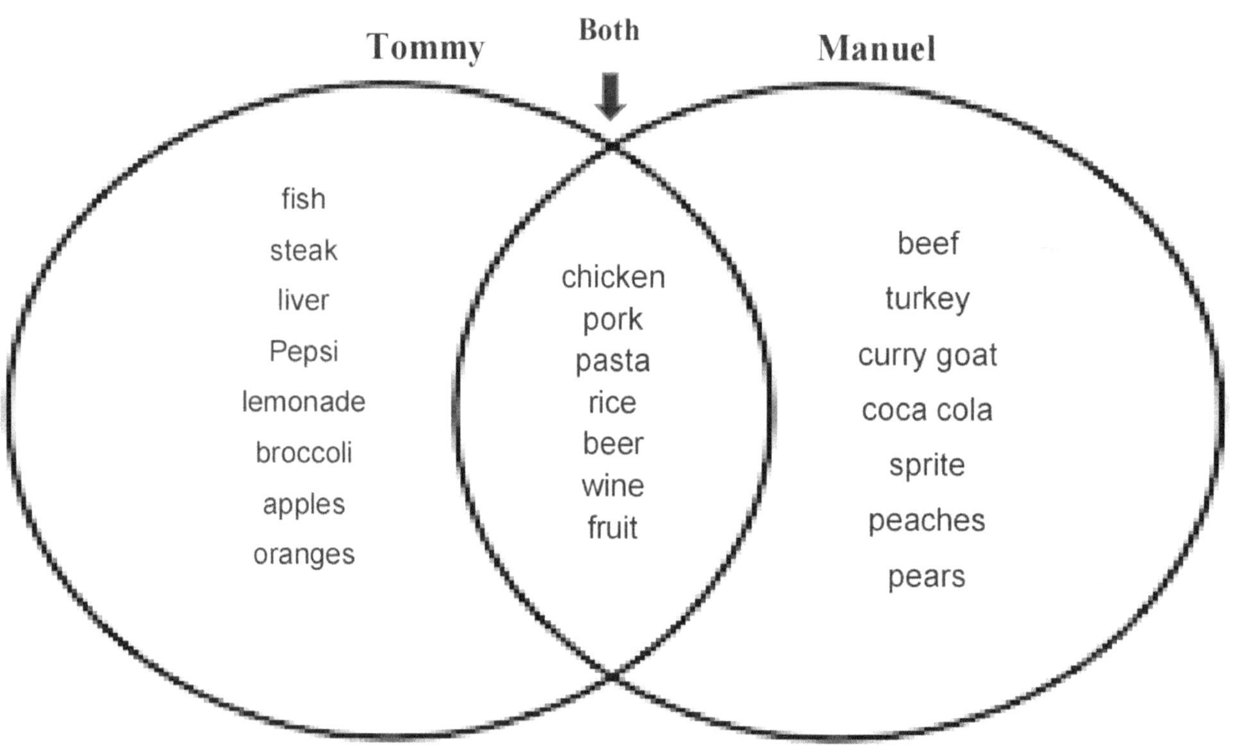

1. Tommy likes to eat __(various answers)__ and likes to drink __(various answers)__ .

2. Manual likes to eat __(various answers)__ and likes to drink __(various answers)__ .

3. Manuel doesn't like to drink __lemonade or Pepsi__ .

4. Both Manuel and Tommy like to drink __beer or wine__ .

5. Tommy doesn't like to drink __coca cola or sprite__ .

6. Tommy likes __(various answers)__ , but Manuel doesn't like __(various answers)__ .

7. Manuel likes __(various answers)__ , but Tommy doesn't like __(various answers)__ .

8. Both Manuel and Tommy like to eat __(various answers)__ and __(various answers)__ .

9. __Tommy__ does not eat turkey or curry goat.

10. __Apples__ and __oranges__ are fruits that Tommy likes.

11. __Beef, turkey__ and __curry goat__ are meats that Manuel likes.

12. __Chicken__ and __pork__ are meats that both Manuel and Tommy like.

REVIEW AND PRACTICE

Directions: Complete each sentence with the correct **past-tense** form of the word.

1. I ____wanted____ to go to the movies this weekend, but I didn't go anywhere. (want)

2. My son ____jumped____ the fence on Friday and sprained his ankle. (jump)

3. On my last job, I ____typed____ every day. (type)

4. I ____liked____ the concert last week, but I don't want to go again. (like)

5. My father ____worked____ ten hours overtime last week. (work)

6. Jose ____solved____ the difficult math problem for me. (solve)

7. We ____tested____ in class on Friday. (test)

8. My cousin ____walked____ home today. (walk)

9. We ____danced____ all night at Lisa's party. (dance)

10. Yesterday, I ____talked____ to my aunt in Paris. (talk)

Directions: Complete each sentence with the past tense form of the verb.

regular = ed	cons + y = (no y) ied	vowel + y = ed	ends with e = d only

11. I ____cried____ all week long when my grandmother died. (cry)

12. My aunt ____carried____ the baby to her crib after she fell asleep. (carry)

13. She ____turned____ the TV on to her favorite show when she got home. (turn)

14. My mom ____washed____ all the clothes in the house on Saturday. (wash)

15. My father ____worked____ seven hours overtime last week. (work)

16. Dad ____worked____ 12 hours straight yesterday and he was tired. (work)

17. I ____copied____ my homework from the board in class today. (copy)

18. My mother ____promised____ to take me on a vacation this summer. (promise)

19. My cousin ____jumped____ the fence on his way home yesterday. (jump)

20. The man ____opened____ the car door for the woman as she was getting out of the car. (open)

Directions: **Circle** the word in each row that does **NOT** belong.

1. chicken — rice — pasta — bread
2. apple pie — cheesecake — pork — chocolate cake
3. coffee — tea — bacon — milk
4. bagel — pancakes — oatmeal — popcorn
5. salad — breakfast — lunch — dinner
6. taste — food — eat — jump
7. corn — chips — asparagus — celery
8. cookies — turkey — ice cream — chips
9. rice — apples — oranges — pears
10. cook — fry — read — bake

Directions: Chose the correct word from the box below to complete the sentences.

nachos & potato skins	dessert	coca cola	drank	eat
restaurant	expensive	hungry	salt	milk
thirsty	steak and potatoes	snacks	ate	hot

11. Yesterday, I did not have lunch and I was very ___hungry___ all day.
12. Diana likes to put ___milk___ in her coffee.
13. Last night we went to a nice ___restaurant___ for dinner.
14. We had ___coughing___ and ___potato sticks___ for appetizers.
15. I ordered ___steak___ and ___potatoes___ for my entree.
16. My daughter had a ___coca cola___ for her beverage.
17. My mother ___drank___ strawberry lemonade for her beverage.
18. For ___dessert___, we had apple pie and ice-cream.
19. I love to ___eat___ at nice restaurants.
20. The restaurant was not very ___stomachache___.

Directions: Choose the category from the box below for each term.

vegetable	entree	snack	meat
utensil	dessert	beans	fruit
lunch	appetizer	beverage	breakfast

1. oranges ____fruit____
2. lemonade ____beverage____
3. chips ____snacks____
4. chicken and rice ____entree____
5. bacon and eggs ____breakfast____
6. fork ____utensil____
7. carrot ____vegetable____
8. chocolate cake ____dessert____
9. spoon ____utensil____
10. tea ____beverage____
11. apples ____fruit____
12. pork ____meat____
13. yogurt ____snack____

Directions: Complete each sentence with a word from the box below:

vegetable	entree	spoon	meat
utensils	dessert	beans	fruit
lunch	appetizer	beverage	breakfast

14. You eat ice-cream with a ____spoon____.
15. I like to drink water for my ____beverage____ with dinner.
16. Broccoli is my favorite ____vegetable____.
17. I like to eat ____meat____ with my meal such as chicken, fish or pork.
18. We need ____utensils____ because there is nothing to eat with.
19. I like to eat pancakes and sausage for ____breakfast____.

Directions: Complete the sentences below with the correct answer.

spoon	fork	knife	coffee cups	cup	bowl

1. I need a _______bowl_______ to put my soup in.

2. Here is a _______spoon_______ for your ice-cream.

3. I need a _______fork_______ to eat my rice and potatoes.

4. We need a _______knife_______ to cut the cake.

5. The _______coffee cups_______ are in the cabinet next to the coffee.

6. Here is a _______cup_______ for your juice.

REVIEW & PRACTICE

Directions: Answer the questions below using a word that represents a word in parenthesis.

7. My daughter is a(n) _______beautiful_______ person. (adjective)

8. Marcos _______is_______ my first cousin. (verb to be)

9. Please give the papers to _____me / her / him_____. (pronoun)

10. My _______shirt_______ is blue and white. (noun)

11. We need to go to _______Walmart_______ today. (proper Noun)

12. What a beautiful _______baby_______! (noun)

13. Your sister lives in _______a_______ big apartment. (article)

14. _____We're / I'm / They're_____ going home early today. (contraction)

15. I _______cleaned_______ all day yesterday. (past tense verb)

16. The baby is _______sleeping_______ right now. (verb)

17. _____I, You, We_____ need a new computer. (pronoun)

18. We _______are_______ going to the store at 3:00p.m. (VTB)

19. My _______white_______ dress is in the cleaners. (adjective)

20. _____Sedanos_____ is my favorite supermarket. (proper noun)

S T U D Y

Irregular Past Tense Verbs

BASE FORM	PAST FORM		BASE FORM	PAST FORM		BASE FORM	PAST FORM
become	became		give	gave		see	saw
begin	began		go	went		sell	sold
break	broke		grow	grew		send	sent
bring	brought		hang	hung		sing	sang
build	built		have	had		sit	sat
buy	bought		hear	heard		sleep	slept
catch	caught		**hurt**	**hurt**		speak	spoke
choose	chose		know	knew		spend	spent
come	came		leave	left		stand	stood
cost	**cost**		lose	lost		sweep	swept
cut	**cut**		make	made		take	took
do	did		meet	met		teach	taught
draw	drew		pay	paid		tell	told
drink	drank		**put**	**put**		think	thought
drive	drove		**quit**	**quit**		throw	threw
eat	ate		read	read		understand	understood
feel	felt		ride	rode		wake	woke
find	found		ring	rang		wear	wore
forget	forgot		run	ran		write	wrote
get	got		say	said		swim	swam

Directions: Answer each question in a complete sentence using an irregular verb.

1. What did you **get** for your birthday? _Students need a sentence with the word GOT._

2. When did you **sweep** the floor? _Students need a sentence with the word SWEPT._

3. What did you **make** for dinner? _Students need a sentence with the word MADE._

4. How much did you **spend** at the mall? _Students need a sentence with the word SPENT._

5. When did you **come** to the United States? _Students need a sentence with the word CAME._

6. How much did you **pay** for groceries? _Students need a sentence with the word PAID._

7. What did you **buy** from the shoe store? _Students need a sentence with the word BOUGHT._

Directions: Write the correct **past tense** form of each verb in the sentences below.

1. I ______went______ to the bank and the post office yesterday. (go)
2. Karen ______needed______ $27 for a black jacket last week. (need)
3. Last night, we ______had______ a party for my mother. (have)
4. My sister ______became______ a nurse in my country last year. (become)
5. My son ______jumped______ the fence on his way home last Friday. (jump)
6. On Tuesday, I ______cut______ my finger on a knife. (cut)
7. My teacher ______taught______ us many things last year. (teach)
8. I am very ______excited______ about my new school. (excite)
9. Last month, I ______wanted______ to go to Orlando. (want)
10. Four years ago, I ______went______ to Japan. (go)
11. My friend ______crashed______ her car in an accident on Wednesday. (crash)
12. I ______put______ my bag on the table and now I cannot find it. (put)
13. My uncle ______ran______ three miles yesterday. (run)
14. I ______worked______ 42 hours last week. (work)
15. My mother ______made______ me a chocolate cake for my birthday. (make)

Directions: Answer each question in past tense. Write in a complete sentence.

16. What did you **eat** for dinner last night? I ate ______________ for dinner last night.

____

17. Where did you **go** yesterday? ____ I went to ______________ yesterday. ___

____

18. When did you **wash** your hair? I washed my hair ______________.

____

PAST-TENSE VERBS

Rules: regular = ed;   x,s,ch,sh = ed;   vowel +y= ed;   consonant + y = ied (no y)   e = d only

1. like ___liked___
2. play ___played___
3. cry ___cried___
4. move ___moved___
5. need ___needed___

6. smell ___smelled___
7. look ___looked___
8. brush ___brushed___
9. try ___tried___
10. copy ___copied___

Directions: Complete each sentence with the correct "past tense" form of the verb in parenthesis.

11. The children ___remained___ quiet while mother was praying. (remain)

12. On Saturday, I ___organized___ my closet. (organize)

13. Last night, we ___finished___ our English homework. (finish)

14. When I worked at the bank, I ___counted___ lots of money. (count)

15. Lisa ___ignored___ her phone when it was ringing. (ignore)

16. I ___tried___ to lift the heavy boxes, but I couldn't. (try)

17. The children ___played___ outside for two hours. (play)

18. Luis ___disagreed___ with his sister about the subject. (disagree)

19. I ___kissed___ my grandmother when she visited me last week. (kiss)

20. Danny ___washed___ my car for me yesterday. (wash)

PRONUNCIATION

Words with "ed" stress	Words without "ed" stress	
celebrated	learned	worked
counted	kissed	liked
needed	practiced	studied
corrected	listened	looked
shouted	prayed	organized
started	talked	loved
decorated	studied	moved
needed	cleaned	walked
invited	cooked	looked

Regular Past-tense Verbs
Past-tense Verbs with **Stress** and "**No Stress**" of "es"

Past tense verbs **NO STRESS**	Past tense verbs **WITH STRESS ("ed")**
1. practiced	1. celebrated
2. danced	2. needed
3. worked	3. decorated
4. learned	4. completed
5. picked	5. counted
6. cooked	6. decided
7. exercised	7. motivated
8. relaxed	8. located
9. baked	9. wanted
10. surprised	10. painted
11. developed	11. voted
12. divorced	12. started
13. finished	13. collected
14. listened	15. invited

Directions: Practice the proper pronunciation of the past-tense verbs.

1. My sister **<u>cooked</u>** a big dinner for our family on yesterday. (no stress)

2. My mother **<u>picked</u>** up my cousin from the airport last night. (no stress)

3. My mother was **<u>surprised</u>** when she saw everyone at surprise party. (no stress)

4. Bianca **<u>started</u>** my homework at 7:00p.m. last night. (stress the "ed")

5. I **<u>wanted</u>** to ask you a question yesterday, but you went home early. (stress the "ed")

6. Carla **<u>practiced</u>** her English for one hour yesterday. (no stress)

7. We **<u>celebrated</u>** my grandmother's birthday on Sunday. (stress the "ed")

8. My father **<u>worked</u>** six hours overtime on his job last week. (no stress)

9. We **<u>danced</u>** all night and had a good time at the party yesterday. (no stress)

FINDING FOOD

q	e	b	q	w	e	r	l	e	m	o	n	a	d	e	q	f	r	u	i	t	i	t	o	p
z	x	r	y	t	r	g	p	a	z	z	x	b	c	v	d	w	e	r	t	y	u	u	k	l
c	v	e	u	i	o	p	o	l	u	n	c	h	b	z	i	a	s	d	f	g	g	r	h	j
b	n	a	a	s	d	f	g	h	j	k	l	m	n	n	n	a	e	a	t	d	f	k	g	h
a	m	k	x	d	r	i	n	k	c	v	n	b	m	l	n	u	i	o	o	p	l	e	k	j
s	y	f	t	r	e	c	h	e	e	s	e	c	a	k	e	s	w	q	a	b	s	v	d	v
e	c	a	v	g	h	j	k	l	q	a	z	x	s	w	r	e	d	c	v	e	f	r	t	e
a	l	s	j	k	t	a	s	t	e	i	u	c	h	e	a	p	j	m	m	v	n	h	y	g
f	o	t	u	p	o	d	c	f	s	w	r	y	a	c	v	b	t	e	q	e	p	e	f	e
o	b	e	i	r	y	c	h	o	c	o	l	a	t	e	c	a	k	e	b	r	d	h	j	t
o	a	d	c	q	t	u	g	r	w	q	w	e	r	t	y	u	i	t	o	a	p	l	s	a
d	z	x	e	e	h	j	b	a	v	w	d	p	g	t	a	p	b	f	i	g	b	f	d	b
z	x	c	v	b	n	m	r	n	a	s	d	f	g	h	j	k	r	i	c	e	q	w	e	l
y	o	g	u	r	s	e	g	h	k	h	u	n	g	r	y	p	o	i	u	y	t	r	e	
z	q	w	e	r	g	s	a	e	u	p	q	a	s	d	f	g	h	u	o	p	w	p	d	s
x	a	k	s	a	l	a	d	s	d	p	z	c	d	s	k	g	w	j	b	e	a	a	t	k
e	w	e	o	e	o	t	y	u	i	o	c	o	f	f	e	e	s	t	r	g	s	s	g	p
g	f	d	u	w	e	q	x	r	t	y	u	a	w	p	l	h	x	s	i	x	d	t	b	l
g	g	j	p	w	d	m	e	a	t	g	k	p	t	u	p	j	d	d	c	c	p	a	d	j
s	h	a	s	d	f	g	h	e	x	p	e	n	s	i	v	e	f	p	e	v	t	w	r	p

WORDS

1. beverage
2. bread
3. breakfast
4. cheap
5. cheesecake
6. chocolate cake
7. coffee
8. dinner
9. drink
10. eat
11. eggs
12. expensive
13. fruit
14. food
15. hungry
16. juice
17. lemonade
18. lunch
19. meat
20. oranges
21. pasta
22. rice
23. salad
24. seafood
25. soup
26. taste
27. turkey
28. vegetables
29. yogurt

Directions: Write the correct **past tense** form of each verb in the sentences below.

1. We ____went____ to the bank last week. (go)
2. I ____needed____ $27 for gas yesterday. (need)
3. Last night, we ____had____ a party for my mother. (have)
4. My sister ____became____ a nurse last year. (become)
5. My son ____jumped____ the fence on his way home last Friday. (jump)
6. On Tuesday, I ____cut____ my finger on a knife. (cut)
7. My teacher ____taught____ us about nouns and verbs last week. (teach)
8. Last month, I ____traveled____ to Georgia. (travel)
9. Four years ago, my family ____drove____ to Tampa. (drive)
10. My aunt ____crashed____ her car in an accident on Wednesday. (crash)
11. I ____put____ my bag on the table and now I cannot find it. (put)
12. Deena ____forgot____ her umbrella today. (forget)
13. Luis told me that he ____quit____ the football team. (quit)
14. Diana ____made____ me a chocolate cake for my birthday. (make)

15. What did you eat for dinner last night? I ATE __________ for dinner last night.

____

16. Where did you go yesterday? ____ I WENT to (the) __________ yesterday.

____

17. How did you sleep last night? ____ I SLEPT __________ last night.

18. What time did you wake up this morning? I WOKE up at __________ last night.

____

***Directions**:*
Answer each question in the affirmative and use the correct past-tense form of the irregular verb.

REVIEW AND PRACTICE

1. How much change did the cashier **give** you? _Students need a sentence with the word GAVE._

2. When did you **go** to the store? _Students need a sentence with the word WENT._

3. What kind of cake did your mother **make**? _Students need a sentence with the word MADE._

4. What did you **have** for dinner last night? _Students need a sentence with the word HAD._

5. What time did you **wake** up this morning? _Students need a sentence with the word WOKE._

6. When did you **come** to the United States? _Students need a sentence with the word CAME._

7. What did your English teacher **teach** you last week? _Students need a sentence with the word TAUGHT._

8. How much did you **pay** for your leather jacket? _Students need a sentence with the word PAID._

9. When did your son **quit** the football team? _Students need a sentence with the word QUIT._

10. How many miles did you **run** yesterday? _Students need a sentence with the word RAN._

***Directions**: Circle the correct part of speech for the words below:*

Parts of Speech:

11. (gerund)	house	play	(singing)	am
12. (article)	is	am	are	(the)
13. (plural noun)	under	(pencils)	Walmart	him
14. (preposition)	school	is	(over)	an
15. (verb-to-be)	and	(are)	worked	playing
16. (past-tense verb)	(listened)	Target	boy	is
17. (proper noun)	(Hollywood Beach)	in front of		practiced
18. (pronoun)	(her)	is	an	work
19. (regular noun)	(dress)	run	working	next to

Directions: Complete each sentence with **much** or **many**.

1. How _______ much _______ are the jeans?

2. How _______ many _______ oranges are left?

3. How _______ many _______ people are in class today?

4. How _______ much _______ ice-cream is left?

5. How _______ much _______ juice is in the refrigerator?

6. How _______ much _______ are the apples?

7. How _______ many _______ boxes of cookies are there?

8. How _______ much _______ are the pencils?

9. How _______ much _______ is the pasta?

10. How _______ much _______ cake is left?

Directions: Complete each sentence with a word from the below:

beverage	eat	fruits	dessert	drink
drinks	vegetable	eats	meat	dinner
desserts	meats	beverages	fruit	breakfast

11. Lemonade and coffee are my two favorite _______ beverages _______.

12. Would you like water to _______ drink _______?

13. Chocolate cake is my favorite dessert _______.

14. What is your favorite _______ meat _______? Turkey or fish?

15. What would you like to drink for your _______ beverage _______?

16. What time do you _______ eat _______ your lunch?

17. I like to eat asparagus as my _______ vegetable _______ with my dinner.

18. Apples and oranges are my favorite _______ fruits _______.

19. My mother eats her _______ breakfast _______ at 7:00a.m. every morning.

20. Fish, chicken and pork are my favorite _______ meats _______.

DIALOGUES: ALL ABOUT FOOD!

1. **Person #1:** What is your favorite food to cook?
   Person #2: I don't have a particular favorite food to cook, but I like to cook many things.
   Person #1: You like to cook things like what?
   Person #2: Well, I like to cook chicken, turkey, seafood and pasta. I can also make roast beef and curry goat. I also like to make rice and beans.
   Person #1: That's very interesting. Not many people can cook all of those things.
   Person #2: I know. My mother taught me how to cook when I was younger.
   Person #1: Does your food taste good?
   Person #2: Of course my food taste good! My food is delicious. Everyone loves my food.
   Person #1: Okay. I would love to taste your cooking.

2. **Person #1:** What is your favorite meal of the day?
   Person #2: Dinner is my favorite meal of the day. Breakfast is my second favorite meal. What is your favorite meal of the day?
   Person #1: Lunch is mine.
   Person #2: What did you eat for lunch today?
   Person #1: I ate a turkey sandwich, some potato chips and I drank some juice.
   Person #2: Oh Okay. I had a salad and some yogurt. I am on a diet. I drank water for my beverage.
   Person #1: Yes, I understand. I need to go on a diet too, but the problem is that I love to eat.

3. **Person #1:** What is your favorite food to eat?
   Person #2: My favorite food? Well, I don't really have a favorite food. I like many different foods. For example, I like to eat chicken with rice, pasta with seafood, pizza with cheese sticks, and I also like fried chicken.
   Person #1: Oh really? Well, I love seafood. I also like fish, shrimp, lobster and crabs, but I also like pork, fish and beef. I like lots of things. I just love to eat.
   Person #2: I love to eat also. What about your favorite beverage?
   Person #1: Well, I like to drink wine, but I also like coffee, tea and mango juice.
   Person #2: Oh. Okay. My favorite beverages are lemonade, sprite, sweet tea and water.

4. **Person #1:** The doctor says that I need to lose weight, so he put me on a diet. I can only eat fruit and vegetables for one month. I cannot eat any meat, rice, bread or sweets.
   Person #2: You are not fat. You are a good size. Will it be hard for you to stop eating meat, rice, bread or sweets? That would be hard for me.
   Person #1: Yes, It will be hard for me not eating meat, sweets and rice for one month because I love to eat all of that.
   Person #2: Yes, I am sure it will be hard for you, but you can do it. I did it before. It was difficult for me at first, but I lost 10 pounds. I was happy afterwards, but it was not easy. I was healthier, I looked better, and I was very proud of myself.
   Person #1: I hope that I lose weight too. I really need to drop some pounds. It will help me to be healthier too.

5. **Person #1:** We took my mother to her favorite restaurant for dinner last night. She loves Italian food, so we went to an Italian restaurant. After dinner, we took her to the mall to buy her a dress.
Person #2: That sounds nice. Was she happy? What was the occasion?
Person #1: Yes, she was very happy. It was her birthday. She turned 67 years old. She had chicken, rice, vegetables, a side salad and chicken soup. She also ordered iced tea for her beverage. She doesn't eat very much, but she ate all of her food last night.
Person #2: How nice. I am glad to hear that she ate her food. That means she liked the food.
Person #1: Yes, she loved the food. I also ate a lot. I ordered fish, a salad, a baked potato and a side order of vegetable soup. I had a coca cola for my beverage.
Person #2: I figured that you ordered fish. You have always liked fish.
Person #1: Yes, you know me well. Fish is my favorite meat. We had a great time. My family made our mother feel good. She was very happy.

6. **Person #1:** Welcome to Rolando's restaurant. May I get you some beverages?
Person #2: Yes, I would like a lemonade. My sister wants a coca cola. She's in the bathroom now.
Person #1: So that will be one lemonade and one coca cola. Would you like to order an appetizer?
Person #2: No appetizers today, but we are ready to order now.
Person #1: No problem. What would you like for your entrée?
Person #2: I would like the chicken/shrimp pasta with a side salad. Caesar dressing please.
Person #1: Okay. One chicken/shrimp pasta with a side salad.
Person #2: Yes, and my sister wants a New York steak with a baked potato and vegetables.
Person #1: How would she like her steak cooked?
Person #2: She wants it well done.
Person #1: Okay, so I have one chicken/shrimp pasta with a side salad and a New York steak with a baked potato and some mixed vegetables.
Person #2: Yes, that is correct.
Person #1: Great. I will be right back with your beverages.
Person #2: Thank you so much.

7. **Person #1:** Do you like to cook?
Person #2: No, I do not like to cook, but I like to eat.
Person #1: That is interesting. What do you like to eat?
Person #2: Well, I like beef, pork, steak, fried and baked chicken, rice, beans and different desserts. I love dessert.
Person #1: I like to eat, but I also like to cook. I love making seafood, but I also like to cook Cuban, Haitian and Venezuelan food.
Person #2: That is interesting. Where did you learn to cook those dishes?
Person #1: Some of my family members taught me. I also learned by watching YouTube. You can learn a lot from YouTube.
Person #2: Very interesting. I need to learn to cook more dishes myself.

8. **Person #1:** Will you go to the supermarket when you get off work today?
Person #2: Sure. What do we need?
Person #1: We need juice, water, vegetables, meat, bread, coffee, breakfast food, pasta and fruit.
Person #2: Okay. Do we need anything else?
Person #1: No. I don't think we need anything else. I think that is all. Where will you go?
Person #2: I think I will go to Walmart. Publix is closer, but Walmart is cheaper.
Person #1: Well, it doesn't matter to me where you go.
Person #2: Okay. I will see you later.
Person #1: See you later.

9. **Person #1:** Your food is always so good. What is your favorite thing to cook?
Person #2: Thank you. Yes, I do love to cook. I like to cook baked and fried chicken, rice, turkey, pasta, lasagna, and seafood. I also like to bake cakes and pies, but I try not to cook so much fried food. Fried food is not good for the body.
Person #1: You are correct. Fried food is not good, but it tastes so good. It sounds like you can cook many things. Can you teach me how to cook a few meals? I would love to cook like you.
Person #2: Yes, I can teach you. When can you come over to learn? I would love to teach you.
Person #1: I can come on Tuesday. That way, I can cook a new meal for my husband/wife on Wednesday or Thursday. I am excited about learning.
Person #2: I will prepare everything for your arrival. Your husband/wife is going to be very surprised when you cook him/her something new.
Person #1: Yes, he/she is. He/she loves eating different things. I can't wait to surprise him/her.
Person #2: OK. Can you come over at 4:00p.m. today? You can watch me cook dinner and then I will let you practice. It is very important that you practice on your own.
Person #1: Yes, I can come today at 4:00p.m. I will be there. Thank you so much.
Person #2: We should be there for about 2 hours. You need time to practice.
Person #1: Ok. Perfect. I will see you then.

10. **Person #1:** Guess what? I am taking a cooking class on Mondays, Wednesdays and Fridays.
Person #2: Wow! That sounds exciting. What kinds of foods are you learning to cook?
Person #1: I am learning to cook pasta, different meats, seafood dishes and desserts.
Person #2: Hmmm. That sounds interesting. What kinds of desserts are you learning to cook?
Person #1: I am learning how to make chocolate cake, lemon cake, red velvet cake, cheesecake, pumpkin pie, apple pie and lemon pie.
Person #2: Wow, you are learning how to make lots of different pies.
Person #1: Yes, I am. I am excited about learning so much.

11. **Person #1:** On Thursday, we went to a nice restaurant to celebrate my friend Silvia's promotion. She is a manager on her job now and she's very excited about her new position. She has worked for the company for 13 years now.
Person #2: Really? Congratulations to your friend. Where did you take her to celebrate?
Person #1: We went to TGI Fridays. There were seven of us. We had a really good time. We ordered many appetizers. By the time the food came, we were already full.
Person #2: What did you order? I know that you love hamburgers and pasta.
Person #1: Yes, I do. I did not order hamburgers and pasta today. This time I ordered buffalo wings and French fries. For dessert, I had a slice of cheesecake. I had a lemonade for my beverage. Some of my friends had wine, but I didn't drink any wine.
Person #2: It sounds like you had a great time.
Person #1: Yes, we did. I'm very happy for my friend Natasha. She works very hard.
Person #2: Awww. That is so sweet of you. You are a good friend.

12. **Person #1:** Mom is going to the grocery store today after work. What do we need?
Person #2: We need fruit, vegetables, meat, snacks, milk, juice, soup, cookies and cereal.
Person #1: Okay. Can you please write a list?
Person #2: Yes, I will do that. I will leave it on the table for you.
Person #1: Perfect. I will give it to mom when she gets home so she will know what to get at the supermarket. Please add chicken, turkey, salmon and pork to your list. Thanks so much.
Person #2: Okay. I will add those items to the list. You're welcome.

13. **Person #1:** Did you go to Lisa and Kevin's wedding on Saturday?
Person #2: Yes, I did, and it was beautiful. The reception was nice too. They were dancing and playing good music. The bride and groom were very happy on their special day.
Person #1: Oh really? I hate I missed it. I was in New York for my cousin's graduation, so I couldn't go. What kind of food did they serve?
Person #2: They served chicken and fish. They also had shrimp salad. For dessert, we had wedding cake and it was delicious.
Person #1: Yes, I heard that the ceremony was beautiful. They said the bride was gorgeous.
Person #2: Yes, she was beautiful. She was wearing a gorgeous white wedding dress. It was long and flowing. I am so sorry you were not able to go.

14. **Person #1:** On Saturday, we celebrated my nephew's birthday. He turned 7 years old. We had a big party for him at my sister's house. We had so much fun.
Person #2: Were there lots of people?
Person #2: Oh yes! There were many people at the party. His aunts, uncles and cousins were there. His classmates from school were there too. His grandparents also came.
Person #1: What kind of food did they have?
Person #2: We had barbeque chicken and ribs, hot dogs, potato chips, baked beans, and macaroni and cheese. We had so much food.
Person #1: Wow! It sounds like you had a good time at your nephew's party.
Person #2: Yes, we did.

15. **Person #1:** I am going to McDonalds. Would you like anything?
Person #2: Yes, I would like two hamburgers, one small fry and a diet coke.
Person #1: Would you like an apple pie?
Person #2: Oh yes. I would love an apple pie.
Person #1: OK. Got it. What should I get for Peter?
Person #2: He likes McDonald fish, so bring him a fish sandwich, a medium fry and a large orange soda. Here is $20.00. That should be enough.
Person #1: Thank you. I will bring you two hamburgers, one small fry, a diet coke and an apple pie. For Peter, I will get him a fish sandwich, a medium fry and a large orange soda.
Person #2: Perfect. You got it. Thank you. I will be right back.
Person #1: OK. See you soon!

ASSESSMENT: FOOD

breakfast	lunch	dinner	coffee
eat	entree	beverage	vegetables
fruits	soup	salad	snacks

1. We will be having bacon, eggs, toast and grits for ___breakfast___.

2. It's not good to eat too many ___snacks___.

3. My favorite ___fruits___ are apples and bananas.

4. My doctor told me to eat more ___vegetables___ such as spinach, broccoli, corn and carrots.

5. I went to ___lunch___ at 12:30p.m. today.

6. My mother makes our ___dinner___ everyday around 7:30p.m.

7. What ___beverage___ would you like to drink with your meal?

8. What would you like to ___restaurant___ for dinner?

9. What kind of dressing do you want on your ___salad___?

Directions: Complete each sentence with the words "cheaper" or "more expensive"

Alexandro's Supermarket		Martha's Supermarket	
bread $2.49	bacon $3.99	bread $2.79	bacon $3.89
milk $3.19	bananas $.89 lb	milk $3.09	bananas $.69 lb
cheese $4.69	apples $.69 lb	cheese $4.59	apples $.79 lb

10. Bananas are ___cheaper___ at Martha's

11. Bread is ___cheaper___ at Alexandro's.

12. Bacon is ___more expensive___ at Alexandro's.

13. Apples are ___more expensive___ at Martha's.

14. Cheese is ___cheaper___ at Martha's.

15. Milk is ___cheaper___ at Martha's.

Directions: Complete each sentence below with the correct form of the verb in parenthesis.

16. I will _________ wear _________ some shorts, a shirt and sneakers to the park today. (wear, wears, wore, wearing)

17. I love to _________ cook _________ fish on Fridays. (cook, cooks, cooked, cooking)

18. I am _________ traveling _________ to California next month. (travel, travels, traveling, traveled)

19. Tomorrow, I will _________ go _________ to the doctor. (go, goes, going, went)

20. Ana and Rosa _________ play _________ at the park in Miramar. (play, plays, playing, played)

21. Yesterday, I _________ baked _________ a chicken for my family. (bake, bakes, baking, baked)

22. Last night, I _________ studied _________ my vocabulary words. (study, studies, studying, studied)

23. Ana _________ plays _________ tennis on weekends. (play, plays, playing, played)

Directions: Complete each sentence with the correct irregular past-tense form of the irregular verb below:

24. We _________ heard _________ about what happened to you. Are you okay? (hear)

25. I _________ woke _________ up feeling sick today. (wake)

26. Sarah _________ did _________ all of her housework yesterday. (do)

27. Mary _________ wrote _________ my uncle many letters when he was in the Army. (write)

28. My English teacher _________ taught _________ us many things last year. (teach)

29. Joseph _________ came _________ to the United States in 2023. (come)

30. I _________ spent _________ all of my money on clothes yesterday. (spend)

31. We _________ saw _________ some beautiful mountains in Colorado last summer. (see)

Directions: Answer the questions in complete sentences.

32. What do you like to eat for breakfast? I would like to eat _________ for breakfast.

____

33. What is your favorite meal of the day? _________ is my favorite meal of the day.

____

Lesson 5: Shopping

Dear ESL Teacher,

As you embark upon teaching Lesson 5: Shopping, you have at your disposal a comprehensive plan designed to foster language acquisition and proficiency among your students. In this lesson, students will learn essential skills for navigating shopping scenarios, such as reading money, identifying various forms of clothing, differentiating between "how much" and "how many", comparing prices, and understanding the concept of pairs (such as a pair of sneakers, pairs of sunglasses, etc.).

Through structured activities such as vocabulary introduction, sentence practice, grammar drills, and conversational exercises, students will build a strong foundation in English language communication related to shopping. The instructional procedures outlined include direct instruction, guided practice, and independent practice, ensuring a balanced approach to learning that supports diverse learning styles and abilities.

Our commitment to differentiation and adaptations provides tools to meet the unique needs of every student, including visual aids for English language learners. Students will engage in reading comprehension, fill-in-the-blank exercises, dialogues, and practice parts of speech. An assessment at the back of the book will allow you to evaluate their understanding and progress.

We encourage you to use this guide as a springboard for engaging and effective teaching, while empowering your students to succeed in their language learning journey. By the end of this lesson, students will be equipped with the vocabulary and grammar necessary to confidently discuss and participate in shopping activities.

OBJECTIVES:

1. Students will identify and use vocabulary related to shopping and clothing.
2. Students will practice constructing sentences using new vocabulary.
3. Students will understand the difference between "how much" and "how many."
4. Students will compare prices using vocabulary for cheaper and more expensive items.
5. Students will learn and use the concept of pairs (e.g., a pair of sneakers, a pair of sunglasses, a pair of gloves).
6. Students will read and comprehend passages related to shopping.
7. Students will demonstrate their learning through a comprehensive assessment.

INSTRUCTIONAL PROCEDURES

Direct Instruction:
    Objective: Present new vocabulary and grammar concepts clearly and explicitly.

Details:

- o Introduce vocabulary related to shopping and clothing using visuals (flashcards, images).
- o Explain and provide examples of "how much" vs. "how many" with various items.
- o Discuss and compare items using "cheaper" and "more expensive."
- o Practice the concept of pairs with examples (a pair of sneakers, a pair of jeans).

Guided Practice:

- **Objective:** Help students apply new knowledge in a supportive environment.
- **Details:**
  - o Conduct structured activities using new vocabulary and grammar.
  - o Provide sentence frames incorporating "how much" and "how many."
  - o Facilitate group activities comparing items (e.g., which item is cheaper or more expensive).

Independent Practice:

- **Objective:** Reinforce learning through individual or paired activities.
- **Details:**
  - o Assign worksheets from the book for vocabulary practice and sentence construction.
  - o Read the reading comprehension passages related to shopping in the lesson.

Differentiation/Adaptations:

- **Provide visual aids and simplified instructions for English language learners:**
  - o Use charts, diagrams, and illustrations to enhance understanding.
  - o Simplify instructions and break down concepts into smaller steps.
  - o Offer bilingual or picture dictionaries.
- **Offer additional practice or alternative assessments for students with diverse learning needs:**
  - o Provide differentiated activities and assignments.
  - o Consider oral presentations or digital projects as alternative assessments.

ACTIVITIES

Vocabulary Introduction:

- o **Objective:** Introduce key vocabulary words related to shopping and clothing.
- o **Details:** Use flashcards, images, and charts. Provide examples in context and practice pronunciation.

Sentence Practice:

- o **Objective:** Construct sentences using new vocabulary.
- o **Details:** Guide students in forming sentences with the new vocabulary. Start with simple sentences and increase complexity.

Grammar Drill:

- o **Objective:** Reinforce understanding of "how much" and "how many."
- o **Details:** Conduct fill-in-the-blank activities and matching exercises focusing on correct usage.

Price Comparison:

- o **Objective:** Compare items using "cheaper" and "more expensive."
- o **Details:** Provide scenarios and have students compare prices of different items.

Reading Comprehension:

- o **Objective:** Enhance comprehension through reading passages related to shopping found in the lesson.
- o **Details:** Call on various students to read the story. As comprehension questions, and instruct students to complete the answers independently.

Dialogues:

- o **Objective:** Foster creativity and application of vocabulary and grammar in context through reading short dialogues in conversational tone.
- o **Details:** Students will get into pairs. Teacher will assign students a dialogue number to read. Students will take five minutes to practice their dialogue silently, then the teacher will call on each dialogue number and the pair of students who were given that number will read.

Assessment:

- **Objective:** Evaluate comprehension and application of lesson content.
- **Details:** The assessment at the end of the lesson includes various tasks covering vocabulary, grammar, and reading comprehension.

MATERIALS AND RESOURCES:

- Book: It's Time to Learn English
- Vocabulary cards
- Whiteboard and markers
- Textbooks or reading materials
- Worksheets for grammar exercises
- Audio recordings for listening activities

TECHNOLOGY NEEDED:

- Projector or screen for displaying visuals
- Computer or tablet for accessing digital resources

This detailed lesson plan ensures that all students actively engage with the lesson content and provides multiple opportunities for practice and assessment.

Lesson 5: Shopping

T - Think Back (Review)

Activity: Begin the lesson by reviewing key concepts and vocabulary from the previous lesson. Use a brief warm-up activity to engage students and assess their understanding of any shopping-related terms they might already know.

Time: 5-10 minutes

E – Entry (Introduction/Beginning)

Activity: Introduce new vocabulary words related to shopping and clothing using visuals such as flashcards and images. Explain the meanings, provide clear definitions, pronunciation examples, and use each word in sentences to demonstrate usage.

Time: 15 minutes

A - Application (Teaching/Presentation/Delivery)

Activity: Present new grammar concepts clearly and explicitly. Use direct instruction to introduce the difference between "how much" and "how many," comparing prices (cheaper, more expensive), and the concept of pairs (a pair of sneakers, a pair of sunglasses).

Time: 20 minutes

C - Collaborative Practice (Student Practice)

Activity: Facilitate guided practice by having students work in pairs or small groups to complete structured activities using sentence frames and prompts. Conduct group activities comparing items (e.g., which item is cheaper or more expensive).

Time: 25 minutes

H - Highlight (Wrap-up/Closing)

Activity: Summarize the key points of the lesson, highlighting the new vocabulary and grammar rules learned. Assign a reading comprehension activity from the book using a passage about shopping. Discuss the main ideas and ask comprehension questions.

Time: 10 minutes

E - Evaluate (Assessment/Evaluation)

Activity: Administer a comprehensive assessment found at the end of the lesson. Assess students on vocabulary, grammar, reading comprehension, and dialogue creation.

Time: 15 minutes

R - Reflect (Final Review)

Activity: End the lesson with a reflective activity where students can share their thoughts on what they learned, how they can use it in real-life situations, and any areas where they need further clarification. Encourage students to share their thoughts on their progress and areas they want to improve.

Time: 5-10 minutes

Shopping

5

	STORES	NEW VOCABULARY	CLOTHING	PAIRS (no a)
1.	department store	buy	shirt/ blouse	jeans
2.	supermarket	bought	pants/slacks	pants
3.	clothing store	purchase	jeans	sneakers
4.	shoe store	customer	dress	socks
5.	bookstore	cashier	skirt	shoes
6.	electronic store	cash	shorts	boots
7.	convenient store	credit card	coat	underwear
8.	boutique	check	jacket	glasses
9.	mall	discount	sweater	gloves
10.	thrift store	sale	suit	earrings
11.	meat store	price	uniform	leggings
12.	jewelry store	items	accessories	shoelaces
13.	hardware store	things	clothes	scissors
14.	uniform store	stuff	scarf	goggles
15.	beauty supply store	spend	sports wear	tweezers
16.	music store	size	tank top	pliers
17.	bakery	subtotal	t-shirt	headphones
18.	shoe repair	tax	swim wear	skates

VOCABULARY PRACTICE

SHOPPING

1. I don't want to **spend** a lot of money at the **mall** today.

2. My cousin wears a **suit** to work every day.

3. I need **a pair of** jeans, **a pair of** sunglasses and a black **jacket**.

4. I need to go to the **uniform** store to buy some uniforms for school.

5. David likes to buy **sportswear** at Walmart.

6. I need to **buy** groceries this weekend.

7. What is the **price** of the blue baseball cap?

8. Yesterday, I **bought** a turkey from the supermarket.

9. My mother needs to **purchase** a new microwave for her kitchen.

10. The **cashier** gave me $3.50 change back.

11. I **bought** many items at the boutique today.

12. My father **paid** for my clothes with his credit card.

13. Macys had a big **sale** on shoes today.

14. **Department stores** like Target, Macys and Ross have a variety of things.

15. The **prices** at Walmart are very good.

16. My father **bought** my mother a beautiful new dress today.

17. I don't like to **buy** a lot of useless **stuff**.

18. The **sales tax** in my county is 7%.

19. The **salesperson** helped me to find a nice shirt today.

20. What **size** do you wear? I wear a medium.

21. Publix has a **discount** on meat this week.

22. I **spent** over $80.00 at the supermarket today.

STUDY

book Store

shoe Store

electronic Store

clothing store

supermarket

convenient store

jewelry store

mall

boutique

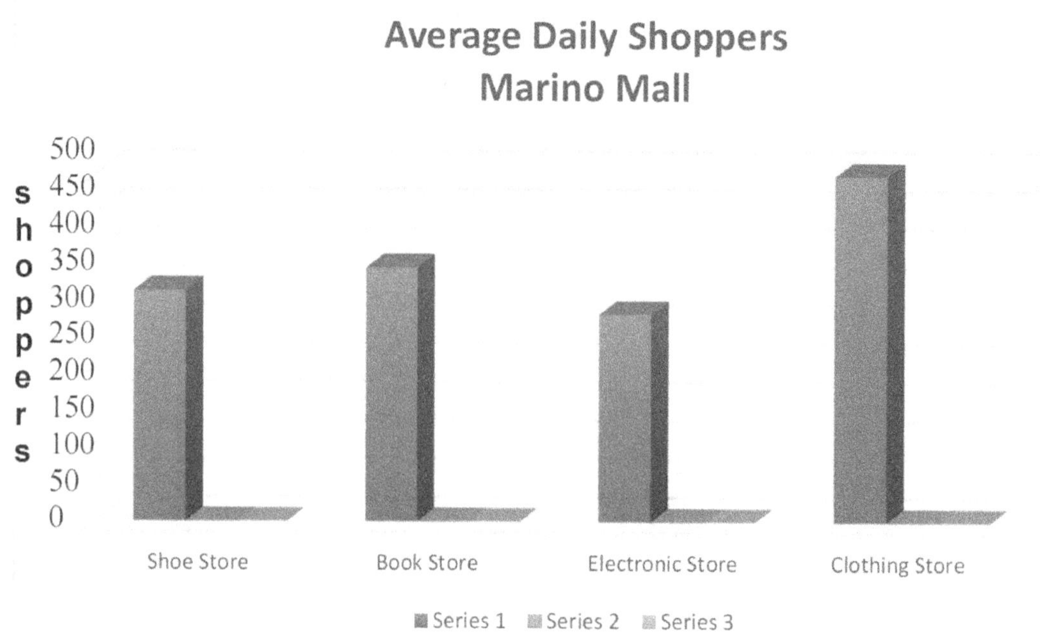

1. How many people shop at the clothing store? _______ shop at the clothing store.

2. How many people shop at the bookstore? 350 people shop at the bookstore.

3. How many people shop at the shoe store? 300 people shop at the shoe store.

4. How many people shop at the electronic store? 300 people shop at the electronic store.

5. Where would you buy a pair of sneakers? I would buy sneakers at the shoe store.

6. Where would you buy a planner? I would buy a planner from the book store.

7. Where would you buy a microwave and a computer? I would buy a microwave at the electronic store.

8. Where would you buy two shirts and a blouse? I would buy them at a clothing store.

9. What is the name of this mall? The name of this mall is called Marino Mall.

10. Where do you shop for groceries? I shop at _______ for groceries.

11. Where do you shop for clothes? I shop at _______ for clothes.

Subject	Verbs	Example Sentences
I, you, we, they	shop	I **shop** at Walmart for groceries on the weekends.
I, you, we, they	shop	We **shop** at the mall for clothes.
I, you, we, they	shop	You **shop** at Burlington for coats?
I, you, we, they	shop	They **shop** at the electronics store for computers.
he, she, it	shops	Victor **shops** at the Nike store for sneakers.
he, she, it	shops	Maria **shops** at the boutique for accessories.
I, you, we, they	buy	I **buy** clothes at Macys.
I, you, we, they	buy	They **buy** turkey and fish at the meat store.
he, she, it	buys	He **buys** toys at the toy store.
he, she, it	buys	She **buys** hair products at the beauty store.

Directions: Complete the sentences below with the correct form of the verb "**shop**".

1. Tina ______shops______ at the mall for clothes.

2. My mother ______shops______ at Walmart for groceries.

3. David and Michael ______shop______ at Footlocker for socks.

4. They ______shop______ at Publix for coffee and juice.

5. My brother ______shops______ at Best Buy for appliances.

6. Lisa ______shops______ at the post office for stamps.

7. My children ______shop______ at Gamestop for video games.

8. Ana and Maria ______shop______ at JCPenny for jeans.

9. My uncle ______shops______ at the tire store for tires.

10. Michael and Angela ______shop______ at the jewelry store for rings.

Directions: Complete the sentences below with the correct form of the verb "**buy**".

11. I ______buy______ my clothes at the mall.

12. Carmen ______buys______ appliances at Best Buy.

13. Darryl ______buys______ chicken and fish at the meat store.

14. Bobby and Charlie ______buy______ tools at Home Depot.

15. We ______buy______ beverages at Winn Dixie Supermarket.

16. They ______buy______ beer and wine at the liquor store.

17. My mother and I ______buy______ cakes from Publix.

Directions: Complete each sentence with the correct form of the words below.

buy	buys	shops	shop

1. We ______buy______ vegetables at Walmart.
2. I like to ______buy______ video games at Best Buy.
3. Lisa ______shops______ at Sedanos Supermarket for her groceries.
4. Brian ______buys______ jeans at the clothing store.
5. When I am in Orlando, I ______shop______ at the outlets.
6. My mother and father like to ______shop______ at Home Depot.
7. I usually ______buy______ meat from the meat store.
8. My mother said that she will ______buy______ a new car for my brother.
9. I want to ______buy______ a new dress for the party.
10. I will ______shop______ at Aventura Mall for my accessories.

baseball cap	shop	bought	buys
accessories	sneakers	sandals	vegetables
purchased	jacket	shirt	Shops

11. I purchased some __(plural noun)__ at the mall today.
12. Yesterday, I ______bought______ a new microwave.
13. Jose is wearing a red __(singular noun)__ today.
14. Tomorrow, I will buy some __(plural noun)__ .
15. Maria wants to ______shop______ at Aventura Mall on Saturday.
16. Yolanda is wearing some beautiful __(plural noun)__ today.
17. Brian has a new __(singular noun)__ .
18. Silvia is wearing a pair of blue ______need a pair______ today.
19. The black __(singular noun)__ is $29.99.
20. Maria ______shops______ at Pembroke Lakes Mall.

Directions: Complete each sentence with the correct form of the verb **shop**.

1. They ___shop___ at the jewelry store for bracelets and rings.
2. We ___shop___ at Sedanos' for groceries.
3. Raquel ___shops___ at Bravo Supermarket for fruits and vegetables.
4. Lauren ___shops___ for accessories at a boutique.
5. I ___shop___ for shoes at Footlocker.
6. Linda, Brenda and Amanda ___shop___ at Amazon for different things.
7. Carlos ___shops___ at Dillards for Jeans.
8. Celeste ___shops___ at Shell for gas.
9. Roberto and Alex ___shop___ for gas at Mobile.
10. We ___shop___ at the downtown mall when we go to Orlando.

Directions: Complete each sentence with the correct subject pronoun.

I	You	We	They	He	She

11. ___I, You, We, They___ shop at Burlington for coats.
12. ___I, You, We, They___ shop for groceries on Saturdays.
13. ___He or She___ shops downtown for clothes.
14. ___He or She___ shops for appliances at the electronic store.
15. ___I, You, We, They___ shop for seafood every Friday.
16. ___He or She___ shops at Walmart for school supplies.
17. ___I, You, We, They___ shop at Office Depot for printer ink.
18. ___He or She___ shops for shoes at Dillards.
19. ___I, You, We, They___ shop for ice-cream at the ice-cream store.
20. ___He or She___ shops at Macys for jeans.

Directions: Practice speaking each line of the information in each box in a complete sentence.

Example: This is Lissette. Her last name is Perez. She is 23 years old. Lissette is wearing a white blouse, a pair of black pants, a pair of white sneakers and accessories.

Paul Smith	**Martha Cuevas**	**Debra Williams**	**David Rodriquez**
23 years old	37 years old	45 years old	19 years old
black shirt	black/white dress	blue pants	white t-shirt
blue jeans	gold earrings	blue belt	white cap
black baseball cap	watch	white shirt	gray sweat pants
sunglasses	gold necklace	sunglasses	white sneakers
black socks	black shoes	black sandals	white socks
black sneakers		accessories	silver watch
			gold necklace
Rosa Caldaron	**Miriam Hernandez**	**John Hawkins**	**Lawanda Scott**
3 years old	19 years old	28 years old	33 years old
pink dress	blue jeans	black suit	red/white skirt
pink socks	white blouse	gray shirt	white shirt
pink headband	black belt	black tie	red blazer
white shoes	sunglasses	black belt	red shoes
	accessories	gold watch	accessories
	black shoes	black shoes	

1. What color is Paul's shirt?   Pauls's shirt is black.

2. How old is Rosa?   Rosa is three years old.

3. Who is 19 years old?   David is 19 years old.

4. Who is wearing a red blazer?   Lawanda is wearing a red blazer.

5. Who is wearing a silver watch?   David is wearing a silver watch.

6. What is John's last name?   John's last name is Hawkins.

7. What color are Debra's pants?   Debra's pants are blue.

8. Who is wearing gray sweatpants?   David is wearing gray sweatpants.

9. Who has a pink headband?   Rosa has a pink headband.

10. Who is wearing red shoes?   Lawanda is wearing red shoes.

11. What color are Martha's earrings?   Martha's earrings are gold.

SHARON LOVES TO SHOP

Sharon is 23 years old, and she lives in her own apartment. Before that, she was living with her parents. After Sharon got a good job, her parents asked her to pay $300 a month to show responsibility, but Sharon did not want to pay her parents any money because she believed that since they are her parents, they should not be asking her for money. The real reason why Sharon did not want to pay anything to her parents is because she loves to shop. She gets paid every two weeks on Friday and when she gets her paycheck, she goes to the mall. She likes to buy clothes, shoes, handbags, accessories and jewelry, but when Monday comes, she has very little money left. Sometimes she has no money for gas. Now that Sharon has her own apartment, she is responsible for the rent, the lights, the water and the cable, but she spends all of her money on shopping and does not pay her bills. One time when Sharon came home, the lights were off because she missed four months of paying the light bill. Another time she came home, the water was off because she did not pay that bill. Another time, she came home and the cable was not working because the bill was not paid. But in November, something very bad happened to Sharon. When she came home from work, the locks to her apparent had been changed and all of her personal items were put outside of the apartment complex next to the trash can. Sharon was evicted because she did not pay her rent for several months. She had to move back in with her parents. They told her that she still needed to pay them $300 a month in order to live with them and she had to be on time with her rent. Sharon moved back with her parents for one year after she was evicted, and she paid them the $300 on time every month. She also stopped shopping so much and she became more responsible with her money and started saving. After 12 months, she found another apartment and moved out again, but to her surprise, her parents gave her a gift. They had saved the $300 a month that Sharon had paid to them and they gave the money back to her. They told her that they were very proud at how responsible she had become and they wanted to encourage her to keep up the good work.

TRUE OF FALSE

1. __F__ Sharon gets paid every week.

2. __T__ Sharon did not want to pay her parents any money because she loves to shop.

3. __T__ When Sharon got her own apartment, she was supposed to pay all the bills.

4. __F__ Sharon was evicted from her apartment because she did not pay the water bill.

5. __F__ Sharon found another apartment after six months.

6. __T__ Sharon did not pay the $300 a month before she moved out the first time.

7. __T__ In November, Sharon was evicted from her apartment.

8. __T__ Sharon paid her parents the $300 on time every month after the eviction.

9. How much did Sharon's parents give her when she moved out the second time?

They gave her $3,600 when she moved out the second time.

Directions: Read each question, then choose the correct answer to the question.

1. What are you wearing today?

a. I wearing today a pair of blue jeans and a white shirt.
b. I am wear a pair of blue jeans and a white shirt today.
c. I am wearing a pair of blue jeans and a white shirt.

2. What is Jorge wearing today?

a. Jorge wearing today a pair of blue jeans and a white shirt.
b. Jorge is wearing a pair of shorts and a red shirt today.
c. Today, Jorge wearing a pair of blue jeans and a white shirt.

3. Where do you buy your bread, eggs and milk?

a. I buy my bread, eggs and milk at the Sedanos Supermarket.
b. I buy my bread, eggs and milk at Sedanos Supermarket.
c. I bought my bread, eggs and milk at Sedanos Supermarket.

4. How much are the jackets?

a. The jacket are $30 each.
b. The jackets is $30 each.
c. The jackets are $30 each.

5. What is your favorite department store?

a. My favorite department store are Walmart.
b. My favorite department store is Walmart.
c. Walmart are my favorite department store.

6. What will you buy at the shoe store today?

a. I buy a pair of sneakers at the shoe store today.
b. I will buy a pair of sneakers at the shoe store today.
c. I bought a pair of sneakers at the shoe store toay.

7. What color are your eyes?

a. My eyes color are brown.
b. My eyes is brown.
c. My eyes are brown.

8. Is Jorge present today?

a. Jorge is absent today.
b. No. Jorge absent today.
c. No. Jorge is absent today.

MICHAEL'S CLOTHING STORE

sandals $23.00	dresses $27.99	sunglasses $12.00	shorts $11.00	T-shirts $7.00
jeans $35.99	sneakers $25.50	belts $9.99	necklaces $13	socks $8.00

1. Yes, the fitting room is around the corner.
2. OK, what about the sneakers? How much are they?
3. Yes, how much are the shorts and the t-shirts?
4. Yes, I would like to try the dark blue pair and the light blue pair.
5. I also like the jeans. How much are they?
6. You are very welcomed. Have a nice day!

Salesperson: Hi my name is Diana. May I help you?

Customer: _______ Yes, how much are the shorts and the T-shirts? _______

Salesperson: The shorts are $11.00 and the T-shirts are $7.00

Customer: Ok. May I try them on?

Salesperson: _______ Yes, the fitting room is around the corner. _______

Customer: _______ Okay, what about the sneakers. How much are they? _______

Salesperson: They are $25.50. Would you like to try them on too?

Customer: _______ Yes, I would like to try the dark blue pair and the light blue pair. _______

Customer: They fit perfectly. I would like the blue sneakers, two packs of T-shirts and one pair of shorts.

Salesperson: Great. Your subtotal is _______ $50.50 _______.

Customer: Thank you so much.

Salesperson: _______ You are very welcomed. Have a nice day! _______

Directions: Answer the following questions in a complete sentence.

1. What is the name of the store? _______ The name of the store is Michael's clothing store. _______

2. What is the name of the salesperson? _______ The salesperson's name is Diana. _______

3. How much are the necklaces? _______ They are $13.00 each. _______

4. What is the total cost of two belts, one necklace and two pair of sandals? _______ The cost of those items is $78.98. _______

Directions: Read the chart and complete each sentence with the information from the chart.

NAME	WALMART	BOOKSTORE	PUBLIX	BURLINGTON	BOUTIQUE
ANA	electronics, groceries	planners	vegetables	coats	jewelry
SUSAN	vegetables, medicine	novels	chicken	-	blouses
HELEN	clothes, shoes	dictionaries	vegetables	dresses	-

Example: Helen buys dictionaries at the bookstore.

1. Ana ______ shops ______ at Publix.

2. ______ Ana and Helen ______ shop for vegetables at Publix.

3. Susan ______ shops ______ at the boutique.

4. Susan shops for ______ vegetables and medicine ______ at Walmart.

5. Ana ______ shops ______ at the bookstore.

6. Who shops at Publix? ______ Ana, Susan and Helen shop at Publix.

7. Who shops for planners? ______ Ana shops for planners.

8. Who buys medicine from Walmart? ______ Susan buys medicine from Walmart.

9. Who shops at Burlington? ______ Ana and Helen shop at Burlington.

Directions: Complete each sentence with **shop, shops, buy, buys**

10. Lisa and Maria like to ______ shop ______ for their makeup at CVS.

11. Jose ______ shops ______ for his shirts from Ross.

12. My mother ______ shops ______ at Macys for her pots and pans.

13. Where do you ______ shop ______ for groceries?

14. Karen and Shanika ______ shop ______ for their shoes at the mall.

15. John ______ shops ______ for his school supplies at Walmart.

16. I want to ______ buy ______ a new car.

17. Claudia, Ana and Lisa like to ______ buy ______ clothes on the weekends.

18. My father is going to ______ buy ______ me a new car.

19. My sister ______ shops ______ for my daughter all the time.

Directions: Answer each question in a complete sentence.

t-shirts: $9.89 a pack	sunglasses: $26.00	umbrella: $10.00	scarf: $17.00	coat: $80.00
blue dress: $45.00	earrings: $15.00	socks $7.99 a pair	black Jacket: $54.00	suit: $150

They are   **It is**   **They're**   **It's**

1. How much are the socks? _____ They are or They're $7.00 a pair. _____

2. How much are the T-shirts? _____ It is or It's $9.89 a pack. _____

3. How much is the black jacket? _____ It is or It's $54.00. _____

4. How much are the sunglasses? _____ They are or They're $26.00. _____

5. How much is the blue dress? _____ It is or It's $45.00. _____

6. How much are the earrings? _____ They are or They're $15.00. _____

7. How much is the umbrella? _____ It is or It's $10.00. _____

8. How much is the scarf? _____ It is or It's $17.00 _____

9. How much is the coat? _____ It is or It's $80.00. _____

10. How much is the suit? _____ It is or It's $150.00 _____

Directions: Answer each question in a complete sentence.

11. What do you need from the supermarket?

    a. I need a black dress.   b. I need turkey and bacon.   c. I need a video game.

12. How much did you pay for your jacket?

    a. I need $75 for my jacket   b. I paid $75 for my jacket   c. I buy $75 for my jacket.

13. Where do you shop for clothes?

    a. I shop at Publix for my clothes.
    b. I shop for clothes at Best Buy Electronics.
    c. I shop for clothes at the mall.

14. What do you want for your birthday?

    a. I want a leather jacket for your birthday.
    b. I want a blue jeans for my birthday.
    c. I want a black jacket for my birthday.

shop		shops	shopping	will shop	shopped
buy		buys	bought	will buy	work
works		working	will work	need	needs

Directions: Complete the sentences with the correct vocabulary word from the boxes above.

1. I like to ___ shop ___ for clothes at Macys.

2. My mother ___ buys ___ new clothes for my children every summer.

3. My sister ___ works ___ at a law office in South Miami.

4. We want to go ___ shop ___ at the mall on Saturday.

5. I ___ will shop ___ for my shoes at Dillards tomorrow.

6. I ___ shopped ___ for three hours in the mall yesterday.

7. Denise ___ shops ___ at Best Buy for her electronics.

8. We want to ___ buy ___ a new microwave for the kitchen.

9. I ___ will buy ___ my son a new car next year.

10. My cousin is not available. He is ___ working ___ now.

Directions: Answer each question in a complete sentence.

11. How many pair of shoes do you want to buy today? ___ I want to buy 2 pair of shoes today. ___

12. What are your favorite two pieces of clothing? ___ They are jeans and T-shirts. ___

13. What would you like to buy today? ___ I would like to buy a ______ today. ___

14. How much money do you have for clothes today? ___ I have $300 for clothes today. ___

Directions: Read the chart and complete each sentence with the information from the chart.

CUSTOMER	MACY'S	BURLINGTON	PUBLIX	ROSS	SPEEDWAY
JOHN	shirts, pants	slacks	fruit vegetables	-	gas
ROSA	accessories	coats	groceries	dresses and shoes	coffee
JULIO	cologne	jackets	groceries	coats, jackets	gas and coffee

Example: John **shops** for **slacks** at Burlington.

1. Rosa _____shops_____ for _____groceries_____ at Publix.
2. Julio _____shops_____ for _____jackets_____ at Burlington.
3. _____Burlington_____ sells coats and jackets.
4. John and Julio_____shop_____ for _____gas_____ at Speedway.
5. Rosa and Julio _____shop_____ for _____groceries_____ at Publix.
6. _____Rosa_____ shops for accessories at _____Macys_____.
7. _____Julio_____ shops for cologne at _____Macys_____.
8. Rosa _____shops_____ for coffee at _____Speedway_____.
9. _____Rosa_____ shops for dresses and shoes at _____Ross_____.
10. Rosa _____shops_____ for _____coats_____ at Burlington.

department stores	electronic store	shoe store	clothing store	supermarket
boutique	convenient store	mall	thrift store	hardware store

11. Sedanos Groceries is my favorite _____supermarket_____.
12. We are going to the _____mall_____ on Saturday to shop at different stores.
13. Chevron gas station is also a _____convenient store_____.
14. I need a pair of sneakers, so I will go to the _____shoe store_____ today.
15. Target and Walmart are _____department stores_____ because they have different departments.
16. I bought a dress and a pair of jeans at the _____clothing store_____.
17. Best Buy is an _____electronic store_____.
18. You buy things cheap at the _____thrift store_____.

Directions: Read the chart and complete each sentence with the information from the chart.

shirt $19	shoes $25	shorts $17	skirt $15	jeans $40
watch $40	necklace $17	sneakers $35	socks $10	suit $150
baseball cap $25	t-shirt $12	jacket $50	bracelet $10	dress $35

	Item	Cost
1.	suit	$150
2.	necklace	$17
3.	shirt	$19
4.	watch	$40
	Total cost:	**$226.00**

What will you wear to the wedding?

I will wear a suit, a shirt, a necklace and a watch.

	Item	Cost
1.	jacket	$50
2.	shorts	$17
3.	shirt	$19
4.	shoes	$25
	Total cost:	**$111.00**

What are you going to wear to school tomorrow?

I will wear a pair of shorts, a shirt, a pair of shoes and a jacket.

	Item	Cost
1.	baseball cap	$25
2.	t-shirt	$12
3.	jeans	$40
4.	sneakers	$35
	Total cost:	**$112.00**

What are you going to wear to the football game?

I will wear a t-shirt, a pair of jeans, a baseball cap and a pair of sneakers.

CHEAPER OR MORE EXPENSIVE

1. Which is cheaper?	baseball cap $12.99	socks $10.99
2. Which is cheaper?	sunglasses $29.99	necklace $19.99
3. Which is more expensive?	black dress $39.99	leather jacket $59.99
4. Which is cheaper?	bread $3.49	cupcakes $4.39
5. Which is more expensive?	sneakers? $55.00	sandals $30.00

LISA AND AMY

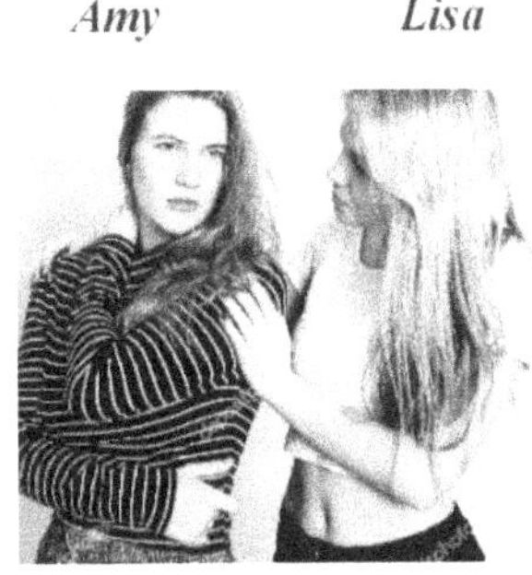

Amy   *Lisa*

Lisa and Amy have been friends since they were in kindergarten. Although they are friends, they are very different. For example, when they were in 5th grade, Lisa asked Amy to join the safety patrols with her, but Amy wasn't interested, so Lisa became a safety patrol and received a nice award at the end of the school year. Amy asked why she didn't get one. Lisa said, *"... because you were not a safety patrol. Only safety patrols got these awards."* When Lisa and Amy went to middle school, Lisa asked Amy to join the dance team with her, but Amy didn't want to, so Lisa joined the team. The danced team traveled to different cities in the state performing, and one time, they were on TV. The dance team was also very popular in the school. When Amy saw them on TV, she said, *"I wish I was on the dance team too."* Lisa said, *"When I asked you to join the dance team, you said no."* When Lisa and Amy went to high school, Lisa asked Amy to join the cheerleading team, but Amy wasn't interested. When the cheerleaders performed at all the football games and sometimes wore their uniforms to school, Amy asked Lisa why she got to perform at the football games and wear her uniform to school. Lisa said, *"... because I am a cheerleader and cheerleaders can wear the uniforms to school if there is a football game after school."* Amy said, *"I wanted to be a cheerleader."* Lisa said, *"I asked you to be on the team, but you didn't want to. You said you were not interested."* When they graduated from high school, Lisa asked Amy to go to college with her so they could be roommates, but Amy did not want to go to college. She wanted to stay home and keep her job at the local supermarket because she was promoted to head cashier. Amy was making $16.00 an hour. Her salary was about $30,000 a year. She was very happy about that, so she was not interested in going to college; so Lisa went to college alone. Four years later, Lisa returned home with a college degree and got a job making $67,000 a year as a bank manager. When Amy asked how Lisa got a good job making so much money, Lisa said, *"because I went to college and earned a college degree. You can get a good job when you have a degree. I asked you to come to college with me, but you didn't want to go."* Amy began to <u>resent</u> Lisa. Amy was also wondering why Lisa had so many wonderful opportunities and she didn't have very many opportunities herself. Amy did not want to be friends with Lisa anymore.

TRUE OR FALSE

1. **T** Lisa and Amy have been friends since they were little girls.

2. **F** Amy participated in many activities with Lisa.

3. **F** Lisa worked at a supermarket as a head cashier when they were in high school.

4. **T** Amy thought that she was making good money until she found out what Lisa was making.

5. **T** Lisa was a cheerleader in high school.

6. **F** The girls were on the safety patrols team together when they were in elementary school.

7. **T** Amy never wanted to do what Lisa wanted to do.

8. **T** Sometimes Lisa would wear her cheerleader uniform to school.

9. **F** Amy wanted Lisa to go to college and be roommates.

10. **T** Lisa went away for four years because she was in college. She returned afterwards.

11. **T** Amy was not interested in going to college because she thought she had a great job.

12. __T__ Amy was not interested in going to college because she thought she had a great job.

13. __T__ Lisa was a dancer, but Amy did not want to be a dancer.

14. __T__ Amy never wanted to do what Lisa wanted to do.

Directions: Answer each question in a complete sentence.

15. In the sentence, "Lisa began to <u>resent</u> Amy." What does the word "resent" mean? ______________

Answers will vary from student to student.

16. How do you think Lisa felt when Amy got an award and she didn't? ______________

Answers will vary from student to student.

17. Why do you think Amy always asked Lisa to do things with her? ______________

Answers will vary from student to student.

18. Do you think Lisa regretted not going to college? Explain. ______________

Answers will vary from student to student.

19. Why do you think Amy always said no to Lisa when she asked her to participate in something?

Answers will vary from student to student.

20. Why do you think Lisa doesn't want to be friends with Lisa anymore? ______________

Answers will vary from student to student.

Directions: Read the chart and complete each sentence with the information from the chart.

CUSTOMER	shoe store	supermarket	electronic store	Walmart
ANA	sneakers sandals	fruit, vegetables deodorant	video games cameras	clothes, shoes
THOMAS	shoes	groceries	cell phones	pants, shirts
DAVID	work boots	deodorant, vitamins	-	t-shirts, underwear

Example: John **buys** bread at the **supermarket**

1. Thomas __________ buys __________ cell phones at the __________ electronic store __________.

2. Ana and David buy __________ deodorant __________ at the supermarket.

3. __________ Walmart __________ sells shoes, pants, shirts and underwear.

4. The __________ supermarket __________ sells groceries.

5. __________ Ana __________ buys video games at the __________ electronic store __________.

6. __________ David __________ buys work boots at the __________ shoe store __________.

7. __________ David __________ doesn't shop at the __________ electronic store __________.

8. Ana and David __________ buy __________ deodorant at the __________ supermarket __________.

9. __________ Ana __________ buys sneakers and sandals at the __________ shoe store __________.

10. David buys __________ t-shirts __________ and __________ underwear __________ at Walmart.

Directions: Choose the correct inflection of **shop**, **shops** and **shopping** for the sentences.

11. Melinda __________ shops __________ at Walmart for clothes.

12. David and John __________ shop __________ for shoes at Footlocker.

13. Lisa is __________ shopping __________ now.

14. We will __________ shop __________ for clothes and shoes tomorrow.

15. Mesha was __________ shopping __________ yesterday.

16. I will __________ shop __________ for a computer at Best Buy on Saturday.

17. Amy __________ shops __________ at Dillards for accessories.

18. My daughters __________ shop __________ at Forever 21 for clothes.

jeans	blouse	T-shirt	dress	jacket
suit	uniforms	shorts	accessories	tank top

shorts

suit

dress

uniforms

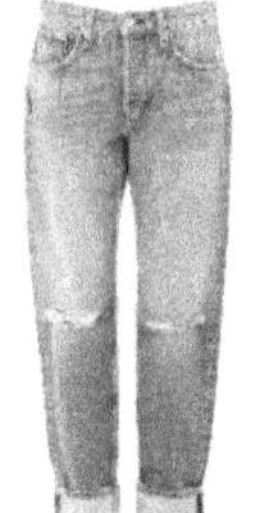

jeans

t-shirt

blouse

jacket

jewelry

Directions: Complete the sentences below with **clothing** that you have learned about in this lesson.

1. Lisa would like a new pair of ___jeans (example)___ for the party.
2. Would you like some___glasses (example)___?
3. Mario needs a new ___jacket (example)___.
4. I love your ___earrings (example)___.
5. My sister bought three pair of ___pants (example)___ at Dillard's today.
6. Joseph has some new ___socks (example)___.
7. I would like a red ___baseball cap (example)___, a white ___t-shirt___, and some black ___sneakers___.
8. Would you like a leather ___coat___ for the winter?
9. I bought my niece a new ___dress___ for her birthday.
10. Joshua needs a new pair of ___shoes___.

PREPOSITIONS

Directions: Complete the sentences below with a preposition.

11. I am going to the movies ___with___ my sister today.   (at, with)
12. I put your water ___on___ the table.   (from, on)
13. Myrna is sitting___next to___ Luisa. (from, next to)
14. I came to the United States ___on___ January 13, 2024. (in, on)
15. Please turn ___on___ the light.   (at, on)
16. I am ___from___ Cuba.   (from, under)
17. Mia is sitting ___behind___ Rosa and Ana.   (under, behind)
18. Your cell phone is ___in___ the car.   (in, together)
19. Mathew came to the United States ___in___ April.   (on, in)
20. Put the cake ___in___ the oven.   (under, in)

SHOP AND BUYS

21. Lisa ___buys___ jewelry at the jewelry store. (shops / buys)
22. Maria likes to ___shop___ at the mall. (shop / buy)
23. My mother ___shops___ for shoes at Burlington. (shops / buys)
24. I will ___buy___ you a leather jacket for your birthday. (shop / buy)

Directions: You use "**are**" when your noun is plural. You use "**is**" when your noun is singular.

1. How much ___is___ the jacket?

2. How much ___is___ the shirt?

3. How much ___are___ the shoes?

4. How much ___is___ the watch?

5. How much ___is___ the rice?

6. How much ___are___ the sunglasses?

7. How much ___is___ the coffee?

8. How much ___are___ the books?

9. How much ___are___ the jeans?

10. How much ___is___ the computer?

sneakers	dress	sandals	watch	cake
computer	jacket	jeans	sunglasses	t-shirt

Directions: Complete each sentence with the correct noun from the boxes above.

11. How much **is** the ___singular noun___?

12. How much **is** the ___singular noun___?

13. How much **are** the ___plural noun___?

14. How much **are** the ___plural noun___?

15. How much **is** the ___singular noun___?

16. How much **are** the ___plural noun___?

17. How much **is** the ___singular noun___?

18. How much **are** the ___plural noun___?

19. How much **is** the ___singular noun___?

20. How much **is** the ___singular noun___?

A BUSY DAY FOR JESSICA

When Jessica woke up at 6:00a.m. this morning, she thought about all the things she had to do today. After she got up, she went running around her neighborhood. She then came back home and made a breakfast sandwich and a cup of tea for herself. Then, she made oatmeal for her husband and daughter before they left the house. Her daughter went to school and her husband went to work at the airport. Jessica jumped in her red truck and started her day. The first place she went was to city hall to pay a traffic ticket. Next, she went to her 10:00a.m. eye doctor's appointment. When she left the eye doctor, she went to the post office, the gas station, and the hospital to visit her cousin who had a baby girl yesterday. At 3:00p.m., she picked up her daughter Jennifer from school. They went to the mall to buy Jennifer some sneakers for PE class. When they left the mall, they went to Publix to buy groceries. When they got home, Jessica cooked chicken, vegetables, and rice for dinner. Jessica, her husband Ricardo, and Jennifer ate dinner at 8:00p.m. Jessica did not watch TV because she was so tired. After she cleaned the kitchen, she took a shower and went to bed because she was so tired.

TRUE OR FALSE

1. Jessica had many things to do today. __T__

2. Jessica ate oatmeal for breakfast. __F__

3. Jessica had a 10:00a.m dentist appointment. __F__

4. Jessica woke up at 6:00p.m. this evening. __F__

5. Jessica jumped in her red truck when she finished running. __F__

6. Jessica cooked chicken, rice and vegetables for breakfast. __F__

7. Jessica and her family ate dinner at 8:00p.m. __F__

8. At 3:00p.m., she picked up Jennifer from school. __F__

9. Jessica's cousin had a baby girl last week. __F__

10. Jessica's husband works at the airport. __T__

Directions: Answer each question in a complete sentence.

11. What is Jessica's husband's name? _His name is Ricardo._

12. What did Jessica drink with her breakfast? _She drank a cup of tea._

13. Why did Jessica and her daughter go to the mall? _To buy some sneakers._

JOHN'S INTERESTING DAY

leather	$200	Publix	breakfast	Speedway
$40	lunch	$60	doctor	hospital
Old Navy	shirt	sneakers	school	truck
house phone	Pollo Tropical	cell phone	girl	baby
boy	teacher	brother-in-law	uncle	post office
25 seconds	7:00p.m.	25 minutes	2:40p.m.	aunt

Yesterday, I had $______$200______, so I bought a black ______leather______ jacket. It was on sale at ______Old Navy______. The regular price of the jacket was $69.99, but it was on sale for $49.00. I had some money left over, so I also bought a pair of blue and white ______sneakers______ for $60.00. It was about 1:30p.m, so I went to ______Pollo Tropical______ and ate ______lunch______. When I was eating in the restaurant, I received a call on my ______cell phone______. It was my mother telling me that my sister Miriam was having her ______baby______ now. I needed to get to the ______hospital______ in a hurry, so I jumped in my red ______truck______ and went to the hospital. It took me ______25 minutes______ to get there. When I arrived, it was ______2:40p.m______. My sister was holding a beautiful baby ______girl______ in her arms. My mother, father and ______brother-in-law______ were all in the hospital room looking at the beautiful baby in the pink blanket. My sister named the baby Ana Maria. I called my wife and told her the good news. I am happy to be a new ______uncle______ today.

Directions: Answer the questions below about the story:

1. Who is telling the story? ______John is telling the story.______
2. Who was having a baby? ______John's sister was having a baby.______
3. Who was in the hospital room? ______John's mother, father and his brother-in-law.______
4. Is the baby a girl or boy? ______The baby is a girl.______
5. What is the baby's name? ______The baby's name is Ana Maria.______
6. What color is the baby's blanket? ______The baby's blanket was pink.______
7. What two items did John buy today? ______He brought a leather jacket and a pair of sneakers.______
8. Who called to tell John that his sister was having the baby? ______His mother called him.______
9. Is John married? ______Yes, he is married.______
10. Is John happy about the baby? ______Yes, John is very happy.______

REVIEW & PRACTICE
Irregular Nouns & Irregular Verbs

1. Two _____thieves_____ broke into the store and stole many items. (thief)

2. I _____put_____ your dinner in the microwave for you. (put)

3. I saw two _____mice_____ in the garage. (mouse)

4. There are too many _____people_____ in the line at the post office. (person)

5. Did your cousin _____quit_____ the soccer team? (quit)

6. Please put the _____knives_____ in the kitchen drawer. (knife)

7. My son has three little _____fish_____ in his fish tank. (fish)

8. I _____saw_____ a beautiful rainbow today. (see)

9. We _____took_____ my grandmother to a restaurant for her birthday. (take)

10. Rosalita _____paid_____ $275.00 for clothes today. (pay)

11. I _____spoke_____ to my daughter's teacher about her grades. (speak)

12. Joseph _____sold_____ his car for $7,500 yesterday. (sell)

13. Three _____men_____ helped me move the tables. (man)

14. I ate nine pieces of _____shrimp_____ at the restaurant. (shrimp)

15. It took seven _____firemen_____ to put the fire out. (fireman)

PRACTICE AND REVIEW

16. My brother loves to _____work_____ on Fridays. (simple verb)

17. Yesterday, I bought two _____shirts_____ for my daughter. (plural noun)

18. Please bring me my _____black_____ jacket. (adjective)

19. I am _____studying_____ now. (gerund)

20. On weekends, we love _____to_____ ride bikes. (infinitive)

21. The children _____are_____ sleeping now. (VTB)

22. _____They / We_____ are very nice people. (subject pronoun)

23. My cousin is _____a_____ news anchor in Colombia. (article)

24. I would like a new _____dresser_____ for my bedroom. (noun)

25. Carlos has three _____notebooks_____. (plural noun)

26. My mother is a _____wonderful_____ person. (adjective)

VOCABULARY PRACTICE

glasses	sweater	accessories	sneakers	watch
skirt	shirt	boots	rice	blouse
milk	jeans	jacket	pasta	dress

1. I need some ___rice___ from the supermarket.

2. Did you buy some ___pasta___ today?

3. That is a pretty ___dress___ that you are wearing.

4. I need a ___sweater___ because it is cold outside.

5. Adidas sells nice ___sneakers___.

6. Carla is wearing a long and beautiful ___skirt___ today.

7. I would like a new pair of ___boots___ for the winter.

8. Patricia has very pretty ___accessories___.

9. I am going to New York. I will need a heavy ___jacket___ because it is cold there.

10. Please get some ___milk___ from Walmart please.

Directions: Write a sentence using "How much is…?" or "How much are…?" for the items below:

Remember your question marks.

11. We ___shop___ at the mall for uniforms.

12. Lisa ___buys___ dishes at thrift stores.

13. I love to ___buy___ sneakers.

14. I will ___buy___ you a bicycle for your birthday.

15. My parents ___buy___ groceries every Sunday.

16. My cousin ___buys___ jeans from Macys.

DIALOGUES: SHOPPING

1. **Person #1:** Good afternoon. How may I help you?
Person #2: Good afternoon. Do you have this blouse in black or red? I really like it, but I need it in black or red in a size medium.
Person #1: I am sorry, but we do not have it in those colors. Would you like to see another color?
Person #2: No, I do not want another color, but do you have these jeans in a medium?
Person #1: Yes, I have them in medium and I also have them in two colors: blue and white
Person #2: Great. I will take a pair of white jeans in a size medium. How much are they?
Person #1: They are usually $35.00, but today they are on sale for $27.00. The sale ends on Wednesday.
Person #2: OK. I will try them on and if they fit me, I will get them.
Person #1: Perfect. The fitting room is around the corner.
Person #2: Thank you. I will be right back.

2. **Person #1:** I went shopping today and I bought so many things. I bought three dresses, two shirts, a sweater, two pair of sneakers, a pair of sandals and a gold watch.
Person #2: Wow! You bought many things!
Person #1: Yes, I did. I needed new clothes because I lost 25 pounds.
Person #2: That is wonderful. Congratulations on losing so much weight.
Person #1: Thank you. I am very happy. I spent $250 today, but I am happy to have new clothes.

3. **Person #1:** We have been learning how to read money in my class. It's been interesting.
Person #2: Do you know how to read money?
Person #1: Yes, I do. For instance, I can read this: $1.29, $45.90, $235.89, $785.16, and $36.00.
Person #2: Ok. Great. You did a good job. I need to learn how to read money in English myself.
Person #1: Yes, you must learn to read money in English if you live in the United States.
Person #2: Thank you. I am going to practice.

4. **Person #1:** Hi. Please tell me how much these items cost.
Person #2: Yes, the black shirt is $15.00, the blue shirt is $20.00, the jeans are $30.00, the red dress is $29.99 and the sunglasses are $18.00.
Person #1: I would like to purchase all of those items please. What is the cost of everything?
Person #2: Yes, your subtotal is $112.99 before tax. With tax, everything will be $119.28.
Person #1: OK. Thank you. Here is my credit card.
Person #2: Thank you. Here is your receipt. Have a great day and please come again.
Person #1: You have a great day too! Thank you.

5. **Person #1:** I have so many places to go this weekend.
Person #2: Really? Where do you need to go?
Person #1: Well, I need to go to the electronic store to look for a new TV, the bookstore to buy a planner, the boutique to buy a nice shirt for a party, the supermarket to buy some groceries, the department store to get a new microwave and the mall to find some nice shoes and blouses.
Person #2: Yes, you do have lots of places to go. I don't have a busy weekend, so I am just going to relax at my house, watch some TV, eat and get fat.
Person #1: OK. Well, that sounds like the good life.

6.

Person #1: Good morning.
Person #2: Good morning. How are you?
Person #1: I am fine. Thank you. Are you going to the store today?
Person #2: Yes, do you need something?
Person #1: Yes, I need some sandwich meat, bread and juice.
Person #2: OK. I will buy you some sandwich meat, bread and juice.

7.

Person #1: I need a new computer, but I don't want to spend a lot of money.
Person #2: How much do you want to spend on a new computer?
Person #1: I don't want to spend more than $400.00 on a computer. I want a good computer for a good price. I'm not sure which brand to get. I may get an Apple Computer.
Person #2: I think Best Buy is having a sale on computers. Also, did you try Walmart and Target? They have computers too.
Person #1: No, I didn't try those stores because they are not electronic stores.
Person #2: No, they are not electronic stores, but they have electronic departments.
Person #1: Yes, you are correct. I may go to those stores and look for a computer. Thank you so much!

8.

Person #1: I am taking my daughter to the mall. She's going to visit my sister in Texas, and she wants some new things.
Person #2: What stores will you go to in the mall?
Person #1: She likes boutiques. She will also go to some of the shoe stores, the clothing stores and the bookstores. She also likes magazines.
Person #2: Yes, I like the mall too. Some of my favorite stores are there. I like shopping at the electronic stores and some of the department stores like Sears, JC Penny, Macys and Dillards. I like buying jeans and jackets from those places.
Person #1: Yes, the mall has nice things, but they can be expensive.
Person #2: Yes, you are correct, but you must buy when they have sales and discounts.
Person #1: I agree. But sometimes the items are not on sale and I spend lots of money on things.
Person #2: Yes, I hate that.

9.

Person #1: Do you like learning English?
Person #2: Yes, I do. It is different. It is a little difficult, but I am getting better every day.
Person #1: What do you like best about learning English?
Person #2: Well, I like the conversation practice because for me, I need more practice in speaking. I understand things on paper, but sometimes it is difficult for me to understand things spoken to me.
Person #1: Oh. That is interesting. You understand on paper, but not always when English is spoken to you? What about reading. Do you read English good?
Person #2: Yes, I read English pretty good. I am happy about that.
Person #1: Do you understand what you read?
Person #2: Yes, I do. I understand what I read most times. Sometimes I don't. But I like learning about pronouns, verbs to be, regular nouns, proper nouns, verbs, gerunds, contractions, adjectives, prepositions, compound words and cardinal and ordinal numbers.
Person #1: You have learned all that? Wow, that is a lot.
Person #2: Yes, it is, and I am happy to have learned so much!

10.
Person #1: I am going to the store in one hour. Would you like anything?
Person #2: Why are you going to the store?
Person #1: ...because we need groceries. There is no food in the house. I am going to Sedanos.
Person #2: Yes, I would like some cookies and meat to make sandwiches.
Person #1: What kind of meat?
Person #2: Please bring some turkey or ham.
Person #1: OK. I will. Do you want anything else?
Person #2: No thank you.

11.
Person #1: Target is having a three-day sale starting today.
Person #2: What items are on sale?
Person #1: Girls and boys clothes are on sale. T-shirts, socks, and jeans are also on sale.
Person #2: Okay. What is the discount?
Person #1: I think everything is 20% off.
Person #2: That is a good sale. I think I will go there after work today.
Person #1: Yes, that is a good idea. See you later.
Person #2: Okay. See you later.

12.
Person #1: I need a new TV. Where should I go?
Person #2: You can go to the electronic store on the corner of Pines Blvd and 127th Street.
Person #1: What is the name of the electronic store?
Person #2: It is called Best Buy. They have lots of electronics.
Person #1: Really? Like what?
Person #2: Well, they have TVs, computers, play stations, DVDs, ipads, cameras, and cell phones. Walmart and Target also have electronic departments.
Person #1: Yes, but I would prefer going to a store that only has electronics.
Person #2: I understand. Go to Best Buy. They have different brands to choose from.
Person #1: OK. I will go there in one hour.
Person #2: Perfect. I hope you find what you need.

13.
Person #1: Did you know that Ross is having a big sale today? Many things are on sale.
Person #2: Really? What things are on sale?
Person #1: Well sneakers are on sale for $30.00, T-shirts are on sale for $10.50 a pack. Jeans for $15.99, different sandals for $12.60, sweaters for under $20.00, blouses for 15.99, and even uniforms are on sale.
Person #2: Wow! I didn't know. I need to go by there. That sounds like a great sale!
Person #1: Yes, it is a really good sale. I'm going today.
Person #2: Okay. I will go tomorrow.

14.
Person #1: Hello my friend. How are you?
Person #2: I am fine and you?
Person #1: What are you doing on Saturday night?
Person #2: I am going to a movie and dinner on Saturday night.
Person #1: That sounds like fun. I was going to invite you to a party that my friend is having.
Person #2: Oh thank you, but I cannot go. I have a busy day on Saturday.
Person #1: No problem. I understand. What about next Saturday?
Person #2: I am not sure. I need to check my calendar.
Person #1: OK. Well let me know after you check your calendar.

WEEKLY ASSESSMENT: SHOPPING

jeans	boots	dress	sneakers
jacket	blouse	belt store	electronic store
accessories	pharmacy	Shoe store	supermarket

VOCABULARY

1. I am going to the __electronic store__ on Saturday to buy a camera and a computer.

2. My sister bought a beautiful black __dress__ from the clothing store last week.

3. Ana's __blouse__ is beautiful.

4. I need a new pair of __jeans__.

5. Did you take your prescription to the __pharmacy__.

6. You should wear some matching __accessories__ with your dress.

7. I will be going to the __supermarket__ to buy some eggs, bread and turkey today.

8. I purchased two pair of __boots__ from the shoe store today.

9. Diana is wearing some beautiful __accessories__.

10. My sister wants a leather __jacket__.

buy	buys	shop	shops	shopping

11. I love to __shop__ at the mall for my handbags.

12. On Saturday, we are going __shopping__.

13. My father says that he will __buy__ me a new laptop for school.

14. My mother __buys__ chicken every week.

15. Liliana loves to __buy__ dolls.

16. I __shop__ at Sedanos and Walmart for my groceries.

17. My brother __shops__ at Nike for his sneakers.

18. Jose __buys__ flowers from the man on the corner.

Directions: Complete each sentence with the correct word.

a	a pair of	some

1. I would like to wear ___some___ accessories with my outfit.
2. Yasmina is wearing ___a___ beautiful scarf today.
3. John is wearing ___a pair of___ blue jeans and ___a___ white T-shirt.
4. We bought ___some___ clothes at Dillards today.
5. I would like ___a___ nice blouse for my skirt.
6. Yesterday, I bought ___some___ sunglasses.
7. Maria is wearing ___a___ blue shirt and ___a___ red skirt.

How much "is"? How much "are"?

41. How much ___are___ the socks?
42. How much ___are___ the jeans?
43. How much ___is___ the jacket?
44. How much ___are___ the dresses?
45. How much ___is___ the scarf?

50. What are you wearing today?

    a. I wearing today a pair of blue jeans and a white shirt.
    b. I am wear a pair of blue jeans and a white shirt today.
    c. I am wearing a pair of blue jeans and a white shirt.

51. What is Jorge wearing today?

    a. Jorge wearing today a pair of blue jeans and a white shirt.
    b. Jorge is wearing a pair of blue jeans and a white shirt today.
    c. Today, Jorge wearing a pair of blue jeans and a white shirt.

52. Where do you buy your bread, eggs and milk?

    a. I buy my bread, eggs and milk at the Sedanos Supermarket.
    b. I buy my bread, eggs and milk at Sedanos Supermarket.
    c. I bought my bread, eggs and milk at Sedanos Supermarket.

53. How much are the jackets?

    a. The jacket are $30 each.
    b. The jackets is $30 each.
    c. The jackets are $30 a pound.

54. What is your favorite department store?

    a.   My favorite department store are Walmart.
    b.   My favorite department store is Walmart.
    c.   Walmart are my favorite department store.

55. Where do you shop for jeans?

    a.   I shops at Macys for jeans.
    b.   I shop at the mall for jeans.
    c.   I shop at Publix for jeans.

Directions: Read the questions below and answer each question in a complete sentence.

56. What is Diana wearing today?   Example: Diana is wearing a red dress, some earrings, a bracelet and some sandals.

57. Where do you shop for groceries? Example: I shop at Aldy's Supermarket for groceries.

58. How much was the jacket, the shirt and the jeans together? Example: They were $120.78 together.

59. What will you wear to the party on Saturday? Example: On Saturday, I will wear a blue shirt, a pair of white pants, a pair of white shoes, a watch and a necklace.

Directions: Answer each question in a complete sentence.

t-shirts: $9.89 a pack	sunglasses: $26.00	umbrella: $10.00	scarf: $17.00	coat: $80.00
blue dress: $45.00	earrings: $15.00	socks $7.99 a pair	black Jacket: $54.00	suit: $150

They are   **It is**   **They're**   **It's**

1. How much are the earrings? They are / They're $15.00.
2. How much is the blue dress? It is $45.00
3. How much is the black jacket and the umbrella together? They are / They're $64 together.

4. How is the suit and the coat? They are / They're $231 together.
5. How much is the blue dress? It is or It's $45.00.

Lesson 6: Managing Sickness

Dear ESL Teacher,

As you embark on teaching Lesson 6: Managing Sickness, you have at your disposal a comprehensive plan designed to foster language acquisition and proficiency among your students. This lesson focuses on essential vocabulary and concepts related to Managing Sickness, a practical and relevant topic for students.

In this lesson, students will learn new vocabulary words specific to the lesson. They will gain the ability to recognize the difference between symptoms and remedies, as well as identify the names of various body parts in English. The structured activities include vocabulary introduction, sentence practice, grammar drills, and conversational exercises. Through these activities, students will build a strong foundation in understanding and using terms related to health and wellness.

The instructional procedures outlined in this lesson include direct instruction, guided practice, and independent practice. This balanced approach supports diverse learning styles and abilities, ensuring all students have the opportunity to engage and succeed. By practicing related sentences on the topic, learning about synonyms, antonyms, and homophones, and focusing on correct grammar and subject/verb agreement, students will enhance their overall language skills.

In addition to vocabulary and grammar practice, students will read a skit, complete a word-finding puzzle, and work in pairs for dialogue activities. This collaborative approach fosters communication skills and reinforces the lesson content in an engaging way. An assessment at the end of the lesson will help evaluate students' comprehension and application of the material.

OBJECTIVES:

1. Students will identify and use vocabulary related to managing sickness.
2. Students will differentiate between symptoms and remedies.
3. Students will identify various body parts in English.
4. Students will construct and practice sentences using targeted vocabulary.
5. Students will demonstrate their learning through a comprehensive assessment.

INSTRUCTIONAL PROCEDURES:

Direct Instruction:

- **Objective:** Present new vocabulary and grammar concepts clearly and explicitly. Teach the meaning of the vocabulary words and explain the difference between symptoms and remedies.
- **Details:** Begin the lesson by introducing new vocabulary words related to Managing Sickness. Explain word meanings using visuals and contextual examples. Provide clear definitions, pronunciation guides, and use each word in sentences to demonstrate its usage. Display visuals,

such as images or diagrams, illustrating each word's meaning. Encourage students to repeat and practice pronouncing the words aloud to reinforce retention.

Guided Practice:

- **Objective:** Help students apply new knowledge in a supportive environment.
- **Details:** Facilitate structured activities where students practice using new vocabulary and grammar concepts from their book with teacher guidance. Provide sentence frames or prompts that incorporate the new vocabulary and grammar structures.

Independent Practice:

- **Objective:** Reinforce learning through individual or paired activities found in the book. Choose activities that students complete independently, then review the answers with students for self-check.
- **Details:** Assign activities from the book that requires students to independently apply what they have learned. This includes completing worksheets or exercises that reinforce vocabulary usage, grammar rules, or conversational skills. Provide clear instructions and examples to guide students. Encourage self-monitoring by asking students to review their work for accuracy and clarity before submitting it. Monitor progress and offer assistance as needed.

Differentiation/Adaptations:

- **Provide visual aids and simplified instructions for English language learners:**
    - **Objective:** Support comprehension for students with varying English proficiency levels.
    - **Details:** Use visual aids such as charts, diagrams, or illustrations alongside verbal explanations. Provide simplified instructions and break down complex concepts into smaller, more manageable steps. Offer bilingual dictionaries or picture dictionaries. Adjust the pace of instruction to accommodate slower processing speeds, allowing extra time for comprehension and practice.

Offer additional practice or alternative assessments for students with diverse learning needs:

- **Objective:** Address individual learning needs and preferences.
- **Details:** Provide differentiated assignments or activities that cater to different learning styles and abilities. Offer extension activities for advanced learners. Consider alternative assessment formats such as oral presentations or digital projects. Use flexible grouping strategies to accommodate social and emotional needs.

ACTIVITIES

Sentence Practice:

- **Objective:** Help students construct meaningful sentences using the new vocabulary and grammar concepts found at the beginning of the lesson.
- **Details:** Guide students step-by-step in forming sentences that incorporate the vocabulary words and target grammar structures. Begin with simple sentences and gradually increase complexity. Provide scaffolded support with sentence starters or frames.

Grammar Drill:

- o **Objective:** Reinforce understanding of grammar rules.
- o **Details:** Guide students to complete the focused exercises where students practice using grammar elements correctly. Include fill-in-the-blank activities, matching exercises, or creating sentences found in the lesson. Provide explanations and examples to clarify misunderstandings.

Conversation Practice:

- o **Objective:** Develop students' ability to engage in spoken communication using learned vocabulary and grammar.
- o **Details:** Pair students or organize small groups for conversational activities. Provide prompts or scenarios requiring the use of targeted vocabulary and grammar in meaningful contexts. Encourage turn-taking and active listening.

Reading Comprehension:

- o **Objective:** Enhance students' ability to understand written English.
- o **Details:** Choose a reading passage from the lesson and listen for proper pronunciation, fluency and comprehension. After reading, ask questions that require students to recall details, make inferences, or summarize key points. Encourage reading aloud to practice pronunciation and fluency.

Dialogues:

- o **Objective:** Foster creativity and application of vocabulary and grammar in context through reading short dialogues in conversational tone.

- o **Details:** Students will get into pairs. Teacher will assign students a dialogue number to read. Students will take five minutes to practice their dialogue silently, then the teacher will call on each dialogue number and the pair of students who were given that number will read.

Assessment:

- o **Objective:** Evaluate students' comprehension and application of lesson content.
- o **Details:** The assessment is found at the end of each lesson. It includes a mix of vocabulary, grammar, and reading comprehension questions, along with a short writing or dialogue creation task.

MATERIALS AND RESOURCES:

- Book: It's Time to Learn English
- Vocabulary cards
- Whiteboard and markers
- Textbooks or reading materials
- Worksheets for grammar exercises
- Audio recordings for listening activities
- Flashcards and visuals

TECHNOLOGY NEEDED:

- Projector or screen for displaying visuals
- Computer or tablet for accessing digital resources

Lesson 6: Managing Sickness

T - Think Back (Review)

Activity: Begin the lesson by reviewing key concepts and vocabulary from the previous lesson. Use a brief warm-up activity to engage students and assess their understanding of any sickness-related terms they might already know.

Time: 5-10 minutes

E – Entry (Introduction/Beginning)

Activity: Introduce new vocabulary words related to managing sickness using visuals such as flashcards, images, or charts. Explain the meanings, provide clear definitions, pronunciation examples, and use each word in sentences to demonstrate usage. Clarify the difference between symptoms and remedies.

Time: 15 minutes

A - Application (Teaching/Presentation/Delivery)

Activity: Present new grammar concepts clearly and explicitly. Use direct instruction to introduce synonyms, antonyms, homophones, and correct grammar structures (subject/verb agreement). Provide examples and demonstrate their usage in sentences.

Objective: Students will construct and practice sentences using targeted vocabulary and demonstrate understanding of grammar rules.

Time: 20 minutes

C - Collaborative Practice (Student Practice)

Activity: Facilitate guided practice by having students work in pairs or small groups to complete structured activities using sentence frames and prompts. Conduct conversational activities where students discuss symptoms and remedies.

Time: 25 minutes

H - Highlight (Wrap-up/Closing)

Activity: Summarize the key points of the lesson, highlighting the new vocabulary and grammar rules learned. Assign a reading comprehension activity using a passage about managing sickness. Discuss the main ideas and ask comprehension questions.

Objective: Reinforce the lesson's content and ensure students understand the material.

Time: 10 minutes

E - Evaluate (Assessment/Evaluation)

Activity: Administer the comprehensive assessment found at the end of the lesson. Assess students on vocabulary, grammar, reading comprehension, and dialogue creation.

Objective: Evaluate students' comprehension and application of lesson content.

Time: 15 minutes

R - Reflect (Final Review)

Activity: End the lesson with a reflective activity where students can share their thoughts on what they learned, how they can use it in real-life situations, and any areas where they need further clarification. Encourage students to share their thoughts on their progress and areas they want to improve.

Time: 5-10 minutes

Managing Sickness

VOCABULARY	SYMPTOMS	REMEDIES	BODY PARTS
1. sick	coughing	cough syrup	face
2. ill	sneezing	cold medicine	nose
3. healthy	runny nose	Flu medicine	mouth
4. hurt	fever	throat lozenges	ears
5. pain	cold	pain relievers	neck
6. ache	Flu	antacids	chest
7. doctor	sore throat	see a doctor	arms
8. appointment	headache	heating pad	hands
9. medicine	stomachache	antibiotics	legs
10. prescription	toothache	medication	knees
11. label	backache	aspirin	eyes
12. emergency	bodyache	get some rest	elbows
13. hospital	infection	checkup	stomach
14. patient	tired	fluids	shoulders

1. When you are **coughing**, you should take some **cough syrup**.

2. I have a **backache**. I need to use a **heating pad** and take some **pain relievers**.

3. My daughter has the **flu**. She needs to **see a doctor**.

4. The baby has an **infection**. He needs **antibiotics**.

5. I have a **sore throat**, so I will take a **throat lozenge**.

6. Roberto has a **fever**. He needs to take a **pain reliver**.

7. I have a **cold**. I need to take some **cold medicine**.

8. When you are **tired**, you should get some **rest**.

9. When you have a **stomachache**, you should take some **antacids**.

Sickness & Heath
Practice Sentences

1. My son is **coughing** and **sneezing** a lot. I will give him some **cold medicine.**

2. I hurt my leg at the gym yesterday. My arms are also **hurting**.

3. I am very **tired**. I need to rest.

4. I have a **bodyache**. I need to use a **heating pad.**

5. I have a **pain** in my right arm.

6. The baby has a **runny nose**. I will give her some baby **medicine**.

7. My grandmother is **sick**. She has been **ill** for a while now.

8. My leg is **aching** very bad.

9. I have a bad **headache**. I need to take a **pain reliever**.

10. The doctor called me in a **prescription** at the pharmacy for my **infection**.

11. I have a doctor's **appointment** at 10:00a.m tomorrow morning.

12. My sister has the **Flu**. She needs to take **cold medicine** or see a **doctor**.

13. When you have a **stomachache**, you should take **antacids**.

14. My brother needs a **throat lozenge** for his **sore throat**.

15. My mouth hurts because I have a **toothache**. I need to see a dentist.

16. When your head hurts, you have a **headache**.

17. You should take **antibiotics** when you have an **infection**.

18. My mother is **coughing** and **sneezing**. She also has a **runny nose**.

19. The baby has a **fever**. She is very warm.

20. My mother never gets sick. She is very **healthy**.

21. You need to take some cold **medicine** for your **cold**.

22. I have an **ache** in my back.

Directions: Complete each sentence using the correct form of the verb "hurt".

hurt	hurts	hurting

1. I ________hurt________ my leg yesterday.
2. My legs and arms ________hurt________ today.
3. Is your back still ________hurting________?
4. My nephew's nose is ________hurting________.
5. My daughter's eyes ________hurt________.
6. My throat ________hurts________ when I talk.
7. My neck ________hurts________ when I turn.
8. My father's back ________hurts________.
9. My husband's legs ________hurt________.
10. My head ________hurts________.
11. My leg ________hurts________ when I walk.
12. My hands are ________hurting________.
13. My stomach and chest ________hurt________.
14. My ears are ________hurting________.

Directions: Complete the sentences below with the correct remedy for the sickness.

He should take a pain reliever.	The baby needs antibiotics.	She needs to take cold medicine.	She needs to take a pain reliever.
They need to take cold medicine.	She needs to take an antacid.	She should see a doctor.	She should use a heating pad.

15. Maria has a stomachache. ________She needs to take an antacid.________
16. Miriam has a cold. ________She needs to take cold medicine.________
17. My brother has a headache. ________He should take a pain reliever.________
18. My mother has a backache. ________She should use a heating pad.________
19. The baby has an ear infection. ________The baby needs antibiotics.________
20. Pedro's sister has a fever. ________She needs to take a pain reliever.________
21. The boys have bad colds. ________They need to take cold medicine.________

They are Sick

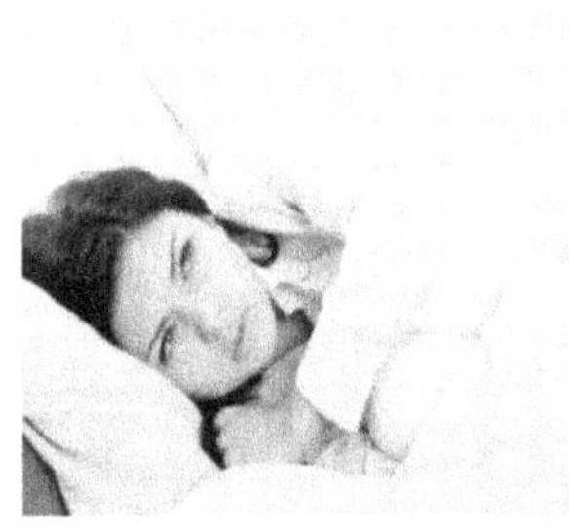

Melissa Cuevas
26 years old
Stomachache
Bodyache
Coughing
Took 2 antacids
Is drinking plenty of
fluids and getting
plenty of rest
Didn't go to the doctor

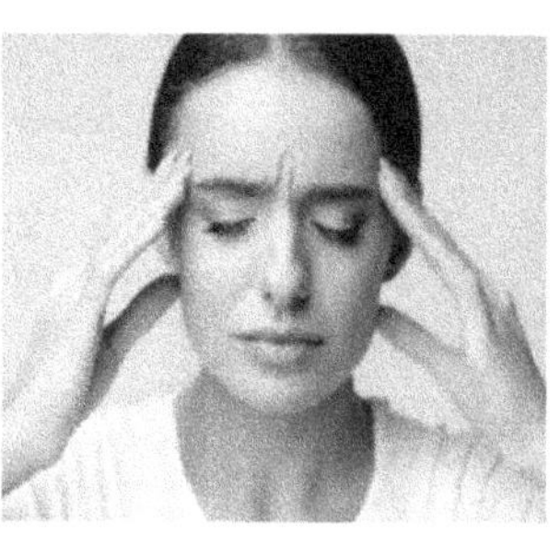

Sharon Taylor
38 years old
Headache
Will take 2 pain
relievers
Will go to the
doctor Monday
10:00a.m.

Jennifer Cooper
31 years old
Toothache
Took 2 Tylenol
Has a dentist's
appointment on
Friday 11:15a.m.

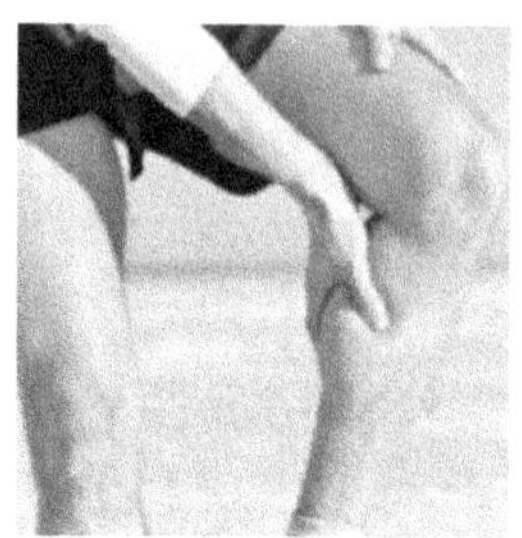

Mark Goldberg
48 years old
His leg hurts
Took 2 pain
relievers
Went to the doctor
yesterday 11:00a.m.

1. Jennifer's __________ mouth __________ hurts.

2. Mark's __________ leg __________ hurts.

3. __________ Sharon __________ has an appointment at 10:00a.m. on __________ Monday __________

4. Did Jennifer go to the doctor? __________ No, she has an appointment on Friday.

5. __________ Melissa's __________ body hurts.

6. __________ Mark __________ is 48 years old.

7. Whose appointment is on Monday? __________ Sharon's appointment is on Monday.

8. Sharon's __________ head __________ hurts.

9. How old is Jennifer? __________ Jennifer is 31 years old. / She is 31 years old.

10. Melissa is __________ coughing / aching / 26 years old.

11. Who has a headache? __________ Sharon has a headache.

12. Did Melissa go to the doctor? __________ No, she did not go to the doctor.

13. Who needs to go to the dentist? __________ Jennifer needs to go to the dentist.

14. Melissa's __________ stomach __________ hurts.

15. How many people have dentist's appointments? __________ only one person

Sickness and Health

has	cold medicine	headache	antacids	don't
rest	doctor	doesn't	antibiotics	have

Directions: Choose a word from the box above to complete each sentence below:

1. David is not sick. He _____ doesn't _____ need a doctor.
2. Maria is very tired. She needs some _____ rest _____ .
3. Marsha's head hurts. She _____ has _____ a headache.
4. We have colds. We need _____ cold medicine _____ .
5. My son has a stomachache. He needs to take _____ antacids _____ .
6. My head is hurting. I have a bad _____ headache _____ .
7. I have an infection in my leg. I need _____ antibiotics _____ .
8. My children are both sick. They _____ have _____ colds.
9. You are very tired. You should get some _____ rest _____ .
10. Michael has the Flu. He will see a _____ doctor _____ tomorrow.

Directions: Answer each question in a complete sentence.

11. Where do you buy your cold medicine? _____ I buy cold medicine at _____ .

12. Debbie is sick. What does she need? _____ Debbie / She needs _____ .

13. Does Kimberly have a cold? _____ Yes, she does. / No, she doesn't _____

14. Do you have a cold? _____ Yes, I do. / No, I don't. (have a cold) _____

15. Carlos has an infection. What does he need? _____ He needs to take antibiotics. _____

16. Maria has a stomachache. What should she take? _____ She / Maria should take antacids. _____

Today is Thursday, October 10, 2024. It is Jennifer's first day working at the Family Medical Center on Cottonroad Street in Chicago, IL. Jennifer is the new medical assistant and she is very excited about her new job. She makes $15 an hour. She is responsible for checking the patients in, taking their weight, temperature and blood pressure. She received her certificate of completion from Chicago Vocational Institute, and she is very happy. Right now, there are four people waiting to be seen by the doctor and Jennifer calls them to the back one at a time and gets them ready to see the doctor. Below is the information on the four patients and why they are at the doctor.

Amy Sanchez age 17 problem: stomachache weight: 123 lbs appt time: 2:00p.m.	**Roberto Collins** age 31 problem: back pain weight: 195 lbs appt time: 11:00a.m.	**Maria Santiago** age 37 problem: the Flu weight: 120 lbs appt time: 1:30p.m.	**Brittany Williams** age 21 problem: bad headache weight: 115 lbs appt time: 10:00a.m.

1. Why is Brittany at the doctor? _____ because she has a bad headache. _____

2. What time is Roberto's appointment? _____ Roberto's / His appointment is at 11:00a.m. _____

3. What is Amy's weight? _____ Amy weight is 123 lbs. _____

4. Who has the Flu? _____ Maria has the Flu. _____

5. What is Maria's last name? _____ Her / Maria's last name is Santiago. _____

6. What time is Brittany's appointment? _____ Her / Brittany's appointment is at 10:00a.m _____

7. Who has a headache? _____ Brittany has a headache. _____

8. What is Amy's last name? _____ Amy's / Her last name is Sanchez. _____

9. Who has back pain? _____ Roberto has back pain. _____

10. Where does Jennifer work? _____ Jennifer / She works at the Family Medical Center _____

11. How much does Jennifer make? _____ Jennifer / She makes $15.00 an hour. _____

12. What city does Jennifer live in? _____ Jennifer / She lives in Chicago. _____

ANSWERING QUESTIONS ABOUT SICKNESS

1. **What is wrong with your sister?**

   a. She has coughing and a runny nose.
   b. She is coughing and has a runny nose.
   c. She has a runny nose and a coughing.

2. **I have an earache. What do I need?**

   a. You need an antacid.
   b. You need to take cold medicine.
   c. You need to see a doctor.

3. **My back is hurting. What should I do?**

   a. You need to see a heating pad and use a doctor.
   b. You need to use a heating pad and take pain relievers.
   c. You need antibiotics.

4. **I have a stomachache. What do I need?**

   a. You should take antacids.
   b. You should take aspirin.
   c. You need to use a heating pad.

5. **Jackie has a toothache. What should she do?**

   a. Jackie should see a dentist.
   b. Jackie should take an antacid.
   c. She needs to take cold medicine.

6. **My son is coughing a lot.**

   a. Your son needs antibiotics.
   b. Your son needs to take cough syrup.
   c. Your son needs a heating pad.

7. **I am going to the pharmacy. What do you need?**

   a. Please bring me some chicken and bread.
   b. Please pick up my prescription.
   c. Please buy me a new pair of jeans.

8. **What did the doctor tell you?**
   a. The doctor said that I have the Flu.
   b. The doctor said that I need a new car.
   c. The doctor said that he has a cold.

9.   I am coughing, sneezing and I have a fever.

    a.   I think you have a stomachache.
    b.   I think you have a backache.
    c.   I think you have a cold.

10. My husband's back is hurting.

    a.   He should use a heating pad, take some pain relievers and get some rest.
    b.   He should use a heating pad, take some pain relievers and take a throat lozenge.
    c.   He should use a heating pad, take some pain relievers and take some antacids.

11. What's the matter?

    a.   I am sick. I do not feel well.
    b.   I am fine. How are you?
    c.   I have sick. I need doctor.

12. My eyes hurt.

    a.   You should take some cold medicine.
    b.   You should use some eye drops.
    c.   You should use a heating pad.

13. The lady is having a heart attack.

    a.   She needs to lie down.
    b.   Please call 911 emergency.
    c.   She should take some cough syrup.

14. I am tired.

    a.   You should see a doctor.
    b.   You should see a doctor and use a heating pad.
    c.   You should get some rest.

15. I have a bodyache.

    a.   You need to take an antacid.
    b.   You should take a pain reliver and get some rest.
    c.   You need to eat something.

16. I have an infection in my leg.

    a.   You need to take pain relivers.
    b.   The doctor needs to prescribe you some antibiotics.
    c.   You need a prescription for some antacids.

SICK PEOPLE

    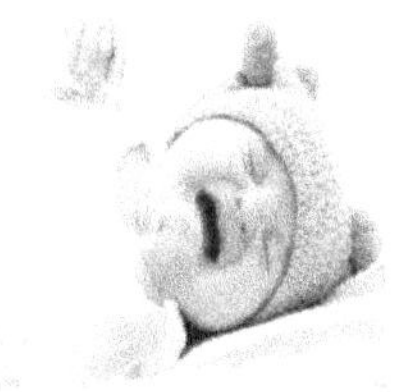

Amy Collins
7 years old

Symptoms:
Headache
Sore throat
coughing
sneezing

Remedies:
cold medicine
throat lozenge
Aspirin

Bertha Goldstein
66 years old

Symptoms:
infection in her
left ear

Remedies:
Antibiotics

Brandon Wilcox
6 years old

Symptoms:
fever
runny nose
coughing

Remedies:
cold medicine
cough syrup

Sheila Gomez
26 years old

Symptoms:
bodyache
Stomachache
fever

Remedies:
pain relievers
heating pad
antacids

Jonathan Huger
7 months old

Symptoms:
ear infection
fever

Remedies:
antibiotics
baby aspirin

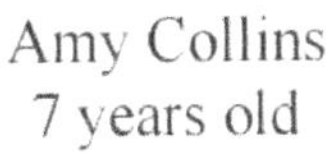

Example: What is Jonathan doing? <u>Jonathan is crying.</u>

1. What does Brandon have? _Brandon has a fever and runny nose._

2. Who has a stomachache? _Sheila has a stomachache._

3. What is Amy doing? _Amy is coughing and sneezing._

4. Who needs to use a heating pad? _Sheila needs to use a heating pad._

5. Who is the elderly person? _Bertha is the elderly person._

6. Who needs antibiotics? _Bertha and Jonathan need antibiotics._

7. Who has a sore throat? _Amy has a sore throat._

8. Who is crying? _Jonathan was crying._

9. Who is under one year old? _Jonathan is under one year old._

THEY ARE SICK

Trin
cold

Fever
Sore throat
Sneezing
Runny nose

Bobby
Stomachache

Bad cough
Bodyache
Sneezing
Eyes hurt

Carmen
Flu
Runny nose
Sore throat
Coughing
Sneezing

runny nose	eyes	throat	Flu	eye
cold	coughing and sneezing	cold medicine	see a doctor	antacid
antibiotics	throat lozenge	cough medicine	pain reliever(s)	oxygen

Example: What does Carmen have? <u>Carmen has a fever, a cold and a sore throat.</u>

1. Bobby's ________ stomach ________ hurt.
2. Trin has a ________ fever, sore throat and runny nose. ________ .
3. Bobby is ________ coughing ________ and ________ sneezing ________ .
4. Carmen has a ________ Flu, runny nose or sore throat ________ .
5. Carmen is ________ coughing ________ and ________ sneezing ________ .
6. Trin needs to take ________ cold medicine ________ for her cold.
7. Bobby needs to take an ________ antacid ________ for his stomachache.
8. Carmen needs to ________ see a doctor ________ for her Flu.
9. Trin should take some ________ pain relievers ________ for her fever.
10. Bobby should take ________ cough medicine ________ for his cough.
11. Carmen should take a ________ throat lozenge ________ for her sore throat.

SICKNESS/HEALTH

back	cold medicine	stomachache	hurts	throat
stomach	hurt	pain relievers	pain reliever	antibiotics
head	ache	see a doctor	infection	aches

1. Your stomach hurts. You have a ___stomach ache___. The problem is in your ___throat___.

2. When you have a headache your head ___hurts___.

3. I have a bad tooth ___ache___. I need to take some ___pain relievers___

4. My legs ___hurt___.

5. When you have a cold. You should take ___cold medicine___.

6. If you have a sore throat. The problem is in your ___throat___.

7. When you have a backache. The pain is in your ___back___.

8. When you have a fever. The pain is in your ___head___.

9. When your leg hurts, you should take a ___pain reliever___.

10. When you have the Flu you should ___see a doctor___.

11. When you have a/an ___various answers___. You should take some ___various answers___.

HOMOPHONES

12. What is the ___serial___ number on the cable box? (cereal, serial)

13. Did you ___hear___ about the new teacher? She is from Colombia. (hear, here)

14. What is your favorite ___meat___? I like turkey and ham. (meet, meat)

15. My right ___eye___ is very red today. (eye, I)

16. Did you ___know___ that you have a hole in your shirt? (no, know)

17. Next ___week___ I will go to Orlando. (weak, week)

18. Is the new baby a ___male___ or female? (mail, male)

19. I flew to Texas on a big ___plane___ last year. (plain, plane)

20. Tomorrow, we will ___be___ in Tampa. (bee, be)

21. Did you ___see___ the new movie? (see, sea)

VIVIAN IS SICK TODAY

Vivian is a 25 year-old successful marketing executive. She lives in South Carolina and she is very intelligent. She graduated from college in her native country Boliva from Universidad Mayor de San Simon. She came to the United States three years ago she got a job immediately because she speaks very good English. Vivian has a big presentation on her job this morning at 11:00, but she woke up feeling terrible. She had a bodyache, a headache, a runny nose and she is coughing and sneezing a lot. She wants to stay in the bed, but she can't because the presentation is very important because it will determine if she will get a new client, which can bring the company lots of money. She forced herself to get up, then she took some cold medicine and drank lots of orange juice. She is sick, but she is still going to work today because the presentation is very important. After the presentation is finished, she will go back home and get into the bed.

Directions: Read each sentence below. If the sentence is correct, write "T" for true. If the sentence is not correct, write "F" for false.

1. F _______ Vivian is not going to work today because she is sick.
2. F _______ Vivian has a bodyache, headache and backache.
3. T _______ Vivian is a successful marketing executive.
4. T _______ Vivian has a college degree.
5. T _______ Vivian forced herself to get up this morning.
6. F _______ Vivian lives in Bolivia now.
7. F _______ Vivian's presentation at work is at 11:00p.m.
8. F _______ Vivian came to the United States three months ago.
9. F _______ Vivian is looking for a new job.
10. F _______ Vivian did not go to work because she is sick.

11. Why is Vivian going to work while she is sick? Because she has a big presentation.

12. Why is the presentation so important? Because it will determine if Vivian will get a new client, which can bring the company lots of money.

13. When will Vivian go back home? She will go back home after the presentation.

SYNONYMS AND ANTONYMS

❖ A **synonym** is a word that means the same as another word. **Example**: lady-woman; college-university; father-dad

❖ An **antonym** is a word that is the opposite of another word. **Example**: run-walk; tall-short; pretty-ugly

Directions: Complete each sentence with an **antonym** for the word in parenthesis.

1. I am very proud of my daughter. She had a very _____good_____ report card. (bad)

2. After class, I asked my teacher an important _____question_____. (answer)

3. Your daughter is very _____pretty_____. (ugly)

4. Please put the dishes _____in_____ the sink. (out)

5. Who is the _____woman_____ with the three children? (man)

6. We need to _____go_____ to the post office today at 3:00p.m. (come)

7. I will _____begin_____ my homework later this evening. (end)

8. My _____sister_____ is a nurse at a hospital. (brother)

9. The test was very _____difficult_____. (easy)

10. I write with my _____right_____ hand. (left)

Directions: Write a **synonym** for each word below:

college: _____university_____	automobile: _____car_____	listen: _____hear_____
mother: _____parent_____	small: _____little_____	begin: _____start_____
lady: _____woman_____	teacher: _____instructor_____	thin: _____skinny_____
big: _____large_____	physician: _____doctor_____	trash: _____garbage_____
gorgeous: _____beautiful_____	go: _____leave_____	correct: _____right_____

REVIEW & PRACTICE

11. My mother is _____tall_____, but my father is _____short_____. (antonyms)

12. I need _____to_____ wash clothes this weekend. (infinitive)

13. I _____worked_____ a lot last year. (past-tense verb)

14. Walmart is _____next to_____ Target. (preposition)

15. I love your _____small_____ car. (adjective)

Homophones

bare	bear		male	mail
be	bea		board	bored
by	bye		hole	whole
die	dye		blue	blew
do	due		would	wood
fair	fare		cereal	serial
flour	flower		no	know
hair	hare		sum	Some
heel	heal		flower	flour
meet	meat		brake	break
new	knew		red	read
sale	sell		hour	our
son	sun		see	sea
steak	stake		for	four
tell	tale		not	knot
there	their, they're		way	weigh
to	two, too		steal	steel
wait	weight		eye	I
week	weak		hear	hear
which	witch		principle	principal
won	one		made	maid

HOMOPHONES

1. I love the color _______ blue _______ on you. (blew, blue)

2. I _______ ate _______ so much at the restaurant last night. (eight, ate)

3. Did you bring the _______ mail _______ in from the box today? (male, mail)

4. _______ Where _______ is Walmart located? (Where, Wear)

5. I love taking walks by the _______ sea _______. (see, sea)

6. Please come. I would love for you to _______ meet _______ my husband. (meat, meet)

7. I walked _______ by _______ your house on my way home today. (bye, by)

8. Did you _______ know _______ that I use to be a dancer? (no, know)

9. The _______ sun _______ is out today and it is very hot. (son, sun).

10. What are you going to _______ wear _______ today? (wear where)

Directions: Think of a word to complete each sentence correctly.

11. We are learning about _______ Sickness _______ in class.

12. _______ Yesterday, _______ I went to the mall, the supermarket and the doctor.

13. Have you seen my _______ cold medicine _______?

14. _______ When _______ are you going to the gym?

15. Lisa's _______ computer _______ is two years old now.

16. We need some _______ pasta _______ and a _______ coffee _______ from the store.

17. My mother _______ cooked _______ a big dinner last night.

18. My _______ English _______ class starts at 6:00p.m. every day.

19. We ate _______ lunch (chicken) _______ at 1:00p.m. yesterday.

20. Tomorrow, I would like to _______ go / drive/ walk _______ to the beach.

play	Maria	The baby	My mother and I	The boys
drive	My neighbors	worked	playing	went
My daughter	jumped	reading	My mother	traveled

Directions: Choose a word from the box above to complete each sentence correctly.

1. __The baby__ needs her bottle.

2. __My daughter__ wants an expensive dress for her prom.

3. The children are __playing__ in the park right now.

4. __My mother (Maria)__ likes to go to church on Sundays.

5. Last week I __worked__ three hours overtime.

6. __My neighbors (The boys)__ go to the beach every weekend.

7. I am __reading__ a good book right now.

8. __The boys__ jump the fence on weekends.

9. __Maria (My mother)__ cooks every day.

10. Yesterday, we __went__ to the bookstore.

Directions: Complete each sentence with a part of speech in the parenthesis.

11. Please put the book __on, next to, etc.__ the bookshelf. (preposition)

12. I really like your __expensive__ car. (adjective)

13. I need to go to __Aventura Mall__ today. (proper noun)

14. In my English class, we __read__ a lot. (verb)

15. My classmate is wearing __a__ pair of blue jeans today. (article)

16. We __are__ going to New York next year. (VTB)

17. I would like a new __car__. (regular noun)

18. Last year, I __exercised__ every day. (past tense verb)

19. __My__ mother is cooking a big dinner now. (pronoun)

20. The girls need three __notebooks__ each. (plural noun)

THE SICK 8 YEAR-OLD LITTLE GIRL

Characters: Receptionist, Patricia, Nurse, Katrina, Doctor, Pharmacist

Receptionist: Good morning
Patricia: Yes. Good morning. My name is Patricia Cuevas. I called this morning to see if I can bring my 8 year-old daughter Katrina in to see the doctor.
Receptionist: Yes. I remember you. I took your appointment over the phone. Please sign in on the sign-in sheet and show me your insurance card when you get a chance.
Patricia: Thank you. Here is my insurance card.
Receptionist: Thank you. That will be $25.00 please.
Patricia: Here is my credit card.
Receptionist: Here is your receipt. The doctor will see you shortly.

*nurse enters the lobby *

Nurse: Katrina Cuevas
Patricia: Yes, that is us. Come on honey. Let's go.
Nurse: Please come with me. I need for you to put her on the scale please.
Nurse: Wow, she's coughing a lot.
Patricia: Yes, she was coughing all night. She didn't get any sleep.
Nurse: Oh no. Well we are going to get you all better. Please sit down on the chair and give me your arm please. Perfect. Now I am going to take your temperature okay Katrina?
Katrina: Okay. (coughing)
Nurse: How are you feeling?
Katrina: I don't feel good. My head hurts and my throat hurts too.
Nurse: We will get you all better okay?
Katrina: Okay. Are you going to give me a shot? I don't want a shot.
Nurse: No sweetheart. I am not going to give you a shot. The doctor will be in shortly.

* Doctor enters the room *

Doctor: Good morning.
Patricia: Good morning Doctor.
Doctor: Okay. What seems to be the problem?
Katrina: I don't feel good. I am sick.
Doctor: What hurts?
Katrina: My head and my throat hurts.
Doctor: What else?
Katrina: I also cough a lot. It hurts when I cough.
Patricia: Doctor, she has a runny nose. She coughs and sneezes a lot and she has a temperature of 102 degrees. She was up all night coughing and sneezing.
Doctor: Yes, I see that she has a slight temperature. (looking at the chart). There is a stomach flu going around and many children are catching it from other students at school. It seems as though she has that. Did she go to school today?
Patricia: No, I kept her home from school because she was coughing and sneezing too much.

Doctor: Okay. I am going to give her a prescription for some medicine and some cough syrup. I am also going to prescribe some throat lozenges. She needs to drink plenty of fluids and get plenty of rest. Do you have any questions for me?
Patricia: Yes. May I have a doctor's note for Katrina to take back to school?
Doctor: Yes, absolutely. The receptionist will give you one. Please pick up your doctor's note and the prescription at the receptionist also and feel better little girl.
Katrina: Okay doctor. Thank you.
Receptionist. Ms. Cuevas, here is your prescription and your doctor's note.
Receptionist Feel better Katrina.
Katrina: Thank you.

** later at the pharmacy **

Pharmacist: Good afternoon may I help you?
Patricia: Yes, I would like to drop this prescription off for my daughter.
Pharmacist: Okay. It will be ready in 15 minutes. Would you like to wait?
Patricia: Yes, I can wait.

15 minutes later

Pharmacist: Patricia Cuevas?
Patricia: Yes, I'm right here.
Pharmacist: Here is her prescription. She must take two tablets every 4 hours. She cannot take this medication on an empty stomach. She also needs to drink plenty of fluids.
Patricia: Okay. Got it. It is 3:00p.m. now. I will give her two tablets now and give her two more at 7:00p.m.
Pharmacist: That's perfect. Then give her two more tablets in the morning. We have your insurance information on file already. That will be $10.00 please. I hope you feel better little girl.
Katrina: Thank you sir.

SYNONYMS

center	end	gift	tired
begin	sick	trash	go
car	listen	correct	university

Directions: Write a synonym for each word below:

hear _____listen_____   leave _____exit_____   middle _____center_____

finish _____end_____   sleepy _____tired_____   college _____univerity_____

start _____begin_____   garbage _____trash_____   automobile _____car_____

right _____correct_____   present _____gift_____   ill _____sick_____

ANTONYMS

Directions: Write an antonym for each word below:

strong	night	young	below
east	answer	wrong	difficult
woman	expensive	single	aunt

uncle _____aunt_____   old _____young_____   above_____below_____

west _____east_____   right _____wrong_____   day _____night_____

easy _____difficult_____   weak _____strong_____   question _____answer_____

married _____single_____   cheap _____expensive_____   man _____woman_____

Directions: Use antonyms to answer the questions below:

1. My brother is _____short_____, but my sister is _____tall_____.

2. Your blue shirt is _____pretty_____, but your red shirt is _____ugly_____.

3. My father is _____fat_____, but my mother is _____skinny_____.

Directions: Practice speaking the information in the boxes below in complete sentences, then answer the questions that follow.

MARIO CUEVAS	DIANA RODRIQUEZ	DAVID HERNANDEZ
job: mechanic **age**: 25 **martial status**: married **native country**: Colombia **lives**: Hollywood, FL **likes**: play soccer, watch TV **children**: 0	**job**: secretary **age**: 27 **martial status**: married **native country**: Venezuela **lives**: Chicago, IL **likes**: sing and read **children**: 2 daughters	**job**: teacher **age**: 31 martial status: married **native country**: Equator **lives**: New York, NY **likes**: watching football & eating **children**: 2 sons
JENNIFER CAMACHO	THOMAS WILLIAMS	BRENDA GREENBERG
job: bus driver **age**: 43 **martial status**: divorced **native country**: Cuba **lives**: Houston, TX **likes**: singing and dancing **children**: 1 son and 1 daughter	**job**: real estate agent **age**: 39 **martial status**: engaged to Diana **native country**: Argentina **lives**: Trenton, NJ **likes**: eat at nice restaurants **children**: 1 son	**job**: model **age**: 24 **martial status**: single **native country**: Puerto Rico **lives**: Ft. Lauderdale, FL **likes**: to travel and do hair **children**: 0

1. Who is from Puerto Rico? _____ Brenda is from Puerto Rico

2. Who is 25 years old? _____ Mario is 25 years old.

3. Who likes to play soccer? _____ Marcio likes to play soccer.

4. Who has two sons? _____ David has two sons.

5. What is Mario's last name? _____ Mario's / His last name is Cuevas.

6. Venezuela is whose native country? _____ Venezuela is Diana's native country.

7. Where does David live? _____ David lives in New York.

8. What does Diana like to do? _____ Diana / She likes to sing and read.

9. Who is Thomas engaged to? _____ Thomas / He is engaged to Diana.

10. What does Brenda like to do? _____ Brenda / She likes to travel and do hair.

REVIEW AND PRACTICE

Directions: Answer each question with the correct answer.

1. **What is your name?**
   a. Name is Kevin.   b. Your name is Kevin.   c. My name is Kevin.

2. **What is your native country?**
   a. My native country Peru.   b. My native country is Peru.   c. Native Country.
   Peru

3. **Are you single?**
   a. Yes, I am.   b. Yes, I do.   c. Yes, I will.

4. **Do you have a social security number?**
   a. No, I don't.   b. No, I didn't.   c. no, I am.

5. **Are you taking English classes?**
   a. Yes, I do.   b. Yes, I am.   c. Yes, I didn't.

6. **What is your marital status?**
   a. I was single.   b. I am not single.   c. I am single.

7. **When is your birthday?**
   a. My birthday is 8th, August
   b. My birthday is August 8, 2000
   c. My birthday is August 8th

8. **Are you cold?**
   a. No, I'm not.   b. No, I don't.   c. No, I am.

9. **What is your last name?**
   a. My last name is Jose.   b. My last name is J.   c. My last name is Cuevas.

10. **How old are you**
    a. I have 27 years old.   b. I 27 years old.   c. I am 27 years old.

11. **What country do you live in now?**
    a. I live in California now.
    b. I live in The United States now.
    c. I live in Chicago now.

12. **What city do you live in?**
    a. I live in Hollywood now.   b. I live in Florida now.   c. I live in the USA now.

Directions: Using the information below, answer each question in a complete sentence.

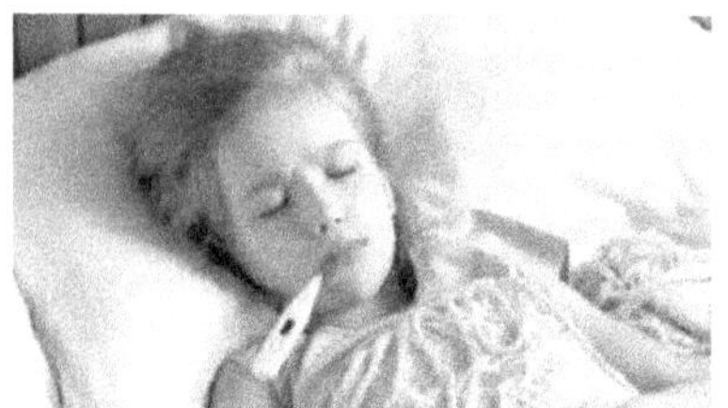

Susie Blackman
9 years old
Stomach Virus

Also: fever, runny nose
coughing, sneezing,
Doctor's appt:
Yesterday at 1:30p.m.

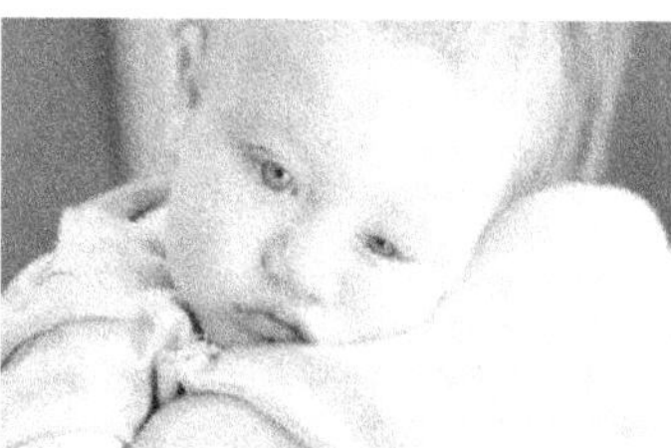

Brandon Greenberg
11 months old
Cold

Also: fever, runny nose
coughing
Doctor's appt:
Today at 9:00.am.

Tom Black
56 years old
Flu
Also: Bodyache,
headache, sore
throat, coughing,
sneezing
Doctor's appt:
Tomorrow at
12:15p.m.

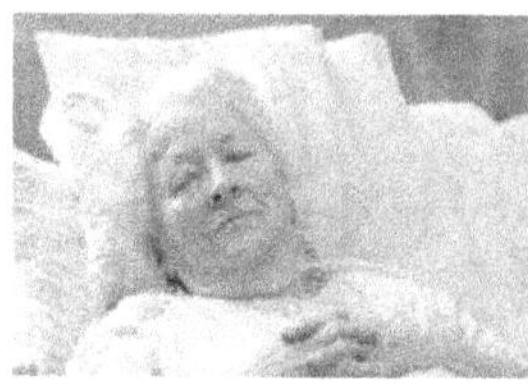

Ms. Emma White
73 years old
Infection in her legs

Also: body ache

Doctor's appt:
yesterday at
2:45p.m.

1. What time is Mr. Black's appointment? His appointment is at 12:15p.m.

2. What is Susie's problem? Susie has a stomach virus.

3. How old is Brandon? Brandon / He is 11 months old.

4. Mr. Tom's body hurts.

5. Who has the flu? Tom has the Flu

6. Susie is coughing and sneezing.

7. Who has an infection and bodyache? Emma has an infection and body ache.

8. Mr. Black's first name is Tom.

9. Who has a stomach virus? Susie has a stomach virus.

10. Emma's leg hurts.

11. Whose appointment is today? Brandon's appointment is today.

12. How old is Mr. Black? Mr. Black / He is 56 years old.

13. Who has a doctor's appointment tomorrow? Tom has an appointment tomorrow.

14. Mr. Black has a Flu and body ache.

15. What is wrong with the baby? The baby has a fever and runny nose.

16. Who is 73 years old? Emma is 73 years old.

17. Susie has a stomach virus.

18. Brandon has a fever.

HOMOPHONES

1. Please ___wait___ for me after class. (weight / wait)
2. I was so ___bored___ at home on Saturday. (board / bored)
3. I have something in my ___eye___. (eye / I)
4. Are you going ___to___ the supermarket today? (to / two)
5. There is a small ___hole___ in my shirt. (whole / hole)
6. Please pick up some bread ___for___ me. (for / four)
7. We will be going to the concert in one ___hour___. (our / hour)
8. Would you like to ___meet___ my son? (meet / meat)
9. The wind ___blew___ the trees down. (blew / blue)
10. The ___plane___ leaves at 2:15p.m. today. (plain / plane)
11. I have a hole in the ___sole___ of my shoe. (sole / soul)
12. What will you ___wear___ to the party? (where / wear)

REVIEW & PRACTICE

Directions: Choose the correct word from the box to complete each sentence below.

was	have	am	were	are	has	is

13. My books ___are___ on the table.
14. I ___have___ three notebooks for school.
15. Your car ___is___ in the garage.
16. Rosa ___has___ a new teacher.
17. Lisa ___has___ blue eyes.
18. I ___was___ a cashier three years ago.
19. We ___were___ dancing at the party on Saturday.
20. Lisa and Robert ___have___ a new house.
21. My school ___is___ on Johnson Street.

DIALOGUES: HEALTH & WELLNESS

1. **Person #1:** I am feeling very bad today. I have a stomachache. I think I had some bad food.
   Person #2: Oh no! What did you eat?
   Person #1: I ate some rice last night, but I think it was bad.
   Person #2: Have you taken anything for your stomach?
   Person #1: Yes, I took an antacid, but I have been running to the bathroom all night.
   Person #2: Oh boy. I think you need to rest and drink plenty of fluids.
   Person #1: Yes, I'm going back to sleep now.
   Person #2: OK. Feel better.

2. **Person #1:** You were not feeling well last week. Are you feeling better today.
   Person #2: Yes, I am feeling a lot better. I was in bed for three days. I had the Stomach Flu.
   Person #1: We missed you. I am glad you are better. We learned some new information in class.
   Person #2: Really, what did you learn about?
   Person #1: Well, we learned about articles, prepositions, infinitives, gerunds and parts of speech.
   Person #2: Wow! I missed all that? What are articles? Please tell me.
   Person #1: Articles introduce nouns. The three articles are "a", "an", and "the". You only use the word "an" before a word that starts with a vowel. For example, an umbrella, an apartment, and an apple.
   Person #2: Well, I am back, and I am excited to learn more English.

3. **Person #1:** How is your brother? Is he still in the hospital?
   Person #2: Yes, but he is doing better. He will be getting out soon. He had an infection in his leg.
   Person #1: I am so sorry to hear that. I heard he was in the hospital, but I didn't know why.
   Person #2: Yes. He has been in the hospital for three days now. His leg was very infected.
   Person #1: Oh no. Is he walking now?
   Person #2: Yes, he is walking. The doctor says he will be going home tomorrow.
   Person #1: That is great. Say hello to him for me.
   Person #2: Okay. I sure will give him your message.

4. **Person #1:** I have been so tired lately. I never seem to have any energy.
   Person #2: Why are you so tired? I noticed that you seem a little slow.
   Person #1: Yes. I am moving slowly because I am so tired. I don't know why. When I come home, I just want to go to sleep.
   Person #2: I you need to exercise and take vitamins. If you exercise, you will have more energy.
   Person #1: Yes, I know. My doctor told me the same thing. Where can I get some vitamins? I'm not sure where to go.
   Person #2: You can get some vitamins at the pharmacy. They have all kinds. They have some for men and some for women. You can also buy some at the supermarket in the pharmacy section.
   Person #1: Okay. I will buy some today. As for the exercise, I think I will start little by little.
   Person #2: Yes. that is a good start.

5. **Person #1:** You look sick. Are you okay?
   Person #2: No. I am not feeling well today. I feel terrible.
   Person #1: Oh no! What's the matter?

Person #2: I have a runny nose, sore throat and a bad cough. My nose hurts, my stomach hurts and my eyes hurt. I woke up feeling like this.
Person #1: Did you go to the doctor?
Person #2: Not yet. I will make an appointment, but I need to call my supervisor first and tell her that I am not going to work today because I am sick.
Person #1: Yes, you must do that right away. I hope you feel better. You need some cold medicine.
Person #2: Thank you. I will call my job first, then take my cold medicine.

6. **Person #1:** The baby cried all night, and I didn't get any sleep.
Person #2: Why was the baby crying all night?
Person #1: I am not sure, but I think she has an ear infection because she keeps pulling on her ear.
Person #2: Are you going to take her to the doctor?
Person #1: Yes, we have an appointment today at 2:00p.m.
Person #2: I hope the baby feels better.
Person #1: Me too. I hate to see her so miserable. Thank you.

7. **Person #1:** My back has been hurting all day and I don't know why. I am in much pain.
Person #2: Oh no! What happened?
Person #1: I am not sure, but it hurts really bad.
Person #2: You should take some pain relievers, then put a heating pad on your back.
Person #1: Yes, my husband/wife said that when he/she gets home from work, he/she will put the heating pad on my back for me. It should make me feel better.
Person #2: Yes, I am sure it will, but if it doesn't help, you should go to the doctor.
Person #1: Yes, I will go if the pain is not better in two days.
Person #2: That's a good idea!

8. **Person #1:** Thank you for calling the doctor's office. How may I help you?
Person #2: Yes, I would like to make an appointment for my son.
Person #1: Okay. What is the problem?
Person #2: He says that his stomach hurts and he cannot eat any food without throwing up. He also has a fever. He has been in the bed all day and he is very hot.
Person #1: I am sorry to hear that. Would you like to come in today?
Person #2: Yes please. He did not go to school today.
Person #1: Can you come in to see the doctor at 11:30 today?
Person #2: Yes, we can come at 11:30.
Person #1: Okay. We will see you at 11:30. I hope your son feels better soon.
Person #2: Thank you so much.

9. **Person #1:** Hello my friend. How are you?
Person #2: I am fine and you?
Person #1: I am doing well. How is your family?
Person #2: My family is good.
Person #1: Well, it was nice seeing you today.
Person #2: It was nice seeing you too!

10.
Person #1: Are you still taking an English class?
Person #2: Yes, I am.
Person #1: What kinds of things are you learning about in English?
Person #2: I am learning many things. Right now, we are learning about sickness and health, symptoms and remedies and also parts of speech.
Person #1: Do you like going to your English class?
Person #2: Yes, I do. I am excited about learning English. I am learning a lot, but it is important for me to practice at my house also.
Person #1: Do you practice a lot at home?
Person #2: Yes. I practice every day when I get home. My family also helps me with my English. I am very happy with my progress. I am learning so much.
Person #1: I have a friend from Colombia who wants to take an English class, but she is afraid.
Person #2: Why is she afraid? There is nothing to be afraid of. English is not difficult.
Person #1: ... because she thinks she will be asked to speak in front of the class.
Person #2: Well, yes sometimes we do speak in front of the class, but it helps us. There is nothing to be afraid of. She will learn a lot. Speaking is very important when learning English.
Person #1: Okay. I will tell her that speaking in English is good for practice.

11.
Person #1: Why are you so sad?
Person #2: Because my grandmother is very ill. She has been in and out of the hospital and she's not doing well. My family is very worried.
Person #1: I am sorry to hear that. What's wrong with her?
Person #2: Well, many things are wrong. She has a very bad Flu. She has high pressure and she also is a diabetic. She has many problems.
Person #1: Oh no! How old is she?
Person #2: She is 86 years old now. She just celebrated her birthday last month.
Person #1: Well, you know when they get older, they begin to have many problems.
Person #2: I know, but I love her so much. I just want her to get better.
Person #1: I understand. I loved my grandmother too, but she died last year.
Person #2: I remember when your grandmother died. You were so sad.
Person #1: Yes, I was, but I am better now. I hope your grandmother gets well soon.
Person #2: Thank you. I appreciate that.

12.
Person #1: My cousin is in school to be a doctor.
Person #2: Wow! That is impressive! What kind of doctor does she want to be?
Person #1: She wants to be a pediatrician. She wants to help the sick babies and children.
Person #2: Your daughter will be a great doctor. She loves the children.
Person #1: Yes, I am very proud of her. She will graduate from college in two years.
Person #2: That is wonderful. You should be very proud of her.
Person #1: Yes, I am. I am so happy for her. She is going to be a great doctor.

WEEKLY ASSESSMENT: Health and Sickness

coughing & sneezing	cold	mouth	stomachache	antibiotics
See a doctor	headache, pain reliver	get some rest	Headache, pain reliever	cold, see a doctor
backache	heating pad	antacids	Sore throat	throat

1. Lisa's stomach is hurting. She has a ___stomachache___.
2. My father's back is aching. He has a ___backache___.
3. My daughter has a runny nose, bad cough and sore throat. She has a ___cold___.
4. I need to take ___antibiotics___ for my infection.
5. Maria has a bad cold. She is ___coughing___ and ___sneezing___ a lot.
6. When you have a toothache, you have pain in your ___mouth___.
7. You should use a ___heating pad___ when your back hurts.
8. When you have a sore throat, your ___throat___ hurts.
9. When you have a ___answers may vary___ you should take some ___answers may vary___.
10. When you have the flu, you should ___see a doctor___.

PRONUNCIATION PRACTICE

Directions: Circle if the pronunciation of the word has stress or no stress when pronouncing it.

11. **worked** — a. stress — b. no stress
12. **baked** — a. stress — b. no stress
13. **celebrated** — a. stress — b. no stress
14. **listened** — a. stress — b. no stress
15. **located** — a. stress — b. no stress
16. **celebrated** — a. stress — b. no stress
17. **wanted** — a. stress — b. no stress
18. **studied** — a. stress — b. no stress
19. **practiced** — a. stress — b. no stress
20. **talked** — a. stress — b. no stress

hurt	hurt	hurting	ache	pain

21. My brother has a bad _____ache or pain_____ in his leg.

22. Roberto _____hurt_____ his back while moving a table.

23. My head is _____hurting_____ now.

24. My eyes _____hurt_____.

25. Denise has an _____ache_____ in her stomach.

26. Mary's back _____hurts_____ now.

27. Both of my arms _____hurt_____ now.

Directions: Read the question on the left. Choose the letter of the correct answer on the right and write it on the line provided.

28. What's the matter? __d__

29. How is your mother? __e__

30. What time is your doctor's appointment? __j__

31. I have an infection. What do I need? __g__

32. My daughter has a stomachache.
    What does she need? __h__

33. What is hurting? __c__

34. Where is the pain? __l__

35. What is the emergency? __i__

36. Who was sick yesterday? __k__

37. Where is the emergency? __b__

a. She needs a heating pad.
b. It is at 4857 Filmore Street.
c. My leg is hurting.
d. I have a headache.
e. She is doing very well.
f. Rosa is sick yesterday.
g. You need antibiotics.
h. She needs to take antacids.
i. My uncle is having a heart attack.
j. It is at 3:00p.m.
k. Ana was sick yesterday.
l. It is in my leg.

Directions: Complete each sentence with the correct tense of the word.

38. My classmates _____read_____ in class every day. They are _____reading_____ now. (read)

39. We _____learn_____ many things in my English class.

40. I love to _____write_____. I am _____writing_____ a poem about my family now. (write)

41. My classmates and I _____practice_____ our English everyday. (practice)

42. Trina _____exercises_____ every day after class. (exercise)

43. My mother and father _____travel_____ to California every year. (travel)

44. Lisa is _____cooking_____ now. She _____cooks_____ every day. (cooks)

mouth	antibiotics	cold	stomachache	coughing/sneezing
runny nose	headache	pain relievers	sick	teeth
backache	heating pad	throat	infection	see a doctor

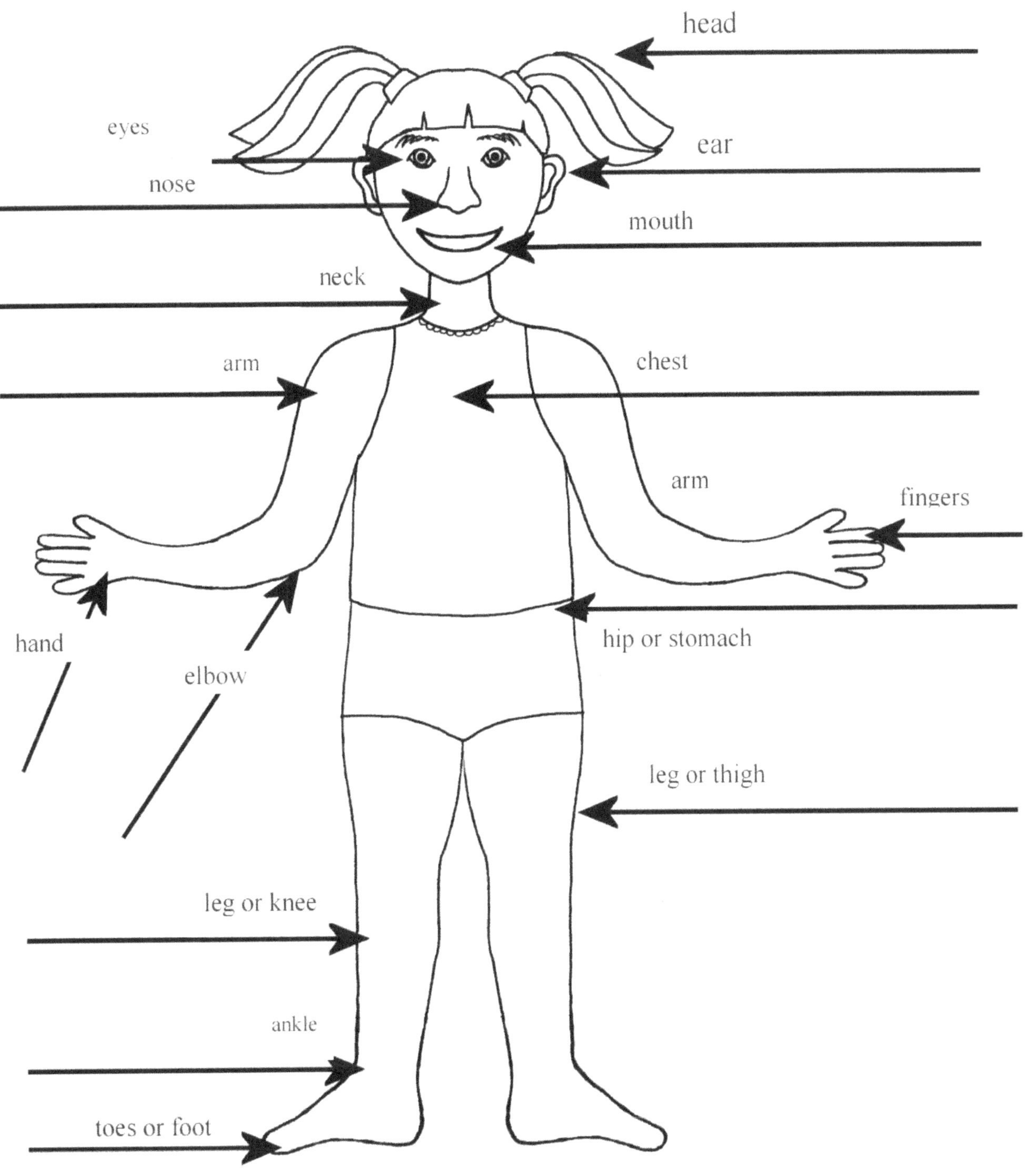

Lesson 7: The Community

Dear ESL Teacher,

As you embark on teaching Lesson 7: The Community, you have at your disposal a comprehensive plan designed to foster language acquisition and proficiency among your students. This lesson focuses on essential vocabulary and concepts related to the community, a vital aspect of everyday life.

In this lesson, students will learn new vocabulary words specific to the community. They will explore compound words, learn to locate places within the community by following driving directions, and engage in oral conversation practice. Additionally, students will read a story, answer comprehension questions, complete a word-finding puzzle, identify the correct answers to questions, and participate in fill-in-the-blank activities.

The instructional procedures outlined in this lesson include direct instruction, guided practice, and independent practice. These methods ensure a balanced approach to learning that supports diverse learning styles and abilities. By practicing related sentences on the topic, focusing on correct grammar and subject/verb agreement, and enhancing reading comprehension skills, students will build a strong foundation in understanding and using community-related vocabulary.

Collaborative activities such as reading dialogues in pairs foster communication skills and reinforce the lesson content in an engaging manner. An assessment at the end of the lesson will help evaluate students' comprehension and application of the material.

We encourage you to use this guide as a springboard for engaging and effective teaching, empowering your students to succeed in their language learning journey. Thank you for your dedication to helping students navigate the complexities of learning a new language while acquiring valuable life skills.

Lesson Plan for Lesson 7: The Community

OBJECTIVES:

1. Students will identify and use vocabulary related to the community.
2. Students will understand and create compound words.
3. Students will locate places within the community by following driving directions.
4. Students will engage in oral conversation practice using learned vocabulary.
5. Students will read a story related to the community and answer comprehension questions.
6. Students will complete a word-finding puzzle and fill-in-the-blank activities.
7. Students will participate in dialogues and demonstrate their learning through a comprehensive assessment.

INSTRUCTIONAL PROCEDURES:

Direct Instruction:

- **Objective:** Present new vocabulary and grammar concepts clearly and explicitly.
- **Details:** Begin the lesson by introducing new vocabulary words related to the community. Explain their meanings using visuals and contextual examples. Provide clear definitions, pronunciation guides, and use each word in sentences to demonstrate its usage. Use the whiteboard or projector to display visuals, such as maps and community landmarks, to aid understanding. Encourage students to repeat and practice pronouncing the words aloud to reinforce retention.

Guided Practice:

- **Objective:** Help students apply new knowledge in a supportive environment.
- **Details:** Facilitate structured activities found within the lesson book where students practice using new vocabulary and grammar concepts with teacher guidance. Provide sentence frames or prompts that incorporate the new vocabulary and grammar structures. Guide students in following driving directions on a map to locate community places. Walk around the classroom, offering support and feedback as students work through the activities. Encourage peer collaboration by having students work in pairs or small groups to complete tasks.

Independent Practice:

- **Objective:** Reinforce learning through individual or paired activities.
- **Details:** Assign tasks that require students to independently apply what they have learned. This includes a Venn diagram found within the lesson, completing worksheets or exercises that reinforce vocabulary usage, grammar rules, or conversational skills. Provide clear instructions and examples to guide students as they work through the tasks. Encourage self-monitoring by asking students to review their work for accuracy and clarity before submitting it. Monitor progress and offer assistance as needed.

Differentiation/Adaptations:

- **Provide visual aids and simplified instructions for English language learners:**
  - **Objective:** Support comprehension for students with varying English proficiency levels.
  - **Details:** Use visual aids such as charts, diagrams, or illustrations alongside verbal explanations. Provide simplified instructions and break down complex concepts into smaller, more manageable steps. Offer bilingual dictionaries or picture dictionaries. Adjust the pace of instruction to accommodate slower processing speeds, allowing extra time for comprehension and practice.

- **Offer additional practice or alternative assessments for students with diverse learning needs:**
  - **Objective:** Address individual learning needs and preferences.
  - **Details:** Provide differentiated assignments or activities that cater to different learning styles and abilities. Offer extension activities for advanced learners. Consider alternative assessment formats such as oral presentations or digital projects. Use flexible grouping strategies to accommodate social and emotional needs.

Vocabulary Introduction:

- o **Objective:** Introduce key vocabulary words essential for understanding community concepts.
- o **Details:** Use visual aids such as flashcards, images, or charts to illustrate each vocabulary word. Provide contextual examples in sentences or short paragraphs. Encourage students to repeat and practice saying the words aloud.

Compound Words Practice:

- o **Objective:** Help students understand and create compound words.
- o **Details:** Introduce the concept of compound words with examples. Have students create their own compound words using community-related vocabulary. Have students complete the exercises in the book focused on identifying and forming compound words.
- o

Map Activity:

- o **Objective:** Develop students' ability to follow driving directions and locate places within the community.
- o **Details:** Provide maps and a set of driving directions. Guide students in following the directions to locate specific places on the map. Discuss the importance of landmarks and directions in navigating a community.

Conversation Practice:

- o **Objective:** Develop students' ability to engage in spoken communication using learned vocabulary.
- o **Details:** Pair students or organize small groups for conversational activities. Provide prompts or scenarios that require the use of targeted vocabulary in meaningful contexts. Encourage turn-taking and active listening.

Reading Comprehension:

- o **Objective:** Enhance students' ability to understand written English through community-related stories.
- o **Details:** Select age-appropriate reading materials or passages that align with the lesson's vocabulary and grammar focus. After reading, ask comprehension questions that require students to recall details, make inferences, or summarize key points. Encourage reading aloud to practice pronunciation and fluency.

2. **Dialogue Creation:**
   - o **Objective:** Encourage students to apply learned vocabulary and grammar by creating dialogues.
   - o **Details:** Guide students in pairs or small groups to develop dialogues that incorporate the lesson's vocabulary and grammar. Provide a scenario or context and encourage creativity. Emphasize natural conversational flow and appropriate language use.

3. **Assessment:**

- o **Objective:** Evaluate students' comprehension and application of lesson content.
- o **Details:** The assessment includes vocabulary, grammar, and reading comprehension questions, along with a short writing or dialogue creation task.

MATERIALS AND RESOURCES:

- Book: It's Time to Learn English
- Vocabulary cards
- Whiteboard and markers
- Textbooks or reading materials
- Worksheets for grammar exercises and compound words
- Maps for the driving directions activity
- Audio recordings for listening activities

TECHNOLOGY NEEDED:

- Projector or screen for displaying visuals
- Computer or tablet for accessing digital resources

Lesson 7: The Community

T - Think Back (Review)

Activity: Begin the lesson by reviewing key concepts and vocabulary from the previous lesson. Use a brief warm-up activity to engage students and assess their understanding of any community-related terms they might already know.

Time: 5-10 minutes

E – Entry (Introduction/Beginning)

Activity: Introduce new vocabulary words related to the community using visuals such as flashcards, images, or charts. Explain the meanings, provide clear definitions, pronunciation examples, and use each word in sentences to demonstrate usage.

Objective: Students will be introduced to, identify, and use vocabulary related to the community.

Time: 15 minutes

A - Application (Teaching/Presentation/Delivery)

Activity: Present new grammar concepts clearly and explicitly. Use direct instruction to introduce compound words and provide examples. Demonstrate how to locate places within the community by following driving directions. Use visuals such as maps and community landmarks to aid understanding.

Objective: Students will understand and create compound words and locate places within the community by following driving directions.

Time: 20 minutes

C - Collaborative Practice (Student Practice)

Activity: Facilitate guided practice by having students work in pairs or small groups to complete structured activities using sentence frames and prompts. Conduct conversational activities where students use learned vocabulary in meaningful contexts.

Time: 25 minutes

H - Highlight (Wrap-up/Closing)

Activity: Summarize the key points of the lesson, highlighting the new vocabulary and grammar rules learned. Assign a reading comprehension activity from the book using a passage about the community. Discuss the main ideas and ask comprehension questions.

Time: 10 minutes

E - Evaluate (Assessment/Evaluation)

Activity: Administer the comprehensive assessment found at the end of the lesson. Assess students on vocabulary, grammar, reading comprehension, and dialogue creation.

Objective: Evaluate students' comprehension and application of lesson content.

Time: 15 minutes

R - Reflect (Final Review)

Activity: End the lesson with a reflective activity where students can share their thoughts on what they learned, how they can use it in real-life situations, and any areas where they need further clarification. Encourage students to share their thoughts on their progress and areas they want to improve.

Time: 5-10 minutes

All about the

7

Restaurant

Gas Station

School

Fire Station

Words to Learn:

1. post office
2. bank
3. pharmacy
4. supermarket
5. gas station
6. clinic
7. fire department
8. library
9. university
10. schools
11. restaurant
12. fast food
13. mall
14. salon
15. DMV
16. hospital
17. cleaners
18. parks
19. hotels
20. doctor's office
21. community
22. neighborhood
23. directions
24. bakery

Park

Supermarket

Hospital

Happy Customer

Bank

1. There are many **parks** in my **neighborhood**.

2. We usually go to the **mall** on weekends.

3. My mother needs to go to the **post office** to mail a package.

4. Are there any **churches** in your community?

5. What city do you **live** in?

6. I need **directions** to the highway.

7. What time are you going to the **bank** to make your deposit?

8. My brother does not like to eat too much **fast food**.

9. We need to go to the **gas station** before we drive to Orlando.

10. I will pick up your prescription from the **pharmacy** today.

11. My sister went to the **library** to check out two books on cooking.

12. Maria will go to the **DMV** (Division of Motor Vehicles) to get her driver's license.

13. Diana had a baby girl. She is in the **hospital** now.

14. We will go to a **restaurant** for dinner tonight.

15. There are some beautiful **hotels** in my city.

16. We need groceries from the **supermarket**.

17. My daughter goes to the local **university** in my city.

18. My father went to the **courthouse** for a traffic ticket.

19. The **doctor's office** is on the corner of Johnson Street and University Drive.

20. You **live** in a beautiful **community**.

Study

1. The **supermarket** is a place where you buy groceries.

2. The **post office** is where you go to mail a package.

3. The **bank** is where you go to cash or deposit a check.

4. The **school** is where children go to learn.

5. The **gas station** is where you go to put gas in a car.

6. The **doctor's office** is where you go when you are sick or when you need a checkup.

7. The **Division of Motor Vehicles** (DMV) is where you go to renew your driver's license.

8. The **pharmacy** is where you go to fill your prescription or buy medication.

9. The **hospital** is where you go to visit a sick person.

10. The **mall** is where you go to shop.

Directions: Look at the information on the left and write the letter of the correct answer on the right.

11. Fruit and vegetables h	a. beach
12. Deposit money g	b. the mall
13. Buy a new shirt b	c. doctor's office
14. My aunt just had a baby. f	d. gas station
15. I have been sick for three days c	e. pharmacy
16. I need to buy some vitamins. e	f. hospital
17. My car is empty. d	g. the bank
	h. supermarket

This is Victoria. She is 57 years old. She is from New York, but she lives in a house in South Carolina now. She likes to play tennis, cook, and go walking. She has lived in her neighborhood for 15 years. When she runs errands, she goes to the supermarket, the park, the post office, gas station and the mall. She likes her neighborhood.

This is Gloria. She is 57 years old. She is from Alabama, but she lives in a house in South Carolina now. She likes to sing, read and go walking. She has lived in her neighborhood for 13 years. When she runs errands, she goes to the supermarket, the mall, the doctor's office, gas station and the pharmacy. She likes her neighborhood.

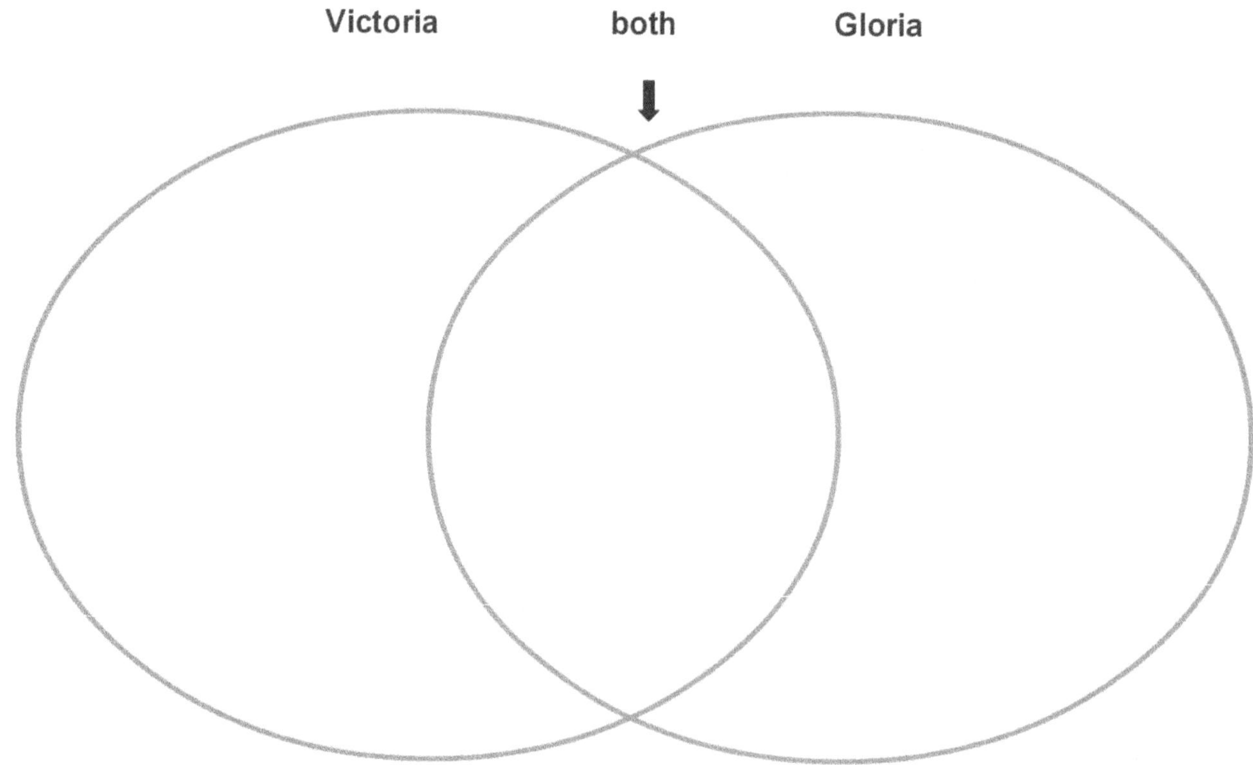

Directions: Read the story below and complete the sentences with the correct answer from the boxes below:

post office	bank	gym	doctor's office	post office
city hall	restaurant	pharmacy	gas station	supermarket

I had a busy day today. I had so many places to go. When I left the house this morning, I went to the __gym__ to exercise. After that, I went to a __restaurant__ to eat some breakfast. Then, I went to the __doctor's office__ for my annual physical. I had three packages to mail, so I went to the __post office__. I also went to __city hall__ to pay a ticket, the __bank__ to deposit a check and the __pharmacy__ to pick up my prescription. Before coming back home, I went to the __gas station__ to get gas and to the __supermarket__ to buy groceries. I returned home around 6:30p.m. I was so tired when I returned home.

Directions: Read the sentences below and answer each question with "Yes, I do or no, I don't".

1. Do you buy shoes at the meat store? ○ Yes, I do ● no, I don't

2. Do you go to the bank to get gas? ○ Yes, I do ● no, I don't

3. Do you mail packages at the post office? ● Yes, I do ○ no, I don't

4. Do you exercise at the gym? ● Yes, I do ○ no, I don't

5. Do you eat dinner at a restaurant? ● Yes, I do ○ no, I don't

6. Do you pick up a prescription at the shoe store? ○ Yes, I do ● no, I don't

7. Do you check out books at the bank? ○ Yes, I do ● no, I don't

8. Do you exercise at the supermarket? ○ Yes, I do ● no, I don't

VOCABULARY

bank	supermarket	courthouse	police station
neighborhood	high school	pharmacy	hospital
gas station	city hall	restaurant	mall

Directions: Complete each sentence with the correct vocabulary word from the box.

1. I need to cash my check at the ______bank______ after work.
2. My car is on "E". I need to get to a ______gas station______ quickly.
3. We took my brother to a nice ______restaurant______ for his birthday.
4. My mom and I visited my aunt in the ______hospital______ after she had the baby.
5. I bought two blouses and one dress at the ______mall______ yesterday.
6. You need to take your prescription to the ______pharmacy______ today.
7. In my ______neighborhood______ there are two churches, a fire department and nice restaurants.
8. My father will pick up my 12th grade son at the ______high school______ today after work.
9. I went to ______city hall______ to report a hole in the street in my community.
10. I went to the ______police station______ to report a crime that I saw the other day.

REVIEW AND PRACTICE

Directions: Complete each sentence with a verb-to-be or past tense verbs.

11. Last night, I ______was______ very tired.
12. We ______practiced______ our English last night.
13. Susan and Diana ______are______ my cousins.
14. On Saturday, I ______cooked______ and______cleaned______.
15. My mother ______is______ sleeping now.
16. I ______am______ going to the supermarket later today.
17. My father ______is______ an accountant.
18. We ______read______ in my English class yesterday.

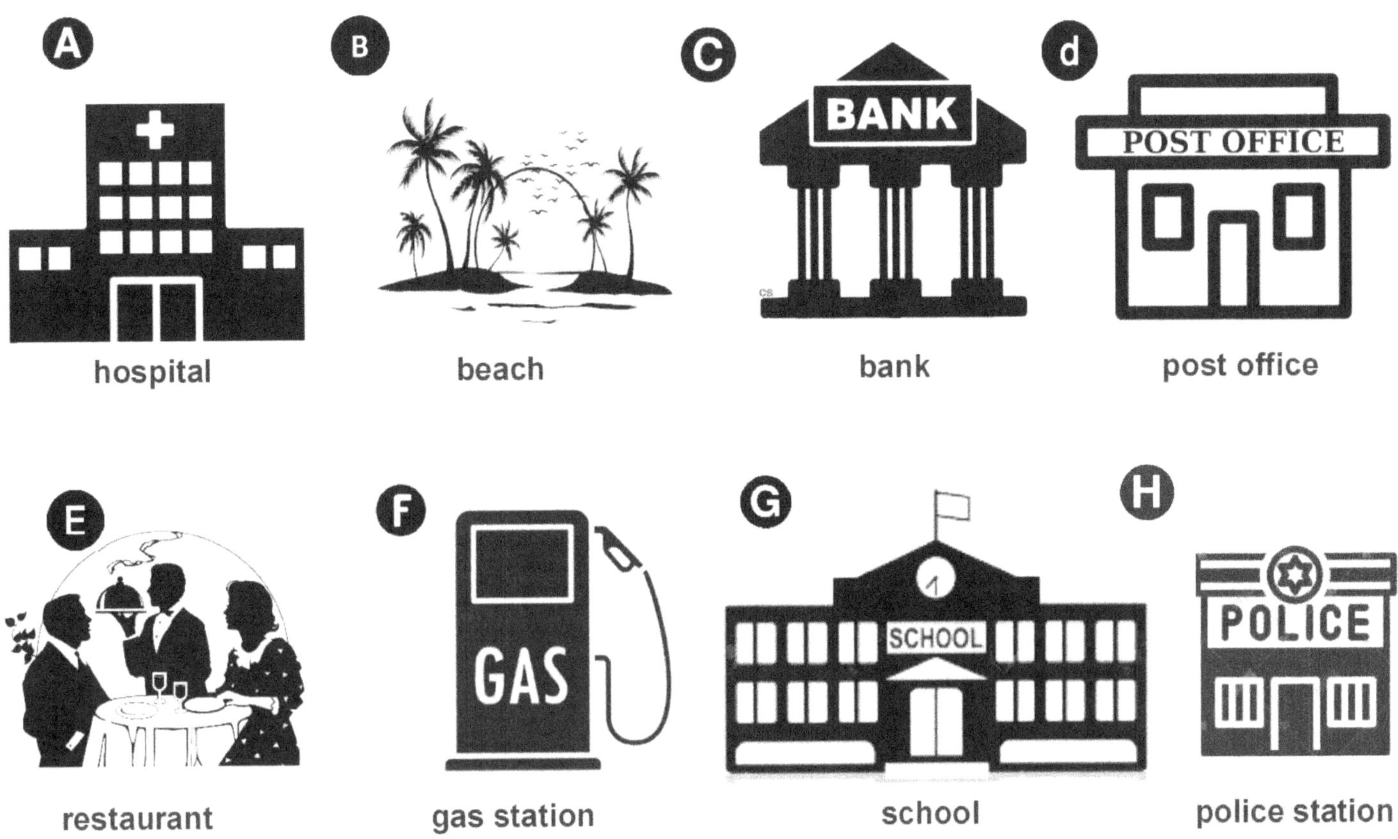

Directions: Complete the sentences below with a place found in a community.

1. We went to a nice ___________ restaurant ___________ for dinner last night.

2. My daughter is learning about plants and animals in ___________ school ___________.

3. I went to the ___________ police station ___________ to file a report about my missing wallet.

4. We visited my grandmother in the ___________ hospital ___________ today.

5. On Saturday, we are going to the ___________ beach ___________ to go swimming.

6. Julia will buy me some postage stamps from the ___________ post office ___________.

7. My car is empty. I need to go to the ___________ gas station ___________.

8. After work, I will go to the ___________ bank ___________ to cash my paycheck.

9. My favorite place to go is the ___________ various answers ___________.

REVIEW AND PRACTICE

Directions: Answer the following questions using the correct part of speech.

1. I will buy you a new _____bike_____ for your birthday. (noun)

2. Sylvia _____was_____ very tired yesterday. (verb to be)

3. Luis lives in _____an_____ apartment on Baker Drive. (article)

4. I am going to _____Orlando_____ this summer. (proper noun)

5. My daughter is going to Orlando for her birthday. _____She_____ is very excited about her trip. (pronoun)

6. Patricia is sitting _____next to_____ Carmen today. (preposition)

7. My uncle is _____an_____ engineer at the airport. (article)

8. My birthday is in _____September_____ (proper noun)

9. Carmen and I _____are_____ going to the gym today after school. (verb to be)

10. I am _____reading_____ now. (gerund)

11. _____What_____ are your favorite colors? (question word)

12. My red _____jacket_____ is dirty. (noun)

13. I need to go to _____Chevron_____ today. (proper noun)

14. I like going to _____Universal Studios_____ in the summer. (proper noun)

Directions: Answer each question below in a complete sentence.

15. Where are you going this weekend? _____I am going to the mall this weekend._____

16. What places are in your neighborhood? _____There is a church, a mall, and a gas station._____

COMPOUND WORDS

bathtub	bathroom	bedroom	football
ladybug	bluebird	blackbird	ice-cream
notebook	bookbag	bookworm	lifetime
sweetheart	businessman	stoplight	nightlight
cellphone	classmate	classroom	schoolhouse
yearbook	cupcake	eyeball	firefly
nightgown	everybody	nighttime	underwater
bookcase	everyone	stepmom	spotlight
lifeguard	earring	basketball	teapot
iceberg	everything	background	sunburn
baseball	everywhere	tablecloth	suitcase
fireball	eyeball	teakettle	girlfriend
weekend	eyebrow	hotdog	workday
underwear	eyelash	tiptoe	wheelchair
mailman	eyeshadow	ladybug	year-end
drugstore	herself	flashlight	cupholder
bulldog	himself	mailbox	placemat
eyeglasses	myself	cheesecake	nightclub
sunshine	sunglasses	sunrise	nightgown

COMPOUND WORDS

Compound Word: A compound word is a word that is formed by combining two words together. For example: hot + dog = hotdog; class + room = classroom

Directions: On the lines below, make compound words using the words below.

1. mailman
2. sunshine
3. nightclub
4. afternoon
5. classmate
6. bedroom
7. cupcake
8. earring
9. notebook
10. carwash
11. underwear
12. oatmeal

1. mail	room
2. sun	ring
3. night	book
4. after	club
5. class	wash
6. bed	noon
7. cup	man
8. ear	mate
9. note	cake
10. car	shine
11. under	wear
12. oat	meal

REVIEW AND PRACTICE

ANTONYMS	SYNONYMS	HOMOPHONES
1. answer question	1. afraid scared	1. rose rows
2. man woman	2. sleepy tired	2. hole whole
3. fat skinny	3. liberty freedom	3. weigh way
4. big little	4. wonderful excellent	4. for four
5. black white	5. teacher instructor	5. eight ate
6. inside outside	6. woman lady	6. ate eight
7. teacher student	7. quiet silent	7. two too, to
8. run walk	8. university college	8. jail gel

<table>
<tr><td>

Glanville Medical Center
Dr. David Dodson
4852 Houston Center Rd.
Houston, TX 77010
281-695-6923

We treat children, adults and seniors
Dr. Dodson is a certified medical doctor and primary care physician specializing in colds, coughs, Flus, fevers, infections, sore throats, aches and pains.

Open Monday through Friday 8:00a.m - 5:00p.m.

</td><td>

Victoria Lakes Cosmetic Surgery
Dr. Dimitri Ivanov
Dr. Adrian Smirnoff
159 Riverdale Drive
Albany, NY 12204
518-962-4563

Dr. Ivanov and Dr. Smirnoff are certified medial doctors. Dr. Ivanov specializes in but enhancements and Botox.

Dr. Smirnoff specializes in breast augmentation, face lifts, and nose jobs.

Open Monday through Saturday from 9:00a.m. - 6:00p.m.

</td></tr>
</table>

Directions: Answer the questions below using the information in the boxes above.

1. What city is Victoria Lakes Cosmetic Surgery located in? _It is in Albany._

2. What does Dr. Smirnoff specialize in? _He specializes in cosmetic surgery._

3. What are the office hours of Glanville Medical Center? _The office hours are 8:00a.m - 5:00p.m._

4. Which office treats colds and Flus? _Glanville Medical Center treats colds and Flus._

5. Where can I go to get a nose job? _You can go to Victoria Lakes Cosmetic Center._

6. Which Dr. specializes in sore throats? _Dr. David Dodson_

7. How many hours is Glanville Medical Center open? _They are open for nine hours._

8. What state is Glanville Medical Center in? _It is in Texas._

9. Which doctor's office performs face lifts? _Victoria Lakes Cosmetic Center._

Directions: Study the map below, then answer the questions that follow.

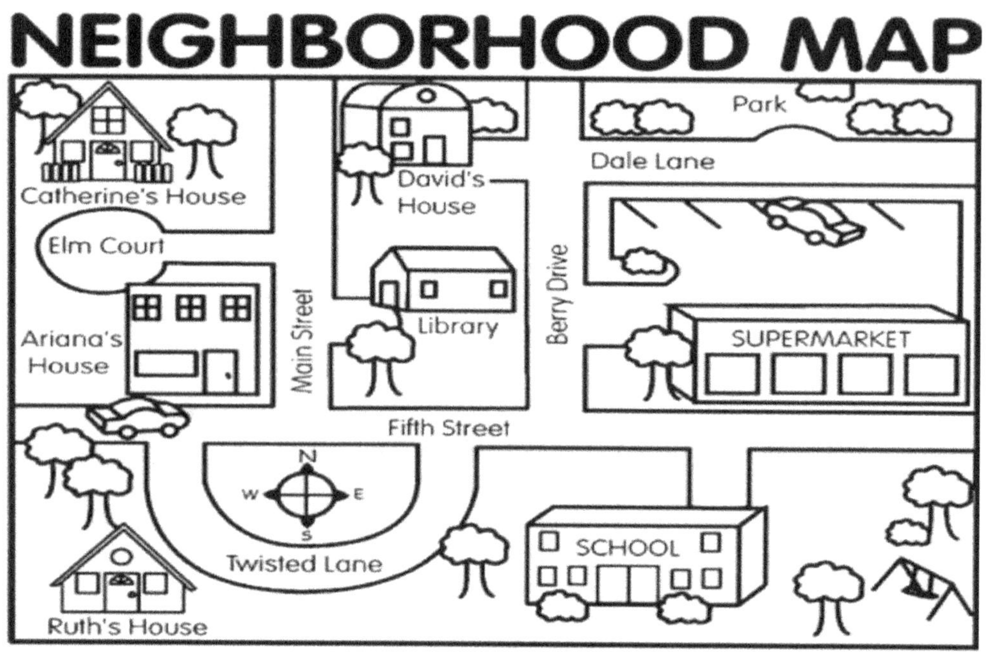

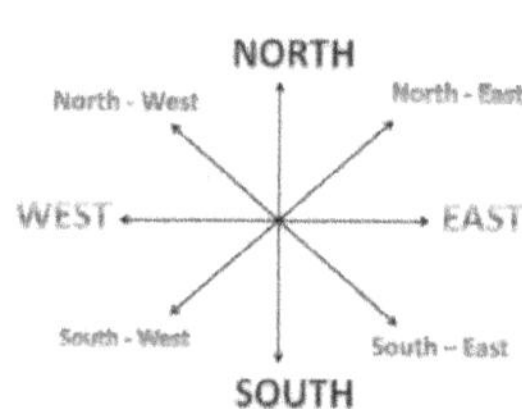

Directions: Follow the directions below, then answer the questions.

1. Start at Ruth's house and go north to Ariana's house. Go east to main street, then go south to fifth street. Go east to Berry Drive, then go North to Dale Lane. Go east about a half mile then turn north. Where are you?

    I am at the park.

2. Start at David's house and go east to Berry Drive. Go South to fifth street, then go west on fifth street to Main Street, then go north on Main Street and immediately go east.   Where are you?

    I am at Ariana's house.

3. Start at the park on Dale Lane and go West to Berry Drive. Go south to fifth street, then go left to Main Street. On Main Street, go North to the end of the road, then go west. Where are you?

    I am at Catherine's house.

4. Start at Catherine's house on Elm Street, then go east to Main Street. Go south on Main Street to Fifth Street. Take Fifth street to Berry Drive and go North about a half mile, then go West. Where are you?

    I am at David's house.

supermarket	fire department	post office	library	cleaners
fast food	bakery	bank	DMV	gas station

Directions: Read the sentences below and on the line provided, write down what is needed.

1. Debbie needs to cash a check. ______________ bank ______________

2. My father's suits are dirty. ______________ cleaners ______________

3. We would like hamburgers, fries and a soda. ______________ fast food ______________

4. There is smoke coming out of the building. ______________ fire department ______________

5. I need a driver's license. ______________ DMV ______________

6. Lisa needs to mail a package. ______________ post office ______________

7. Mom needs to buy groceries. ______________ supermarket ______________

8. We want cakes and cookies. ______________ bakery ______________

9. Brenda wants to read a book about dogs. ______________ library ______________

10. Luis needs gas for his car. ______________ gas station ______________

Directions: Complete each sentence with the correct part of speech in the parenthesis

11. We are going to ______ McDonalds ______ today at 3:00p.m.   (proper noun)

12. ______ We ______ need to buy some groceries today.   (pronoun)

13. Maria is a lovely person. ______ She ______ is my best friend. (pronoun)

14. Gabriela ______ writes ______ every day in her English class. (verb)

15. I am ______ going ______ to the doctor's office today. (gerund)

16. Jose ______ is ______ going to the bank today. (VTB)

17. The baby needs ______ to ______ eat now. (infinitive)

18. I like to ______ study ______ every Saturday. (simple verb)

19. Please buy me a ______ soda ______ at the store. (noun)

Conversation Practice

Directions: Let's practice speaking in English. Read the first paragraph below out loud. Then, fill in information about yourself in the second paragraph. Practice reading it with a partner. After you read the information about yourself, fill in the information in the third paragraph about your partner, then practice reading that out loud.

Practice:

Good morning. My name is Alina and I live in Los Angeles California in a big community. My community has a bank, a post office, a mall, and a church. On Saturdays, I like to go to the mall and on Sundays, I like to go to church. There are many nice people in my community. I like my community.

About you:

Good morning. My name is ______ Mia ______ and I live in ______ Miami ______ in a big community.

My community has a ______ mall ______, a ______ cleaners ______, a ______ hospital ______, and a

______ supermarket ______. On Saturdays, I like to go to (the) ______ malll ______, and on Sundays, I like to

go to (the) ______ church ______. There are many nice ______ parks ______ in my community. I like my

community.

About your partner:

This is my partner ________________ and he/she lives in a ________________ community. His/Her

community has a ________________, a ________________, and a ________________. On Saturdays,

he/she likes to go to (the) ________________ and on Sundays, he/she likes to go to (the)

________________ . There are many ________________ people in her/his community. He/She

likes his/her community.

More Practice

I have many places to go today. I need to go to the ________________, the ________________,

and the ________________. I also want to go to ________________ to buy a new

________________ and some ________________. I have a busy day today.

MIA & TIA THE TWINS

Mia and Tia Caldwell are 15-year-old identical twin sisters. They look so much alike that it is difficult for people to tell them apart. Even their parents have a hard time telling them apart. They are in 9th grade, but they only have three classes together. Although they are twins, they are very different. Mia doesn't like math and she does not do very well on her math tests. Tia is not good in Language Arts. She makes Cs on her assignments in Language Arts. When Mia has a math test, her sister Tia goes to her class and takes the test for her. When Tia has a Language Arts test, Mia goes to her class and takes the test for her. The teachers never know the difference since they look exactly alike. Mia likes to sing and dance. She is outgoing and has lots of friends. Tia likes to read books and watch movies. She is introverted and doesn't have many friends. Mia likes boys. Tia doesn't care about boys. Mia loves to eat pizza. Tia doesn't like pizza. Mia loves the color blue. Tia's favorite color is black. Mia likes to wear lipstick. Tia doesn't like makeup. Also, Tia is a little bit taller than Mia. Mia and Tia are very close. Although they are different, they love each other very much.

1. What is the last name of the twins? _____ Their last name is Caldwell. _____

2. What grade are they in? _____ They are in the 9th grade. _____

3. What does Mia like to eat? _____ Mia likes to eat pizza. _____

4. What subject is Tia <u>not</u> good in? _____ Tia is not good in Language Arts. _____

5. How many classes do Mia and Tia have together? _____ They have three classes together. _____

6. Who likes to sing and dance? _____ Mia likes to sing and dance. _____

7. Which twin does not have many friends? _____ Tia does not have many friends. _____

8. What is Tia's favorite color? _____ Tia's / Her favorite color is black. _____

9. Which twin does not wear makeup? _____ Tia does not like to wear makeup. _____

10. How old are the twins? _____ The twins are 15 years old. _____

11. Which twin likes to watch movies? _____ Tia likes to watch movies. _____

12. Which twin is good in math? _____ Tia is good in math. _____

Directions: Circle the words from the bottom of the page in the puzzle below.

r	e	s	t	a	u	r	a	n	t	g	g	n
a	s	d	f	g	g	e	q	w	e	u	a	e
q	a	z	x	c	v	b	n	m	c	n	s	i
c	o	m	m	u	n	i	t	y	h	i	s	g
d	d	f	g	o	h	j	k	l	u	v	t	h
h	o	s	p	i	t	a	l	h	r	e	a	b
q	f	g	h	h	c	e	g	a	c	r	t	o
a	q	n	o	m	b	w	l	n	h	s	i	r
z	v	b	t	d	a	s	f	g	h	i	o	h
s	u	p	e	r	m	a	r	k	e	t	n	o
m	a	l	l	h	y	d	i	p	o	y	m	o
c	o	u	r	t	h	o	u	s	e	m	j	d
y	u	o	p	b	n	e	h	c	l	h	w	o
c	i	t	y	h	a	l	l	h	d	g	m	c
a	c	a	r	w	a	s	h	o	i	k	n	t
m	e	r	d	v	g	t	f	o	n	n	b	o
r	q	w	k	j	M	y	g	l	e	a	v	r
a	s	r	d	q	v	D	d	s	r	b	c	z
h	a	l	i	b	r	a	r	y	R	f	x	a
p	o	s	t	o	f	f	i	c	e	d	c	s

post office	community	hotel	university
bank	neighborhood	motel	church
pharmacy	mall	city hall	courthouse
supermarket	schools	park	doctor
gas station	library	restaurant	hospital
DMV	car wash	diner	

1. Where do I go to put gas in my car? _______ doctor's office

2. Where do you go to mail a package? _______ post office

3. Where do you go to pick up a prescription? _______ city hall

4. Where can I buy some bread, chicken, and rice? _______ bank

Directions: Read the story and choose a word from the boxes below to complete the sentences in the story.

sixteen	dolls	color	food		daughter
girl	February 3rd	bedroom	grade	July 15th	New York
summer	living room	seven	video games	animals	July
son	Georgia	radio	Florida	music	colors

Hello. My name is Ana. I would like to tell you about my niece Natasha. She is ___seven___ years old and is in the second ___grade___. Natasha lives in New York, but she came here to Georgia in July for her ___summer___ vacation to visit my family and me. She will be going back home on ___July 15th___. Natasha is a very sweet little ___girl___. She loves to play with ___animals___ especially cats and puppies. Her favorite ___color___ is yellow and her favorite ___food___ is spaghetti. She likes to listen to ___music___, watch TV, and relax on the sofa in the ___living room___. She also likes to play ___video games___. My three-year-old ___daughter___, Rosa loves Natasha. She likes to follow her around the house. Natasha will be here for two weeks and then she will go back to ___New York___.

Directions: Choose the letter of the correct answer to answer each question.

1. Who did Natasha go to visit?

    a. Her grandmother   b. her aunt   c. her friend

2. Where is Natasha from?

    a. Florida   b. Georgia   c. New York

3. How old is Natasha?

    a. seven years old   b. 17 years old   c. three years old

4. How old is Natasha's cousin?

    a. seven years old   b. 17 years old   c. three years old

5. Where does Ana live?

    a. Florida   b. Georgia   c. New York

6. When is Natasha going back home?

    a. In July   b. On July   c. In June

7. What does Natasha like to play with?

    a. music   b. animals   c. dolls

Directions: Choose the letter of the correct answer.

1. **Do you have a small family or large family?**
   a. I has a medium family.   [b. I have a medium family.]   c. I medium family.

2. **How many brothers and sisters do you have?**
   a. I has 2 brothers and 1 sister.   [b. I have two brothers and one sister.]   c. I have two brother

3. **How old is your grandmother?**
   a. She 73 years old.   [b. She 73 years old.]   c. She is 73-year-old.

4. **Do you have cousins?**
   a. Yes, I don't   [b. Yes, I do]   c. No, I don't

5. **How old is your baby sister?**
   [a. She is 7 years old.]   b. She has 7 years old.   c. She is 7 year olds.

6. **Where does your family live?**
   a. I live in Hollywood now.   b. They lives in Colombia   [c. They live in Colombia.]

7. **Who do you live with?**
   [a. I live with my family.]   [b. I lives with my family]   c. I with my family

8. **What time is your appointment?**
   a. It at 3:00p.m.   b. It 3:00p.m.   [c. It is at 3:00p.m.]

9. **What is your native country?**
   [a. My native country is Venezuela.]   b. My is Venezuela.   c. My native country is Florida.

10. **What is your last name?**
    a. My last name Flores.   b. My last name is Ana.   [c. My last name is Flores.]

11. **What is your first language?**
    [a. My first language is Spanish.]   b. My first language is Cuba.   c. It Spanish.

12. **Where are you going?**
    [a. I am going to Walmart]   b. I is going to Walmart   c. I going to Walmart.

13. **What is your favorite color?**
    a. Me color favorite color is red.   [b. My favorite color is blue.]   c. My favorite color green.

14. **Where are you going?**
    a. I going to the store now.   [b. I am going to the store now.]   c. I going store.

15. **How are you?**
    a. I am 25 years old.   [b. I am fine. Thank you.]   c. I am in the classroom.

COMMUNITY RESOURCES

1.
Person #1: I am very excited. I just moved into my first apartment. It has two bedrooms and one bathroom. I really like it because it is very nice.
Person #2: Congratulations on your new apartment. How much do you pay in rent each month?
Person #1: The rent is $975 a month. I just received a raise on my job, so I can afford it.
Person #2: Do you have furniture yet?
Person #1: No, not yet, but I brought my bedroom set from my mother's house. I will get furniture for the other rooms later.
Person #2: Yes, the most important room is your bedroom. I am so happy for you. I cannot wait to see it.
Person #1: You can come over on Saturday to see it. You can help me organize things.
Person #2: I can help you clean a little, but not a lot.

2.
Person #1: I just moved into the area, and it is hard for me to find many places.
Person #2: What places do you need to find?
Person #1: I need to find the supermarket, the post office, the pharmacy, the library and the gas station. I have to find so many places.
Person #2: Those places are not hard to find. There is a gas station nearby and the post office is around the corner. The pharmacy is five blocks from here and the library is three blocks away. The bank is also on the corner of Johnson Street and 56th street.
Person #1: Thank you. I guess I just need to get familiar with the area.
Person #2: Please ask me for help. I will be more than happy to help you, or you can put the addresses in your navigator. Your navigator will help you to find different places.
Person #1: Thank you so much. I appreciate your help.
Person #2: You're welcome.

3.
Person #1: I am going to take my puppy to the park after work today. He likes to run around and play. He loves going to the park.
Person #2: Yes. Animals love to play in the park. How old is your puppy?
Person #1: My puppy is four years old and yes, she loves going to the park. She likes to play with the other puppies.
Person #2: I like to take my dog for walks too, but we only walk in my neighborhood. We go in the evenings.
Person #1: Really? Sometimes I walk my puppy around my neighborhood, but she likes the park better.
Person #2: Maybe I will begin to take my dog to the park sometimes too.
Person #1: Yes, I think your dog will like that.

4.
Person #1: I have to go many places after English class today.
Person #2: Where do you need to go?
Person #1: I need to go to the bank, the supermarket, the post office and the library.
Person #2: Wow! You do have lots of places to go. When will you be finished with everything?
Person #1: I will be finished this evening after 6:00p.m. I will cook dinner when I return home.
Person #2: Well, I will talk to you later. I am busy today too.

5. **Person #1:** Hi. My name is _________________. I am from _____________. What is your name?
Person #2: My name is _________________. I am from _________________.
Person #1: That is interesting. Where do you live now?
Person #2: I was living in California, but my family moved. I am living in Pembroke Pines now.
Person #1: Oh. Okay. I live in Miami Gardens nearby Family Dollar on 3rd Street and 122 Ave.
Person #2: I live behind the bank close to the post office. It is around the corner from Walmart.
Person #1: I know where that is. My cousin lives near you. Well, it was nice to meet you.
Person #2: It was nice to meet you too. Have a nice day!

6. **Person #1:** I went to a really nice birthday party on Saturday. We had a wonderful time.
Person #2: Who had a birthday party?
Person #1: It was my friend's party. She just turned 22 years old. We had an amazing time.
Person #2: Did the party have lots of food?
Person #1: Oh yes, there was lots of food and drinks. There was also dancing, singing, good music and lots of people. Many people were there. We had so much fun.
Person #2: It sounds like you had a wonderful time. I didn't do anything on Saturday. I just stayed home. I cleaned, cooked, watched some movies, washed the dishes, and went to sleep.
Person #1: Next time I will take you with me. I think you will have a good time.
Person #2: Wonderful. I think I will like that.

7. **Person #1:** Good morning. Are you taking an English class?
Person #2: Yes, I am. I like my English class. I am learning many things and I have made many friends.
Person #1: Oh really? Why do you want to learn the English language?
Person #2: I want to learn to speak English so I can get a good job in this country. It is important to be able to communicate with people in the United States. English is the official language in this country.
Person #1: Yes. That is true. Why did you come to the United States?
Person #2: I came here to be with my family. My brothers and sisters are here, so I came to be with them. My father and mother are still in Argentina.
Person #1: Okay. I understand. I came to the United States for better job opportunities, but I need to learn English too. I will register to take an English class on Monday.
Person #2: That is good. I think you will learn a lot. Learning English is not that difficult. You just need to study and practice every day both in class and at your house.
Person #1: Thank you. I will study hard.

8. **Person #1:** I need to go to the post office because I need to mail some packages to my family in Mexico. I also need to send some things to my sister in Cuba.
Person #2: Why do you need to mail things to your family?
Person #1: ...because I take care of them. I send them money, medicine, supplies and other things. I hope that they can come to the United States soon.
Person #2: Yes, I understand. I send things to my family in Colombia. I want my family to come to the United States too. I want them to be here with me.

ASSESSMENT: Community Resources

bank	supermarket	post office	neighborhood
library	clothing store	pharmacy	hospital
gas station	restaurant	restaurant	university

1. I need to cash my check at the _______ bank _______ after work.
2. My car is on "E". I need to get to a _______ gas station _______ quickly.
3. I took my husband to a nice _______ restaurant _______ for his birthday.
4. My daughter is working on her college degree at the _______ university _______.
5. I checked out three books at the _______ library _______ today.
6. I visited my sister in the _______ hospital _______ after she had the baby.
7. I need to take my prescription to the _______ pharmacy _______ today.
8. We have no food. I need to go to the _______ supermarket _______.
9. There are many parks in my _______ neighborhood _______.
10. I will go to the _______ post office _______ to mail a letter today.

Directions: Read the sentence on the left and match the community resource on the right to the sentence by writing the letter of the correct answer.

11. You need to mail a package. __g__
12. You need to fill a prescription. __k__
13. I want to earn a college degree. __d__
14. We are eating dinner out tonight. __a__
15. Bill needs to cash his paycheck. __b__
16. I need to pay my traffic ticket. __f__
17. I want to go running. __j__
18. My mother has been sick. __h__
19. Your cousin just had a baby. __i__
20. My daughter is learning about civics. __u__
21. I want to check out two books. __e__
22. I need to buy groceries. __c__

a. restaurant
b. bank
c. supermarket
d. university
e. library
f. city hall
g. post office
h. doctor
i. hospital
j. park
k. pharmacy

Directions: Read the sentences below and choose the compound word from the box to complete the sentence.

COMPOUND WORDS

earthquake	cupcake	hairbrush	bathroom	beachball
sunflower	eyebrow	carwash	downtown	roastbeef
birthday	cheeseburger	cellphone	catfish	earrings

1. Please bring the ___pharmacy___ for me to do my hair.
2. Sheba bought a pair of ___earrings___ from the mall today.
3. We saw a beautiful yellow ___sunflower___ in the garden today.
4. I had a ___cheeseburger___ and fries for lunch today.
5. I will be back. I need to use the ___bathroom___.
6. My uncle went fishing and caught a ___catfish___ on Saturday.
7. John ate one ___cupcake___ for dessert after dinner.
8. The children were in the pool playing with a ___beachball___.

Directions: Answer each question with the correct answer: Yes, I do or No, I don't

9. Do you buy groceries at the shoe store. ⚪ Yes, I do ⚫ no, I don't

10. Do you buy shoes at the hardware store? ⚪ Yes, I do ⚫ no, I don't

11. Do you buy cookies at the bakery? ⚫ Yes, I do ⚪ no, I don't

12. Do you buy appliances at the electronics store? ⚫ Yes, I do ⚪ no, I don't

13. Do you buy clothes at the mall? ⚫ Yes, I do ⚪ no, I don't

14. Do you buy gas at the bank? ⚪ Yes, I do ⚫ no, I don't

15. Do you buy books at the library? ⚫ Yes, I do ⚪ no, I don't

16. Do you have surgery at a hospital? ⚫ Yes, I do ⚪ no, I don't

Directions; Answer the question below in a complete sentence.

17. Where do you need to go today? ___I need to go to the supermarket today.

Lesson 8: Employment

Dear ESL Teacher,

As you embark on teaching Lesson 8: Employment, you have at your disposal a comprehensive plan designed to enhance your students' understanding of employment-related vocabulary and concepts. This lesson focuses on essential topics such as learning new vocabulary words related to the workplace, understanding past, present, and future tenses, comprehending pay stubs, understanding taxes, benefits, and overtime. Students will also review and practice subject-verb agreement, read stories and practice comprehension, work in pairs while reading dialogues, and take an assessment at the end of the lesson.

Through structured activities such as vocabulary introduction, sentence practice, grammar drills, and conversational exercises, students will build practical skills for discussing employment and workplace scenarios in English. The instructional procedures outlined include direct instruction, guided practice, and independent practice, ensuring a balanced approach to learning that supports diverse learning styles and abilities.

OBJECTIVES:

1. Students will identify and use vocabulary related to employment and the workplace.

2. Students will construct and practice sentences using targeted employment vocabulary.

3. Students will demonstrate understanding of basic grammar concepts (subject-verb agreement, past, present, and future tenses).

4. Students will read and comprehend pay stubs, understand taxes, benefits, and overtime.

5. Students will engage in conversations using learned vocabulary and grammar related to employment.

6. Students will participate in dialogues to practice communication skills in a workplace context.

7. Students will demonstrate their learning through a comprehensive assessment.

INSTRUCTIONAL PROCEDURES:

Direct Instruction:

- **Objective:** Present new vocabulary and grammar concepts clearly and explicitly.
- **Details:** Introduce new employment-related vocabulary words (e.g., job, occupation, interview, salary, wage, etc.) using visuals and contextual examples. Explain the meanings, provide pronunciation guides, and use each word in sentences. Display visuals such as images or diagrams illustrating each word. Encourage students to repeat and practice pronouncing the words aloud.

Guided Practice:

- **Objective:** Help students apply new knowledge in a supportive environment.

- **Details:** Facilitate structured activities where students practice using new vocabulary and grammar concepts. Provide sentence frames or prompts incorporating new vocabulary and grammar structures. Walk around the classroom, offering support and feedback. Encourage peer collaboration by having students work in pairs or small groups.

Independent Practice:

- **Objective:** Reinforce learning through individual or paired activities.
- **Details:** Assign tasks from the book for students to independently apply what they have learned. This could include worksheets or exercises reinforcing vocabulary usage, grammar rules, or conversational skills. Provide clear instructions and examples. Encourage self-monitoring by asking students to review their work before submission. Monitor progress and offer assistance as needed.

Differentiation/Adaptations:

- **Provide visual aids and simplified instructions for English language learners:**
- **Objective:** Support comprehension for students with varying English proficiency levels.
- **Details:** Use visual aids such as charts, diagrams, or illustrations alongside verbal explanations. Provide simplified instructions and break down complex concepts into smaller steps. Offer bilingual dictionaries or picture dictionaries. Adjust the pace of instruction to accommodate slower processing speeds.

ACTIVITIES

Vocabulary Introduction:

- **Objective:** Introduce key employment-related vocabulary words.
- **Details:** Use flashcards, images, or charts to illustrate each vocabulary word. Provide contextual examples in sentences or short paragraphs. Encourage students to repeat and practice saying the words aloud.

Sentence Practice:

- **Objective:** Help students construct meaningful sentences using new vocabulary and grammar concepts.
- **Details:** Guide students in forming sentences that incorporate vocabulary words and target grammar structures. Begin with simple sentence structures and gradually increase complexity. Provide scaffolded support with sentence starters or frames if needed.

Grammar Drill:

- **Objective:** Reinforce understanding of grammar rules (subject-verb agreement, tenses).
- **Details:** Have students complete exercises where students practice using grammar elements correctly. This can include fill-in-the-blank activities, matching exercises, or creating sentences, all exercise found within the lesson. Provide explanations and examples to clarify misunderstandings.

Conversation Practice:

- **Objective:** Develop students' ability to engage in spoken communication using learned vocabulary and grammar.
- **Details:** Pair students or organize small groups for conversational activities. Provide prompts or scenarios requiring the use of targeted vocabulary and grammar structures. Encourage students to take turns speaking and actively listen to peers.

Reading Comprehension:

- **Objective:** Enhance students' ability to understand written English through reading passages found in the lesson.
- **Details:** After reading, ask comprehension questions requiring recall of details, making inferences, or summarizing key points. Encourage students to read aloud to practice pronunciation and fluency.

Dialogues:

- **Objective:** Foster creativity and application of vocabulary and grammar in context through reading short dialogues in conversational tone.

- **Details:** Students will get into pairs. Teacher will assign students a dialogue number to read. Students will take five minutes to practice their dialogue silently, then the teacher will call on each dialogue number and the pair of students who were given that number will read.

ASSESSMENT:

- **Objective:** Evaluate students' comprehension and application of lesson content.
- **Details:** The assessment is found at the end of each lesson.

Materials and Resources:

- Book: It's Time to Learn English
- Vocabulary cards
- Whiteboard and markers
- Textbooks or reading materials
- Worksheets for grammar exercises
- Audio recordings for listening activities

Wrap-up

Technology Needed:

- Projector or screen for displaying visuals
- Computer or tablet for accessing digital resources

Employment

8

Vocabulary	Occupations	Industries
1. work	cashier	all industries
2. job	cook/chef	restaurant
3. occupation	teacher/professor	education
4. employment	doctor	medical
5. employer	nurse	medical
6. employee	lawyer/attorney	legal
7. interview	server/waiter/waitress	restaurant
8. position	bank teller	banking
9. salary	security guard	all industries
10. full time	accountant	financial
11. part time	pilot	aviation
12. skill	actor/actress	entertainment
13. experience	salesman	all industries
14. shift	mechanic	automotive repair
15. schedule	politician	political
16. company	pharmacist	pharmaceutical
17. organization	realtor	real estate
18. business	journalist	journalism
19. hire	news anchor	media
20. fire	secretary	all industries
21. temporary	police officer	law enforcement
22. permanent	bus driver	transportation
23. benefits	computer technician	technology

EMPLOYMENT SENTENCES

1. I **work** at Bank of America. Where do you **work**?

2. If you are late to work everyday, your **supervisor** may **fire** you.

3. What are your **skills** for the **position**?

4. I have an **interview** at 2:00p.m. today. I hope I get the **job**.

5. Do you have **experience** for the **position**?

6. Are you **full time** or **part time**?

7. Do you get **benefits** on your job?

8. My **employer** is Walmart Corporation.

9. My son's new job is **temporary**. He will work for only six months.

10. What is your sister's **occupation**? Is she a teacher?

11. What **industry** is an actress in?

12. I had an **interview** for a secretary's position today. I hope they **hire** me.

13. My brother has his own **business**.

14. I am on the **schedule** to work three days this week.

15. Do you have a **job**?

16. There is a new **employee** in my department.

17. I will make $17.00 **an hour** on my new job.

18. My **salary** is $89,000 a year.

19. Broward County Schools is a big **organization**.

20. My sister works for a retail **company**.

21. A bus driver is in the transportation **industry**.

22. My father works the second **shift** from 2:00-10:00p.m.

24. What are your **skills** for the position that you are applying for?

25. A **full time** job is 40 hours or more a week.

APPLICATION FOR EMPLOYMENT

Name ____
      First   Last   Middle Initial

Address: ____
                                City   State   Zip

Telephone: _____________________ Email: ____________________________

Position Applied For: ______________________________ ___Full Time ___Part Time

Salary Desired: _________________ (per year) _________________ (per hour)

Date you can start? ___________________________________

Days and Hours Available: _________________ Days you **cannot** work: ________________

___Temporary   ___permanent

WORK HISTORY

Position: ___________________	Position: ___________________
Company: ___________________	Company: ___________________
City, State: __________________	City, State: __________________
Number of years: ___________	Number of years: ___________
Duties/Responsibilities: ___________	Duties/Responsibilities: ___________
_______________________________	_______________________________
_______________________________	_______________________________
_______________________________	_______________________________

Skills: ____
____
____

REFERENCES

Name: _____________________	Name: _____________________
Company: ___________________	Company: ___________________
Phone Number: _______________	Phone Number: _______________
Relationship: ________________	Relationship: ________________
Number of Years Known: _________	Number of Years Known: _________

work	works	don't work	doesn't work

1. I am an attorney. I _____work_____ in a law office.
2. My niece is a college professor. She _____works_____ at a university.
3. Carmen is an actress. She _____doesn't work_____ in a courthouse.
4. I am a bus driver. I _____don't work_____ in a school.
5. I am a mechanic. I _____don't work_____ in a hospital.
6. Julio is a cashier. He _____works_____ in a store.
7. I am a secretary. I _____work_____ in an office.
8. David and John are security guards. They _____work_____ outside.
9. Lissette is a carpenter. She _____doesn't work_____ in a daycare center.
10. My son is a computer specialist. He _____works_____ on computers.

Directions: Answer each question in a COMPLETE SENTENCE.

11. What is your occupation? _____I am a teacher._____

12. Where do you work? _____I work in a school._____

13. Who is your employer? _____My employer is Home Depot._____

14. Who is your supervisor? _____Rosa Garcia is my supervisor._____

15. How much do you make on your job? _____I make $14.00 an hour on my job._____

teacher	restaurant	school Bus Driver	cashier	nurse

16. I want to take care of sick patients. I want to be a _____nurse_____.
17. I would like to take orders and be kind to customers. I want to work in a _____restaurant_____.
18. I want to safely take students to and from school. I would like to be a _____bus driver_____.
19. I want to teach students different things. I want to be a _____teacher_____.

CARLA'S JOB AT THE SUPERMARKET

Carla works at Publix supermarket. She is 24 years old and lives with her aunt Tina. She is a part time cashier and makes $14.00 an hour. Carla works the second shift from 2:00-7:00p.m. She works on Tuesdays, Wednesdays, Saturdays and Sundays. She gets a 30-minute break three hours after she starts work and she usually has a sandwich or a salad on her break. She meets lots of people at Publix. Sometimes she sees her friends and neighbors. One time, she saw the cashier from the gas station next to her school. Carla was hired nine months ago, and she was very happy to be able to get a job because she had just come to the United States from Colombia. She speaks and understands a little English and that is why she was able to get a job, but she is still learning English. She goes to her English class in the mornings for four hours each day. Her English class finishes at 12:30p.m. everyday. She's very happy to in the United States.

Directions: Answer each question in a complete sentence.

1. When was Carla hired? _______ Carla / She was hired nine months ago. _______

2. What time does Carla's English class begin? _______ Her English class begins at 8:30a.m. _______

3. How much does Carla make on her job? _______ Carla / She makes $14.00 an hour. _______

4. Who does Carla live with? _______ Carla / She lives with her Aunt Tina. _______

5. What is Carla's occupation? _______ Carla / She is a cashier. _______

6. How many hours a day does Carla work? _______ Carla / She works five hours a day. _______

7. What time does Carla take her break? _______ She takes her break at 5:00p.m. _______

8. What does Carla usually eat on her break? _______ Carla / She usually eats a salad or a sandwich. _______

9. How old is Carla? _______ Carla / She is 24 years old. _______

10. Is Carla full time or part time? _______ Carla / She is part time. _______

Directions: Answer each question correctly using the answers from the box below:

I am nurse	My interview is at 3:00p.m.	No I don't work overtime
I work Memorial Hospital	I am a nurse	I go to lunch at 12:30p.m.
My benefits are medical, dental, vision and sick days	Yes, I get benefits on my job.	I work at Memorial Hospital
My hours are from 8:00a.m. -- 4:30p.m.	Rosa Garcia is my supervisor.	No, I wasn't hired.
No, I was hired.	Interview in 3:00p.m.	I am full time.
I am full time.	Days off Sunday and Monday	My days off are Sundays and Mondays.

1. What is your occupation? _______ I am a teacher. _______

2. Where do you work? _______ I work in a school. _______

3. What are your hours? _______ My hours are from 8:00a.m. to 4:30p.m. _______

4. What time is your interview? _______ My interview is at 3:00p.m. _______

5. Who is your supervisor? _______ Rosa Garcia is my supervisor. _______

6. What time is your lunch? _______ I go to lunch at 12:30p.m. _______

7. Do you get benefits on your job? _______ Yes, I get benefits on my job. _______

8. What are your benefits? _______ My benefits are medical, dental, vision and sick days. _______

9. Do you work overtime? _______ No, I don't work overtime. / Yes, I work overtime. _______

10. Were you hired? _______ No, I wasn't hired. _______

11. Are you full time or part time? _______ I am full time. _______

12. What are your days off? _______ My days off are Sundays and Mondays. _______

Directions: Match the definition on the left with word it describes on the right.

full time ___f___		a. total amount before deductions
occupation ___c___		b. take-home pay after deductions
industry ___h___		c. teacher, bus driver, engineer
gross pay ___a___		d. Less than 40 hours
net pay ___b___		e. medical, dental, vision, vacation, etc.
benefits ___e___		f. 40 hours or more
FICA ___g___		g. Social security
		h. medical, banking, education, hotel

Past, Present & Future

Past:

- LAST YEAR, I learned many things in my English class.
- I took a Spanish class LAST YEAR.
- I was very sick THREE WEEKS AGO.
- THREE WEEKS AGO, I was very sick.
- The children were punished because they jumped in the bed LAST NIGHT.
- When I was younger, I played the piano.
- My sister exercised for two hours YESTERDAY.
- I worked at the mall three years ago.
- Three weeks ago, the track team were running down the street.
- I was learning how to speak English LAST YEAR.
- I typed 50 words per minute on my last job.
- 5 YEARS AGO, I worked at a computer company.
- ON THURSDAY, I went to the beach.

Present:

- I am learning a lot in English class. (continuous)
- I cook for my husband every day. (continuous)
- I am driving now.
- He reads in his class every week. (continuous)
- We are writing our sentences now.
- Right now, I am working.
- I watch TV every day at 4:00p.m. (continuous)
- The baby is sleeping now.
- The students are listening to their teacher.

Future:

- TOMORROW, I will go to my doctor's appointment.
- I am taking my mother to the airport NEXT WEEK.
- You will take your test TOMORROW.
- NEXT MONTH, I will start my new class.
- I am looking for a new job NEXT YEAR.
- 5 YEARS FROM NOW, I will be getting married.
- I am going to the store TOMORROW.
- I will go to shopping THIS WEEKEND.
- I will be going to school at Hispanic Unity NEXT MONTH.
- On Thursday, I will go to the beach.

NAME	PRESENT	PAST
Ronald	salesman/sells computers	salesman/sold office supplies
Angela	actress/appears on TV shows, commercials and movies	receptionist/answered phones, filed papers and ran errands
Beth	computer technician/fixes computers	teacher's assistant/helped the students and the teacher
Derrick	plumber/unstops sinks & toilets	plumber's assistant/assisted the plumbers
Lisa	college professor/teaches college students	teacher/ taught 3rd and 4th grade students
Renee	cashier/takes money from customers at Walmart	waitress/served customers at a restaurant

Directions: Write complete sentences about the people above and their present and past work history. See example below:

PAST & PRESENT

Example: <u>Renee is a cashier. She takes money from customers at Walmart. She was a waitress. She served customers at a restaurant.</u>

1. Derrick: Derrick is a plumber. She unstops sinks and toilets. He was a plumbers assistant. He assisted the plumbers.

2. Lisa: Lisa is a college professor. She teaches college students. She was a teacher. She taught 3rd and 4th grade students.

3. Beth: Beth is a computer technician. She fixes computers. She was a teacher's assitant. She helped the students and the teacher.

4. Ronald: Ronald is a salesman. He sells computers. He was a salesman. He sold office supplies.

5. Angela: Angela is an actress. She appears on television shows. She was a receptionist. She answered phones, files papers and ran errands.

Directions: Answer each question in a complete sentence.

1. **Where do you work?**
   a. I working at a bank.   b. I work a bank.   c. I work at a bank.

2. **What is your occupation?**
   a. I am a chef at a restaurant.   b. I am in the restaurant industry.   c. I am chef.

3. **What is your salary?**
   a. I make $15.00 an hour.   b. I am $15.00 for hour.   c. I make $15.00 per year.

4. **What time is your interview?**
   a. It at 2:00p.m.   b. It is in Hollywood.   c. It is at 2:00p.m.

5. **Who is your supervisor?**
   a. My supervisor Juan Hernandez
   b. She is Juan Hernandez
   c. Juan Hernandez is my supervisor.

6. **Where is your job located?**
   a. It is in Miami Gardens.   b. It is located in Johnson Street.   c. It located in Tampa.

7. **What are your days off?**
   a. I am off at 8:30-5:00p.m.   b. I am off on Saturdays and Sundays   c. I am off at 5:00p.m.

8. **Are you full time or part time?**
   a. I are full time.   b. I full time.   c. I am full time.

9. **Do you get benefits on your job?**
   a. Yes, I get benefits.   b. Yes, I don't get benefits.   c. Yes, I did get benefits.

10. **Do you like your job?**
    a. Yes, I do.   b. No, I didn't.   c. No, I did.

11. **How many people are in your department?**
    a. 6th people are in my department   b. 6 people only   c. My supervisor is in my department.

12. **How much vacation time do you get on your job?**
    a. I two week's vacation   b. I get two week's vacation.   c. two years vacation.

13. **What is your work schedule?**
    a. I work Tuesday through Sunday from 8:30a.m. – 4:00p.m.
    b. Tuesday through Sunday my work.
    c. 8:00a.m.

Writing past, present and future sentences

work

Past: _______________ Last year, I worked at Walmart. _______________

Present: <u>I work at Walmart.</u>

Future: _______________ Next year, I will work at Walmart. _______________

type

Past: <u>I typed 50 words per minute on my last job.</u>

Present: _______ I type 50 words per minute on my job now. _______

Future: _______ I will type 50 words per minute on my next job. _______

drive

Past: _______ I drove trucks on my last job. _______

Present: _______ I drive trucks on my job. _______

Future: <u>I will drive trucks on my new job.</u>

learn

Past: _______ I learned a lot in my English class last year. _______

Present: <u>I am learning many things in my English class.</u>

Future: _______ I will learn a lot of English in my new English class. _______

watch

Past: _______ I watched a great movie last night. _______

Present: <u>I am watching a great movie right now.</u>

Future: _______ I will watch a good movie tomorrow evening. _______

practice

Past: ____

Present: _______ I practice my English every day. _______

Future: <u>I will practice my English vocabulary tonight.</u>

JACKIE MORALES' INTERVIEW

Jackie Morales has an interview today at 9:30a.m. She is interviewing for a secretary's position at a law office. Jackie completed the application online and she is bringing her resume with her today. She will wear a dark blue suit, a white shirt, a pair of heels and modest accessories. She has six years' experience as a secretary in Brazil. Brazil is her native country. She has many skills. She can type 55 wpm. She can answer phones professionally. She can file papers, and she can work on the computer. The position pays $52,000 per year and the hours are from 8: 30a.m - 4:30p.m. with a 30 minute lunch break. The position is fulltime, and she will get many benefits: medical, dental, vision, life insurance, vacation and sick days. The job would be located only 15 minutes from her house in east Atlanta. Jackie has studied the company and she is ready for her interview. She hopes she gets the job because it would really help the family with bills. Her husband and two children will also be happy for her.

TRUE OR FALSE:

1. Jackie is from Brazil. __T__

2. Jackie has three children. __F__

3. Her interview is at 9:00a.m. __F__

4. The position does not pay benefits. __F__

5. Jackie is ready for the interview. __T__

6. Jackie doesn't have any experience. __F__

7. The job would be far from her house. __F__

8. Jackie wants to get the job. __T__

9. The job is located in downtown Ft. Lauderdale. __F__

10. Jackie has skills for the position. __T__

Directions: Answer each question in a complete sentence.

11. Does Jackie have children? __Yes, Jackie has two children.__

12. How many hours a day is the position? __The position is eight hours a day.__

13. What position is Jackie interviewing for? __a secretary's position__

14. How much does the position pay? __The position pays $52,000 a year.__

WORK SCHEDULE FOR SEDANOS' SUPERMARKET

Work Week: November 15, 2023 - November 21, 2023

	Sun.	Mon.	Tues.	Wed	Thur.	Fri.	Sat.
Angela	off	3:00-11:00	3:00-11:00	3:00-11:00	3:00-11:00	3:00-11:00	off
Ricardo	7:00-12:00	off	7:00-12:00	7:00-12:00	3:00-9:00	3:00-9:00	off
Claudia	9:00-2:00	off	off	9:00-2:00	9:00-2:00	off	9:00-2:00
Luis	off	8:30-5:00	8:30-5:00	8:30-7:00	8:30-7:00	8:30-5:00	off
Maria	off	off	12:00-8:00	12:00-8:00	off	off	12:00-8:00

Directions: Study the work schedule above. Answer the questions from the work schedule.

1. How many people are working this week? Five people

2. Who is off on weekends? Angela and Luis

3. How many people are full time? Two people

4. How many hours does Claudia work this week? 20 hours

5. How many people are off on Friday? One person is off on Friday.

6. Where do these employees work? They work at Sedanos' Supermarket.

7. What s the start date of this work week? The start date is November 15th.

8. Who is off on Fridays? No-one is off on Fridays.

9. How many people are part time? Three people are part time.

10. Who is off on Wednesday? No-one is off on Wednesday.

11. How many hours does Maria work this week? 24 hours

12. What kind of position would you like to have? I would like to have a chef's position.

13. How many hours would you like to work? I would like to work six hours a day.

PEOPLE INFORMATION

Angelica **Last name**: Smith **age**: 27 years old **Occupation:** Bank Teller **Employer**: Bank of America **Years**: 7 **Duties**: count money, deposit checks, process loans **Hours**: 9:00-5:30pm **Salary**: $56,000 a year	Barbara **Last name**: Cuevas **age**: 47 years old **Occupation:** 3rd grade teacher **Employer**: Riverside Elementary School **Years**: 23 **Duties**: teach students, plan lessons, talk to parents **Hours**: 8:15-3:30p.m **Salary**: $54,000 per year	Derrick **Last name**: Mitchell **age**: 22 years old **Occupation:** Bus Driver **Employer**: Dade County Schools **Years**: 17 **Duties**: drive students to and from school **Hours**: 7:30-4:30p.m **Salary**: $17.00 an hour
Evelyn **Last name**: Goldman **age**: 56 years old **Occupation:** Cashier **Employer**: Walmart Corp. **Years**: 6 **Hours**: 9:00-2:00p.m. **Salary**: $13.00 per hour	Franciso **Last name**: Hernandez **age**: 23 years old **Occupation:** Stock Person **Employer:** Home Depot **Years**: 4 **Duties**: Stocking the shelves **Hours**: 2:00-7:30p.m. **Salary**: $14.00 an hour	Tina **Last name**: Johnson **age**: 39 years old **Occupation:** Medical Assistant **Employer**: Memorial West Hospital **Years**: 9 **Duties**: take blood pressure, take weight and take blood. **Hours**: 8:30-5:30p.m **Salary**: $17.00 per hour

1. What is Barbara's salary? ___Barbara / Her salary is $54,000 a year.___

2. How many hours a day does Evelyn work? ___Evelyn / She works five hours a day.___

3. What is Tina's salary? ___Tina's / Her salary is $17.00 an hour.___

4. What are Derrick's responsibilities? ___Derrick drives students to and from school.___

5. Who is the employee of Memorial West Hospital? ___The employee is Tina Johnson.___

6. Who is the employer of Francisco? ___It is Home Depot.___

7. Who is Evelyn's employer? ___Evelyn's / Her employer is Walmart Corp.___

8. What is Tina's last name? ___Tina's / Her last name is Johnson.___

9. How many years have Francisco worked at Home Depot? ___He has worked there for four years.___

Name	Hospital	Bank	School	Law Office	Book Store	Pharmacy
Alicia and Ben	X					
Thomas		X				
Jennifer, Amy, Mia						X
Sandra			X			
William	X					
Tina, Sam				X		
Jorge, Carlos					X	

Directions: Use the correct form of the word "work" in the sentences below.

work, works, working

1. William ______works______ at a hospital.

2. Sam ______works______ at a law office.

3. Jennifer, Amy and Mia work at a ______pharmacy______.

4. Thomas ______works______ at a ______bank______.

5. ______Jorge______ and ______Carlos______ work at a bookstore.

6. Alicia and Ben ______work______ at a ______hospital______.

7. Jennifer, Amy and Mia ______work______ at a pharmacy.

8. Jorge is ______working______ at a ______bookstore______.

9. Sandra ______works______ at a ______school______.

10. Ben and William are ______working______ at a hospital.

11. ______Jorge______ works at a bookstore.

12. ______Thomas______ works at a bank.

Directions: Complete each sentence with the correct vocabulary word below:

hire	benefits	job	work
schedule	salary	interview	industry

13. My ______schedule______ this week is from 9:00a.m.-2:00p.m.

14. What time is your ______interviewe______ today?

15. Your son and daughter both ______work______ at the airport?

16. My ______salary______ is $19.00 an hour.

17. Lisa has a new ______job______.

Employment Vocabulary
Week 2

1. payroll tax	A payroll tax is a tax that employers deduct from their employees' paychecks and send directly to the government.
2. paycheck	A paycheck is a check that an employee is given as payment for services rendered.
3. paystub	A pay stub is part of a paycheck that lists details about the employee's pay. It itemizes the wages earned for the pay period and year-to-date payroll. The pay stub also shows taxes and other deductions taken out of an employee's earnings. And, the pay stub shows the amount the employee actually receives (net pay).
4. net pay	The "actual" amount after deductions are taken out.
5. gross pay	The "total" amount BEFORE deductions.
6. schedule	The days and hours that an employee works.
7. FICA	Social security deduction. It stands for Federal Insurance Contributions Act
8. federal withholding	This is the amount of federal income tax withheld from your paycheck and sent to the federal government. The amount you pay depends on how much you earn.
9. Medicare	Medicare is a tax that employees pay that provides health insurance coverage to individuals who are age 65 and over
10. Medicaid	Medicaid is a tax that employees pay that provides medical benefits to groups of low-income people, who may have no medical insurance or inadequate medical insurance.
11. taxes	These are fees that every taxpayer must pay in order to fund the federal government.
12. IRS	The IRS is a government organization that's in charge of collecting taxes from every tax payer.
13. deductions	Money taken out of your paycheck for different things such as federal withholding, FICA, Medicaid, medical, dental, vision, etc.
14. direct deposit	This is a deposit of money by a payer directly into an employee's bank account.
15. hours	The number of hours work in a payroll period.
16. overtime	Time worked "after" 40 hours.

CRYSTAL LAKE SECURITY FIRM

Name: David Mendez
Check Date: March 23, 2024
Employee Number: 435789
Period From: 03/05/2024
Tax Status: S2
Period Thru: 03/16/2024

Location: Payroll

Position: Security Guard

NET PAY	GROSS INCOME	DEDUCTIONS	TAXABLE INCOME
Current 1,107.19	1,311.50	204.31	976.45
Year-to-date 7,568.34	7,984.34	625.89	867.90
Annual Salary	31,720.00		

DEDUCTIONS SUMMARY

TAXES	CURRENT	YEAR-TO-DATE
Fed. With	125.35	1,518.66
FICA	38.45	1,391.77
Medicare	13.25	325.49
Life Insurance	13.98	227.76
Vision	5.25	36.75
Dental	8.03	56.21
Overtime	68.62	274.44

Position	Rate	Hours	Overtime	Total Overtime	Current	Check Total	Net Pay
6789900	15.25	80	3	68.62	1,220.00	1,311.50	1,107.19

Total Gross	1,311.50	**Total Net:**	1,107.19

End Bal	Beg. Bal	Adjust	Earned	Used
Vacation 0.00	0.00	0.00	0.00	0.00
Sick 62.53	62.53	0.00	0.00	0.00
Overtime 0.00	12.00	0.00	0.00	0.00

Direct Deposit to: **Wells Fargo** **Acct:** **5479097435** **Deposit Amount:** **1,107.19**

READING DAVID'S PAYSTUB

Directions: Study the paystub on the previous page, then use the information from the stub to answer the questions below.

1. What is the employee's rate per hour? _His rate is $15.25 an hour._

2. What is the name of David's bank? _David's / His bank is Wells Fargo._

3. What is the employee's complete name? _The employee is David Mendez._

4. How many hours of overtime does this employee have on this paycheck? _3 hours_

5. How much has this employee paid in year-to-date federal withholding taxes? _$1,518.66_

6. What is David's yearly salary? _His yearly salary is $31,720.00._

7. When did this pay period begin? _This pay period began on 03/05/2024._

8. What is David's take-home pay on this paycheck? _His takehome pay was $1,107.19._

9. What is David's gross pay on this paycheck? _David's gross pay was $1,311.50._

10. How much has David paid in year-to-date life insurance? _He has paid $227.76 in YTD life insurance._

11. What is David's net pay on this paycheck? _His net pay on this check is $1,107.19._

12. What date did David get paid? _David was paid on March 23, 2024._

13. How much has David paid in year-to-date vision? _David has paid 36.75 in YTD vision._

14. What is David's occupation? _David is a Security Guard._

VOCABULARY

federal withholding taxes	paystub	promotion	overtime
Medicare	gross pay	Medicaid	retirement

15. Taxes paid for people who do not have insurance is called _medicaid._

16. The total amount of your paycheck before taxes is your _gross pay_.

17. When you are given a higher position, it is called a _promotion_.

18. Money paid to the government is called _Federal Withholding taxes_.

19. The paper with all of your employment information is called your _paystub_.

20. Extra money you get after 40 hours is called _overtime_.

Name	Mall	College	Restaurant	Shoe Store	Book Store	Pharmacy
Lisa and Diana	X					
David		X				
Mia, Amy, Rosa						X
Jennifer			X			
William	X					
Tia, Susie, Carlos				X		
Alex					X	

1. Jennifer works at a __restaurant__.

2. __Mia, Amy & Rosa__ work/works at a pharmacy.

3. __Alex__ works at a bookstore.

4. William and Diana __work__ at a mall.

5. David __works__ at a college.

6. Jennifer, Amy, Rosa and Mia __work__ at a __pharmacy__.

7. Thomas, Susie, and Carlos work at a __shoe store__.

Medical Assistant
FT, 2 years exp. required
2 years college
Medical, dental, vision,
vacation, sick $45,000
Call 897-984-5890 for duties
8:30-5:00p.m.   M-F

Police Officer
FT, no exp required. Will train.
  High school diploma required
Overtime available
City of Hollywood
$55,750 Full Benefits
12:00-8:30a.m.   Sun-Thur

Chef
PT, 2 years exp. required
High school diploma required
6 hours a day
10:00a.m-4:00p.m.
$13.00 an hour
Bilingual preferred   M-F

---

8. Which position prefers bilingual speakers? __It is the chef's position.__

9. Which position offers overtime? __The police officer's position offers overtime.__

10. Which position requires college? __The Medical Assistant's position requires college.__

11. Which position requires 8 hours a day plus a 30 minute break? __The police officer & Medical assistant.__

12. Which position does not require experience? __The police officer__

13. Which position is off on weekends? __The Medical Assistant and the Chef's position__

14. Which position pays $4,645.83 a month? __The police officer's position__

15. Which position pays $390 a week? __The chef's position__

NAME	NOW	BEFORE
Dana	doctor / helps patients	student / studied to become a doctor
Charles	teacher / teaches students	teacher's assistant / helped the teacher
Raquel	secretary / types letters & answers phones	receptionist / helped customers and filed documents
Charlene	school bus driver / drives students to and from school	uber driver / drove customers to different places
Jenny	chef / prepares exotic meals for customers at an expensive restaurant	cook / cooked food at a fast food restaurant
David	bank teller / cashes checks and deposits money	cashier at Sedanos' supermarket /counted money and helped customers
Brenda	police officer / enforces the law	security guard / protected people

PAST & PRESENT

Directions: Write complete sentences about the people above and their present and past work history. See example below:

Example: <u>Charlene is a bus driver. She drives people around. She was an Uber driver. She drove people to different places.</u>

1. Brenda: <u>Brenda is a police officer. She enforces the law. She was a security guard. She protected people.</u>

2. Dana: <u>Dana is a doctor. She helps patients. She was a student. She studied to become a doctor.</u>

3. David: <u>David is a bank teller. He cashes checks and deposits money. He was a cashier at Sedanos. He counted money and helped customers.</u>

4. Raquel: <u>Raquel is a secretary. She types letters and answers phones. She was a receptionist. She helped customers and filed documents.</u>

5. Charles: <u>Charles is a teacher. He teaches students. He was a teacher's assistant. He helped the teacher.</u>

JULIO'S INTERVIEW

Julio has been looking for a job in the United States for three weeks now. He is from Peru. He came to the United States in August of 2023. He lives with his brother Luis and his sister Diana. Luis and Diana came to the United States in February 2021 with Diana's husband and her two children. When Julio came in 2023, he registered for an English class. He took the class for one year and he learned lots of English. Now, he can speak and understand enough English to get a job. Back in Peru, his occupation was a construction worker, so he has been interviewing for construction jobs. So far, he has not found a job, but he continues to interview for construction jobs at different companies. He has an interview today at 9:30a.m. at Holmes Construction Company. He will wear a nice black suit with a tie. He hopes that he will get the job because he needs money. His family is very supportive of him and they are happy that he is in the United States with them, but he wants a job so he can help with the bills. The schedule for this job is 6:00a.m – 3:00p.m. with one hour for lunch Monday through Friday. This job would be perfect for him because he wakes up early anyway.

True or False

1. Julio's interview is at 8:30a.m. ___F___

2. Julio's family does not support him. ___F___

3. Julio is from Peru. ___F___

4. Julio has two children. ___F___

5. Back in Peru, Julio owned a construction company. ___F___

6. He came to the United States in August 2024. ___F___

7. Julio understands enough English to get a job. ___T___

8. Julio likes to sleep late. ___F___

9. He has been looking for a job for three weeks now. ___T___

Directions: Answer the following questions correctly.

10. What will Julio wear to his interview today?

He will wear a nice black suit with a tie.

11. What company is Julio interviewing for? ___Holmes Construction Company.___

REVIEW AND PRACTICE

Directions: Answer each sentence with the correct part of speech in the parenthesis.

1. Yesterday, I ___went___ to Miami to visit my aunt. (go)
2. I bought my mother two ___cakes___ today. (plural noun)
3. We ___are___ going to Tampa this weekend. (VTB).
4. Your ___dress___ is beautiful. (noun)
5. My sister's puppy is ___eating___ now. (gerund)
6. I am going ___to___ Walmart today after school. (infinitive)
7. I live ___at___ 9956 NW 78th Street in New York. (preposition)
8. You need a new pair of ___shoes___. (plural noun)
9. Please buy some ___fruits___ from the supermarket today. (noun)
10. Your mother is my teacher. ___She___ a great person. (contraction)
11. My cousin is ___a___ teacher, but my brother is ___an___ engineer. (articles)
12. The baby is ___ini___ the bed now. (preposition)
13. The woman at the desk is very ___nice___. (adjective)
14. My son is going to ___Universal Studios___ this weekend. (proper noun)
15. I ___prepared___ my family a big dinner last night. (past-tense verb)

16. What is your occupation? ___I am a medical assistant.___

17. Where are you going after school today? ___I am going to the mall today after school.___

18. Who is your new employer? ___My new employer is Memorial Hospital.___

19. What time is your interview today? ___My interview is at 2:30p.m today.___

REVIEW & PRACTICE

Directions: Writing the missing tense for the words.

Past: ______ I went to the comedy show last night.

Present: ______ I go to the comedy show every year.

Future: I <u>will be going</u> to the comedy show on Saturday.

Past: ______ I had cake with my dinner last night.

Present: I am <u>eating</u> cake right now.

Future: ______ I will eat cake later today.

Past: ______ I talked to my my friend on the phone two days ago.

Present: I <u>talk </u>to with my friend on the phone every day.

Future: ______ I will talk to my friend on the phone later today.

Past: ______ I ran a marathon last year.

Present: ______ I run a marathon every year.

Future: My brother <u>will run</u> in a marathon next month.

Past: I <u>sang</u> a beautiful song in church on Sunday,

Present: ______ I sing in church on Sundays.

Future: ______ I will sing a song in church on Sunday.

Past: ______ I made you a cake for your birthday.

Present: ______ I am making you a cake for your birthday now.

Future: I <u>will make</u> you a cake for your birthday tomorrow.

Past: ______ I did my homework yesterday.

Present: I am <u>doing</u> my homework now.

Future: ______ I will do my homework later today.

WESTBROOK FURNITURE STORE

Name: Diana Garcia   **Location**: Payroll   **Check**
Date: June 27, 2021
Employee Number: 206478   **position**: Payroll Clerk   **Period**
From: 06/05/2021
Tax Status: S1   **Period**
Thru: 06/18/2021

	Gross Income	Deduction	Taxable Income
Net Pay			
Current	1,932.67	363.72	1,587.93
1,211.51			
Year-to-date	26,584.78	4,364.64	22,447.90
16,984.02			
Annual Salary	50,442.77		

Deductions Summary

Taxes	**Current**	**Year-to-Date**
FED W/H	235.97	3,518.66
FICA	98.45	1,391.77
MEDICARE	23.02	325.49
LIFE INSURANCE	18.98	227.76

Description	Position	Rate	Hours	Current
Check Total **Net Pay**				
	678990000	25.77	75	1,932.67
1,932.67 1,211.51				

Total Gross	**1,932.67**

	Beg. Bal	Adjust	Earned	Used
End Bal				
Vacation	0.00	0.00	0.00	0.00
0.00				
Sick	62.53	0.00	0.00	0.00
62.53				
Overtime	0.00	0.00	0.00	0.00
0.00				

Direct Deposit	Bank of America	97474657690
1,211.51		

Understanding a Paystub

1. What is the current amount of social security tax deductions? ___$98.45___

2. What is the net pay amount of this check? ___$1,211.51___

3. How many regular hours were worked on this pay stub? ___75 hours___

4. What is the rate per hour on this pay stub? ___$25.77___

5. What is the gross amount earned (before taxes)? ___$1,932.67___

6. What is the pay period end date? ___06/18/2021___

7. What is the year-to-date amount for life insurance? ___227.76___

8. What is Diana Garcia's employee number? ___206478___

9. What is the position of this employee? ___Payroll Clerk___

10. What is the year-to-date federal withholding amount on this check? ___3,518.66___

deductions	paystub	overtime
full time	FICA	federal withholding taxes

11. A person who works at least 40 hours per week is ___full time___.
12. Everyone must pay ___federal withholding taxes___.
13. ___FICA___ is the same as social security taxes.
14. Some people have many ___deductions___ on their paycheck.
15. ___Full time___ is more than 40 hours a week.
16. Your ___paystub___ has all of your information about your pay.

Directions: Answer each question in a complete sentence.

17. How many hours a week do you work? ___I work _____ hours a week.___
18. Who is your supervisor? ___My supervisor is _____.___
19. Are you full time or part time? ___I am _____.___
20. What are your days off? ___My days off are _____ and _____.___

REVIEW AND PRACTICE

Directions: Choose a word that will complete each sentence below:

1. I would like a cold glass of ___lemondade___.
2. ___Your___ new ___niece___ is beautiful.
3. Yesterday, I bought a ___black___ jacket.
4. Would ___you___ like some ___coffee___?
5. ___I___ will take the ___test___ on Friday.
6. I will travel to ___Mexico___ on ___Friday___.
7. My ___mother___ and father are ___divorced___.
8. Leidy's son came in ___2nd___ place in the competition.
9. My son likes to cut his hair ___himself___.
10. Is your brother ___an___ accountant?
11. I love ___your___ new computer.
12. On Friday nights I like to ___grill___.
13. Nicolas is ___exercising___ now.
14. Let's go to ___Burger King___ after class today.

Directions: Answer each question in a complete sentence.

15. Are you full time or part time? _______ I am _______.

16. How much do you make on your job? _______ I make _______ and hour / a year.

17. Who is your employer? _______ _______ is my Employer.

18. When is your lunch break? _______ My lunch break is at _______.

19. What are your days off? _______ My days off are ____ and ____.

20. What department to you work in? _______ I work in the _______ department.

DIALOGUE: EMPLOYMENT

1. **Person #1:** You have worked for your organization a long time.
   Person #2: Yes, I have worked on this job for 27 years now. I love it.
   Person #1: Wow! It is nice to love what you do. It is important to work for an organization that you like. If not, you will not be happy.
   Person #2: That is true. I have a great employer. My supervisor is wonderful, and I really like my coworkers. We are like a family here.
   Person #1: I want to find a job like that. I would like a job that pays well, has good benefits, and makes me happy. I also hope I have good coworkers like you.
   Person #2: You will find a good job like mine too. Just keep looking. Do not give up.

2. **Person #1:** Good morning my friend. How are you?
   Person #2: I am fine. I am finally working now. I work security at a bank from 8:00p.m. - 4:30p.m. I have a 30-minute lunch break.
   Person #1: Oh wow! Congratulations. How long have you had that job?
   Person #2: I was hired three weeks ago. I am full time and I make $18.50 an hour.
   Person #1: I am so happy for you. Do you like it?
   Person #2: Yes, I like it very much. I am full time. I get benefits plus a 2-week vacation.
   Person #1: That is wonderful. I am a manager at Walmart now. I got a promotion about three months ago.
   Person #2: That is great! Congratulations. How is your family?
   Person #1: Everyone is good. It was nice seeing you.
   Person #2: It was nice seeing you too! Have a great day!

3. **Person #1:** Are you making a good salary on your new job?
   Person #2: Yes, I am. I make $48,500.00 a year. I also get benefits.
   Person #1: What are some of your benefits? Some jobs have different benefits than others.
   Person #2: Yes, that is true. Well, I get medical insurance, dental insurance, vision insurance, sick time and vacation days. I also get life insurance and holidays.
   Person #1: That is wonderful. I am very happy for you. Do you get bonuses?
   Person #2: No. I don't get bonuses, but I am happy with my salary and my benefits.

4. **Person #1:** Good afternoon. My name is ______________. What is your name?
   Person #2: My name is ______________. Good afternoon to you too.
   Person #1: Well, it is nice to meet you. What is your occupation?
   Person #2: I am a legal secretary. I work for an attorney at a law firm. What is your occupation?
   Person #1: I am a teacher at an elementary school. I teach 1st grade.
   Person #2: A teacher? That sounds interesting. Do you like working with children?
   Person #1: Yes, I do. I love working with children. I like teaching them new things.
   Person #2: That is great. Children can be fun to work with. Well, have a nice day.
   Person #1: You have a nice day too.

5.

Person #1: I have an interview at 9:30a.m today. I will be interviewing for a postal worker position at the post office. I have always wanted to deliver mail.
Person #2: That's wonderful! Did you prepare for the interview? It is important to prepare properly. They are going to ask you many questions about your experience.
Person #1: Yes, I did some research and I asked myself some practice questions.
Person #2: How are you getting to the interview? Are you taking the bus?
Person #1: My brother is taking me. He will pick me up at 8:45a.m. I want to be early in case there is traffic. I want to be early so I can prepare and get my mind right.
Person #2: Yes, you do not want to be late on your interview. Do you have your resume?
Person #1: Yes, I do. Wish me luck. I'm very excited about it.
Person #2: Ok. Good luck!

6.

Person #1: I got my new schedule today. I will be working four days next week.
Person #2: Which four days will you work? I hope you will have weekends off.
Person #1: I will work on Tuesday, Wednesday, Thursday, and Friday from 9:00a.m. – 4:00p.m. I will work 6.5 hours a day with a 30-minute lunch break. I am off on Saturday and Sunday.
Person #2: Good. You have the weekends off. You are part time? That sounds like part time because you do not work 40 hours per week.
Person #1: Yes, I am permanent part-time. I hope to be made fulltime in about a year. Then, I will get 40 hours a week, make more money and get benefits.
Person #2: Yes, that would be great for you. I hope they make you full time too.
Person #1: Thank you.

7.

Person #1: Are you excited about the holiday coming up?
Person #2: No, I am not excited because I have to work.
Person #1: Why do you have to work on a holiday? That is not good.
Person #2: Because I work at the airport and it is open 24 hours a day, 7 days a week.
Person #1: Oh. That's true. Will you be paid overtime?
Person #2: Yes, I will be getting overtime, so I am happy about that. I could use the extra money.
Person #1: Well, at least you can look forward to the extra money.
Person #2: Yes, that's true.

8.

Person #1: I really need a job. I need money, but I need to learn English first.
Person #2: There are classes that teach you how to speak English. You should register.
Person #1: It sounds like what I need. Where do I go?
Person #2: There is an English school on Johnson Street. They have two classes – one for beginners and one for more advanced English speakers.
Person #1: That sounds perfect for me. Can you please provide me with the information?
Person #2: Absolutely. I will give it to you in a moment.
Person #1: Thank you so much!

9.

Person #1: What are you learning about in your English class?
Person #2: We are learning about past tense verbs, employment, the 5 Ws and adjectives.
Person #1: It sounds like you are learning a lot. What have you learned already?
Person #2: We have learned about regular nouns, proper nouns, pronouns, verbs to be, articles, and past-tense verbs. We have learned other things too. We have learned so much.
Person #1: Do you ever practice reading or writing?
Person #2: Yes we practice reading and writing every day in class with my teacher, Mrs. Merritt.
Person #1: That is awesome. Good luck learning English.
Person #2: Thank you very much.

10.
Person #1: I am trying to find employment. I need a job.
Person #2: How are you trying to find employment?
Person #1: Well, I have been looking on the computer every day. I would like to be a nurse's assistant in the medical industry.
Person #1: Did you try looking in the newspaper?
Person #2: No, I didn't. I have just been looking on the computer.
Person #1: You should try the newspaper also.
Person #2: Okay. I will do that. Thank you.
Person #1: You are welcome.

11.
Person #1: My daughter just got a new job at the local supermarket. She is a cashier.
Person #2: That is great! Is she fulltime?
Person #1: No. She is part time. She only gets 25 hours a week. They pay her $13.00 an hour. She doesn't get any benefits, but she likes the job, and she is happy there.
Person #2: At least she can still go to school.
Person #1: Yes, she still has time to study.
Person #2: Well congratulations to her.
Person #2: Thank you. I am proud of her. She is starting to show some responsibility.

12.
Person #1: I just found out that Walmart is hiring for cashiers and stock people.
Person #2: Are you going to complete an application?
Person #1: Yes, I need to apply on the computer because the application is online I want to be a cashier.
Person #2: How much does the position pay?
Person #1: I don't know yet, but I will find out later. May I borrow your computer to complete the application? I would like to do it today.
Person #2: Yes, you may come over and use it.
Person #1: Thank you so much. I hope I get the job. I really need the money.
Person #2: Yes. I understand. I hope you get the job too!

13.
Person #1: Good morning my friend. Where do you work now?
Person #2: I work at an office. I am a file clerk.
Person #1: What do you do as a file clerk?
Person #2: I file papers. I type and sometimes I answer phones and talk to customers. I make $14.00 an hour. I work Monday – Friday.
Person #1: That's really good. Are you fulltime or part time?
Person #2: Right now I am part time, but I hope that they will make me full time.
Person #1: Are you temporary or permanent?
Person #2: I am permanent.
Person #1: Good luck becoming full time.
Person #2: Thank you so much.

ASSESSMENT: Employment

bank teller	chef	full time
job	FICA	part time
employer	shift	mechanic

1. The ______bank teller______ deposited the money into my checking account.

2. Since I am only working ______part time______ I worked 32 hours this week.

3. The ______mechanic______ said that my car needed an oil change.

4. The ______chef______ at the expensive restaurant cooked a delicious meal for us.

5. My ______employer______ is Broward County Public Schools.

6. My sister just got a new ______job______ working at Bank of America.

7. A ______full time______ job is 40 hours or more each week.

8. I paid $77.98 in ______FICA______ taxes. That was for social security.

Directions: Read the occupations on the left and write the industry that it belongs to on the right.

entertainment	restaurant	education	transportation	medical	legal

Occupation	Industry
9. chef	restaurant
10. bus driver	transportation
11. teacher	education
12. nurse	medical
13. actor/actress	entertainment
14. lawyer/attorney	legal

Directions: Look at the clue words given and choose the occupation from the box that matches the keyword.

painter	cashier	dentist	nurse
Flight attendant	teacher	bartender	engineer

15. Students, board, books ______teacher______

16. Needles, blood, patients ______nurse______

17. Teeth, mouth, cleaning ______dentist______

18. Paintbrush, paint, ladder ______painter______

19. Money, register, customers ______cashier______

Directions: Complete each sentence with the correct word or phrase.

1. Shelly's occupation is ______a______ bank teller. (a / an / the)

2. A full-time job is ______40______ hours a week. (30,35,40)

3. A doctor is in the ______medical______ industry. (education / medical)

4. I make $43,000 ______a year______ on my job. (an hour / a year)

5. My ______employer______ is Wells Fargo Bank. (employment / employer / employee)

6. Do you have a ______job______? (occupation / employment / job)

7. I am ______interviewing______ for a position as a medical assistant today. (interview/interviewing)

8. I only work 35 hours a week. I am ______part time______. (full time / part time)

9. I worked 43 hours this week. I made three extra hours in ______overtime______. (schedule / overtime)

10. I work the ______3rd______ shift from 2:00-10:00p.m. (1st/2nd/3rd)

11. Were you ______hired______ for the new job? (hired / fired / interview)

Directions: Answer each question in a complete sentence.

31. Where do you work?
 a. I working at Publix.   b. I work Publix.   c. I work at Publix.

32. What is your occupation?
 a. I am a chef at a restaurant.   b. I am in the restaurant industry.   c. I am chef.

33. What is your salary?
 a. I make $15.00 an hour.   b. I am $15.00 for hour.   c. I make $15.00 per year

34. What time is your interview?
 a. It at 2:00p.m.   b. It is in Hollywood.   c. It is at 2:00p.m.

35. Who is your supervisor?
 a. Mi supervisor Juan Hernandez
 b. She is Juan Hernandez
 c. Juan Hernandez is my supervisor.

36. Where is your job located?
 a. It is in Miami Gardens.   b. It is located in Johnson Street.   c. It located in Tampa.

37. What are your days off?
 a. I am off at 8:30-5:00p.m.   b. I am off on Saturdays and Sundays   c. I am off at 5:00p.m.

Dear Teacher,

As you reach the conclusion of this Teacher's Edition, we hope that the journey through each lesson has been as rewarding for you as it has been for your students. This ESOL/ELL book was crafted with the aim of providing comprehensive and interactive lessons that not only teach the English language but also engage students in meaningful and practical ways.

Throughout the lessons, covering topics such as Basic Communication, Family, Housing, Food, Shopping, Sickness, Community Resources, and Employment, students have been exposed to essential vocabulary and foundational concepts. Each lesson has been designed to integrate the key learning domains of reading, writing, speaking, listening, and comprehension, ensuring a holistic approach to language acquisition.

By effectively teaching and engaging students in the interactive activities outlined in this book, you have guided them towards a significant understanding of the English language. Your dedication to using diverse instructional procedures and differentiation strategies has empowered students to confidently navigate real-world scenarios in English, both in reading and speaking.

We believe that your students now possess a solid foundation in English, equipped with the skills to communicate effectively and understand complex concepts.

Thank you for your dedication to teaching and for making a positive impact on the lives of your students. We hope this book has been a valuable resource for you and that it continues to support your teaching endeavors in the future.

Best regards,

Mia Y. Merritt